D0585870

Prince Edward

In memory of my father

PRINCE EDWARD

Ingrid Seward

CENTURY

First published by Century in 1995

First published in the United Kingdom in 1995 by Century Ltd
Random House UK Limited
20 Vauxhall Bridge Road, London, SW1V 2SA

Random House Australia (Pty) Ltd
20 Alfred Street, Milsons Point, Sydney, NSW 2061, Australia

Random House New Zealand Ltd
18 Poland Road, Glenfield, Auckland 10, New Zealand

Random House South Africa (Pty) Ltd
PO Box 337, Bergvlei 2012, South Africa

Random House UK Limited Reg. No. 954009

A CIP catalogue record for this book is available from the British Library

Papers used by Random House UK Ltd are natural, recyclable products made from wood grown in sustainable forests. The manufacturing processes conform to the environmental regulations of the country of origin.

ISBN 0 71267 5566

Typeset by Deltatype Ltd, Ellesmere Port, Cheshire
Printed and bound in the United Kingdom by
Mackays of Chatham, PLC, Chatham, Kent

Acknowledgements

I WOULD LIKE to thank His Royal Highness The Prince Edward for speaking so openly and honestly to me and for allowing me to meet so many of his colleagues, including members of the Royal Household, past and present. The contributions of these and the other people I spoke to were invaluable, but I would like to point out this is not an authorised biography and unless otherwise stated the opinions expressed are entirely my own.

I would also like to thank all of those who gave up their time to talk to me, in particular former senior Royal Marines officers, Ewen Southby-Tailyour, Robert Tailyour, Ian Moore and Alan Hooper and those others who helped me understand the complexity of their élite fighting force. I hope I have, as they wished, terminated any further debate as to what happened during Prince Edward's time with the Royal Marines.

For helping me understand Prince Edward's life, from his birth to his emergence as a television producer and managing director of his own company, I have many people to thank. Amongst them my late father's close medical colleague and friend, Sir John Peel, my own friends Betty Parsons, Peter Brown, and Abel Hadden, Prince Edward's Private Secretary, Lt Col Sean O'Dwyer, his former Private Secretary, Air Commodore Adam Wise and his Press Secretary, Geoff Crawford.

Amongst the other people who have helped me I would like to thank James and Belinda Edwards, Jill Holland, James Thomas, Sir Alan and Lady Cottrell, Dr Gavin Mackenzie, Lord Renfrew of Kalmsthorn, Richard Gozney, Paul Arengo Jones, Michael Hobbs, Kevin Morley, Biddy Hayward, Sir Tim Rice, Jeremy James Taylor, Jayne Fincher, Marina Mowatt, Malcolm Cockren, Christopher and Lesley Ronaldson, Tim Wilcox and Brian MacLaurin.

Finally I would like to thank my agent Mike Shaw and Kate Parkin, my editor from Century, for all their encouragement and for being so patient while awaiting delivery of this book.

Contents

Introduction

PRINCE EDWARD IS the first member of the Royal Family to try and make his way in the real world.

It has not been easy. He has had to wage a battle royal against the constraints of his background, the misgivings of his parents and the scepticism of his mother's subjects to establish himself as plain Edward Windsor. Along the way he has been ridiculed, had his manhood and masculinity and temperament called into question, examined and found wanting. He has suffered the indignity of unemployment.

He still has much to prove – to a public increasingly distrustful of its reigning family, but also to himself. It was his decision and his alone to live his life outside the protective cocoon of his royalty and he knows that he will be judged by the same competitive and often ruthless standards that apply to everyone else.

That he should even wish to is remarkable in itself. For Edward was always the most 'royal' of all the Queen's children. It was something everyone remarked on throughout his childhood. 'He was the one who always wanted to do the right thing,' said his prep school headmaster, James Edwards.

Yet it is Edward, more so even than his sister Anne he so adores, who chose to turn his back on the royal tradition. In doing so he has won the hardest battle of all – to be himself.

To achieve that he not only had to learn to take responsibility for his own decisions but also how to let his emotions show and how to respond to them.

'I am not as normal as I would like to be because I can't give,' he once plaintively wrote to a girlfriend, Romy Adlington. But slowly, gingerly, he started to learn how to share his feelings. Five years later, when his boss Biddy Hayward remarked that 'girls need hugs,' he was able to reply, 'Boys need hugs, too!'

Showing emotion is not something that comes easily to the Royal Family. On most occasions it is actually discouraged. A fuss is to be avoided, even on birthdays.

One birthday morning Edward joined his mother at her breakfast table in her private dining room overlooking Constitution Hill. The Queen ate her toast and marmalade and sipped her special blend of tea which she makes for herself with her own electric kettle. Her radio was tuned to the morning news on Radio 4. Her Pipe Major who plays beneath her window every morning was working his way through his repertoire. If Edward was expecting something, nothing was forthcoming. There was no card, no present, not even a birthday greeting. When Edward kissed his mother goodbye, still nothing was said.

A couple of hours later a senior member of the Royal Household asked the prince what his mother had given him for his birthday. He replied, with an amused smile, that he did not think she knew it was his birthday as he had breakfasted with her that morning and she had not mentioned it.

A hasty telephone call was put through to the Queen's Page, to remind Her Majesty that it was her youngest son's birthday. By lunchtime Edward had his present. To anyone else such remoteness might have seemed callous indifference but at the time Edward thought nothing of it. If it had been his twentieth or his thirtieth his mother would not have forgotten. But Edward was then in his late twenties; this was just another birthday and the Royal Family has an anniversary of some kind to celebrate almost every day of the year.

Not even the threat of death seemed to disturb this dispassionate routine. In June 1981 blank shots were fired at the Queen as she rode on horseback to the Trooping the Colour ceremony. Edward was on half-term which he was spending at Craigowan on the Balmoral estate. No one thought to contact him to tell him what had occurred or that his mother was all right. The first he knew about it was when he saw it on the television news that evening. It was Edward who then telephoned his mother.

His relationship with Charles could be equally detached.

After the Duke of Windsor died in 1972 some of his kilts were returned to Buckingham Palace. They were in the tartans that went with the subsidiary titles belonging to the Prince of Wales and were duly given to Charles. The previous Prince of Wales was a much smaller man than the present incumbent, however, and the kilts were packed away. A few years later they were found by the teenage Edward. He tried them on and they fitted. Pleased with his acquisition, Edward waited until the summer holidays at Balmoral for a suitable moment to wear them. He proudly appeared at dinner one evening in a kilt in the tartan of the Duke of Rothesay.

By law anyone can wear any tartan they wish. By custom, however, only members of the clan or those to whom the clan chief has given specific permission are allowed to wear the clan tartan. Charles, as Prince of Wales, was also the Duke of Rothesay and he had most definitely not given Edward permission to wear either the kilt or the tartan. He pompously ordered Edward to leave the room and go back upstairs and change. His little brother slunk away. He voiced no complaint and nobody would have expected him to. His family is determinedly hierarchical and Edward had got above himself.

But all was not as it seemed on the placid surface. As Alan Hooper, the Royal Marine colonel who was his commanding officer when he went on manoeuvres in Belize noted in his diary: 'There is steel in there and doubtless considerable determination.' Edward's view of himself and his position would soon start to change. The inner man no longer knitted neatly with the princely show.

As he grew up he started to question who he was and, more pertinently, what he was and what he was supposed to do with his life. When he discovered that he did not like the answers, he broke royal ranks and decided to do something about it.

There was a price to pay. As a prince he could have lived the sybaritic life of a playboy. Instead he went off in pursuit of a career. Michael Hobbs, the chairman of the Duke of Edinburgh Award, said, 'He should have been out having a good time.'

He was immensely proud of his heritage even as he became increasingly frustrated with some of the pomp and more archaic aspects of the monarchy. At the same time, he is concerned about the damage to Britain's pride and prestige the ferocious criticism of his family and the institution is causing.

He once asked of me: 'What do people expect of the monarchy? Or the Royal Family? What is it? Nobody can answer; everybody has got different advice and that's always been the problem.'

He sometimes hides his concern behind a mask of black humour. When Buckingham Palace was being cleaned, it was covered in scaffolding and plastic sheeting. Kevin Morley, the former managing director of Rover cars, recalled: 'He said, "What we're doing is dismantling it stone by stone. When we remove the scaffolding there will be nothing there."'

There are those who would accuse Edward of contributing to the process – by the way he quit the Royal Marines and his involvement in projects like *It's a Royal Knockout* and the decidedly un-Royal worlds of theatre and commerce. Edward would discount the criticism. He is working to his own set of values. If they sometimes run contrary to the more traditional modes of behaviour then that is only to be expected because Edward is a prince of contradictions.

He is a heterosexual accused of being a homosexual. He lives in a palace surrounded by the trappings of an Edwardian lifestyle and works in an insalubrious quarter of town. He enjoys the traditional pursuits of the country but lives in the city. He has been brought up surrounded by beautiful things but has few possessions of his own.

He has his friends and is immensely loyal to them – 'They would have to rob the Bank of England before he would let them down,' said Malcolm Cockren, the chairman of his television production company – but there is a solitary air about him. 'I sometimes feel he must be lonely, going back to Buckingham Palace – second floor, top left-hand corner,' said Michael Hobbs.

He is a member of one of the richest families in the world but chooses to earn his own living. He has dined off gold plate and supped pints of bitter in his local public house.

He was born into a family and an institution in which playing for the team is everything. He was sent to Gordonstoun which places great emphasis on individual fulfilment.

'I'm still a member of the Royal Family and there are still things I feel I can help with,' he told me. But he is no longer prepared to put royal duty before personal aspirations. He will no longer, he said, 'have time for many royal tours, not until I've got my company up and running. That's my priority and that's my commitment.'

He is a prince of the realm. He is happier as plain Edward Windsor.

One

An Age of Change

PRINCE EDWARD WAS born on the evening of Tuesday 10 March, 1964. It was a most unusual confinement, for there at the bedside, holding the Queen's hand, was the Duke of Edinburgh. It was the first time he had seen one of his children born.

He was there at the express invitation of his wife.

The Queen was thirty-seven. She had not found childbearing easy and her first-born and heir, Prince Charles, had been delivered by Caesarian section. But sixteen years had passed and fashions had changed in the interim, even in matters as primary as obstetrics.

When she had given birth to Charles the emphasis had been on using the advances in medical science to help relieve the discomfort of the mother's labour. The father was an unnecessary appendage, to be kept as far out of the way as possible. Now the accent was more on the relationship between mother and baby and how that could be enhanced, both physically and emotionally, by the mother being aware of what was happening – and how important it was to involve the father in the process.

As a keen reader of women's magazines which had been devoting an increasing number of their pages to articles expounding these new theories, the Queen had become fascinated by this new approach. It struck a timely chord. Her life had always been subject to the advice of others. Even in matters as intimate as how they were delivered of their own children, the Royal Family had had to submit to checks and scrutiny. Since the reign of the Stuarts it had been customary for a selection of Privy Councillors and Ladies-in-Waiting to be in attendance at

Royal births to ensure that the baby was not switched. In 1894 Queen Victoria ruled that henceforth only the Home Secretary need be summoned. In 1948, shortly before the birth of his grandson, Prince Charles, George VI did away completely with the archaic law.

Now, for the first time in 300 years, the royal woman in labour was mistress of her own confinement room. The Queen, for whom having children had been an impelling dynastic duty, was determined to enjoy the experience, and she wanted her husband to share it with her. How quickly social mores had changed. Prince Philip had been barred from the birth of Charles, Anne and Andrew. The idea of having him there with her would have been incomprehensible if not distasteful in an age so decorous that it forbade the publication of any photographs of the Queen in her pregnancy and never officially acknowledged that she had delivered her first-born by Caesarian section. But now even the Queen had caught the change in mood, and decreed that Philip would be in attendance at the birth – the first time, certainly in modern history, that any royal father had been allowed in to see his progeny born.

More sensitive on occasion than his abrasive public image sometimes suggests, Philip took a concerned interest in the proceedings and when the spirit of others started to wane, his cheerful banter would revive them.

The baby was delivered in the bathroom of the Belgian Suite which had been converted into a delivery suite. Named in honour of King Leopold of the Belgians, it is situated on the ground floor of Buckingham Palace next door to the swimming pool. During the Queen's confinement black drapes were hung over the floor-to-ceiling French windows which look out over the terrace to the Palace gardens and the lake.

Attending the Queen that day were five doctors – her surgeon-gynaecologist Sir John Peel, who had been present at the birth of her three older children; her new family doctor, Dr Ronald Boldey Scott; Sir John Weir, 82, who had been one of her physicians since 1952; John Brudenell, a consultant at King's College Hospital; and Dr Vernon Hall, Dean of the Medical School at King's College Hospital – plus two midwives, Sister Annette Wilson and Sister Helen Rowe.

Also there was Betty Parsons, whose relaxation techniques and no-nonsense advice have helped thousands of women to deal with the concerns of childbirth. Betty paid particular attention to breathing and in one of her most famous exercises, would exhort both the expectant mothers and the many fathers-to-be who attended her ante-natal classes to pant like a dog.

Relations were not of the smoothest between Parsons and the doctors, who, most conventional in their methods as befitted their eminent positions, had little empathy with Betty's newer, 'alternative' approach. The Queen, however, had enjoyed her training sessions with the former midwife and insisted that she be there at the birth. Philip, too, was supportive. He had drawn the line at attending her pre-natal classes – lying on his back panting 'doggy doggy, doggy' was hardly the Duke of Edinburgh's style – but when Betty had arrived at the Palace the morning the Queen went into labour, it was Philip who had quickly ushered her into the delivery room before the doctors could lock her out.

By this stage, though, the doctors were too involved in looking after their patient to worry about Betty. The baby was not due for another week and only the previous morning the Queen had been out walking in the palace grounds with her corgis and her four-year-old son, Andrew, seemingly on course for a full-term pregnancy. But the contractions had started early the following day and by the evening she was in full labour.

The delivery was slower than they might have hoped for. It was at this point that Philip's good humour proved so valuable.

'It's a solemn thought that only a week ago General de Gaulle was having a bath in this room,' he remarked when he walked into the bathroom and saw all the glum faces.

It was said in a jocular way which helped ease the tension that had been building up amongst the doctors and the nurses attending their Sovereign.

The Queen did not have what today would be called a 'natural' childbirth, though by the standards of the time it was regarded as very straightforward. The anaesthetist Vernon Hall, administered gas and oxygen as necessary. She also had pethidine, a pain reliever with properties similar to morphine, which was popular at the time.

There was never any danger (the real risk had been with Anne, as this was the first birth after the Caesarian with Charles) and the Queen did not suffer a lot of pain. The birth, however, was 'a bit slow'. Finally, at 8.20pm, to the relief of all involved, the Queen was delivered of 'a delicate child, small but healthy'.

Philip would later declare: 'People want their first child very much when they marry. They want the second child almost as much. If a third comes along they accept it as natural but they haven't gone out of their way to get it. When the fourth child comes along, in most cases it is unintentional.'

His wife took a keener view of the process. As a young girl she had declared that, when she grew up, she wanted to marry a farmer, live in the country and have lots of animals. Above all, she wanted four children – two boys and two girls. She had married a sailor, not a farmer but her other wishes had been fulfilled. So why not a second daughter to go with the two sons she now had? So convinced was she that she was going to have a little girl, she had not bothered to think of boys' names. Only girls' names had been discussed.

This was one matter, though, over which even a Sovereign had no say and, much to the Queen's surprise (if not to that of her doctors who throughout had taken the more pragmatic medical view) the baby was a boy. Philip telephoned the news to the Queen Mother at Clarence House then interrupted Prince Charles doing his prep at Gordonstoun and finally spoke to Princess Anne at school at Benenden in Kent.

Sir John Weir called Edward 'a bonny baby'. Dr Vernon Hall said he was 'a very serious looking boy'. He added, 'Everything went well – no problems.'

By comparison with his siblings, Edward was a small child. Charles had weighed in at 7lb 6oz, Andrew at 7lb 3oz. Anne's birth weight was 6lb. The Queen's youngest was only 5lb 7oz. He was, however, very pretty. As the Queen remarked to Cecil Beaton: 'It's most unfortunate that all my sons have such long eyelashes while my daughter hasn't any at all.'

He was finally named Edward Antony Richard Louis after his godfathers Lord Snowdon, Richard, Duke of Gloucester and Prince Louis of Hesse, prefixed by the old royal name of his great-great-grandfather, Edward VII. The choice had been a long time in the selection and his names were not officially announced until twenty-four hours short of the forty-two day deadline which, if it is exceeded, can result in a fine (though not in this case; the Sovereign, as the embodiment of the law, is above the law). He was christened on Saturday 2 May and Beaton first saw the new-born three weeks later when he went to the Palace to take the official photographs. 'The infant,' he noted, 'showed bonhomie and an interest in the activity that was going on.' He was 'alert and curious and already a character'.

His mother was very taken with him. As Beaton observed in his diary: 'His adult behaviour pleased the Queen who was in a happy and contented and calm mood.'

What the Queen called 'my second family' was now complete. Sixteen years separated her eldest and youngest children. But whereas Andrew, born half a generation after his sister, Anne, had been an unexpected and, initially at least, inconvenient arrival (he was conceived shortly before his mother embarked on a tiring 16,000-mile, nine-week tour of Canada), Edward had been very much on the Queen's maternal agenda.

She had seen little of Charles and Anne when they were young. Always a princess first, she had put duty before more personal commitments, her children included. That pressure only increased when she was brought to the Throne at the age of twenty-five by the premature death of her father, George VI. The responsibility of office had overwhelmed her and the children sometimes went for months without seeing her. Shortly after her Accession, Elizabeth and Philip toured Canada for six months. When she was eventually reunited with Charles and Anne she said: 'I don't think they really knew who we were.' She was right; they did not.

Her second family was a second opportunity – and a chance to make amends, for it was not just the royal schedule that was to blame for the distant state of her family relationships.

The Queen belonged to a class and generation which believed that children belonged in the nursery, to be brought out for their parents' inspection for half an hour in the morning and then again before they said their prayers and went to bed at night. That was the way she had been brought up and nothing in her sheltered young life had happened to challenge that view.

Philip, for his part, was the product of a broken home who had been left to fend for himself and saw no reason why he should treat his own children any differently. He was a promising young officer in the Royal Navy when he married Princess Elizabeth. No less a personage than Admiral of the Fleet Lord Lewin, Chief of the Defence Staff during the 1982 Falklands War who served as a midshipman with Philip, believed that had Philip been able to continue his naval career he, and not Lewin, would have been First Sea Lord. That glowing appraisal was never put to the test. When Elizabeth became Queen, Philip found himself sucked into the royal vortex. He was still young – he was thirty-one when his wife became his Sovereign – but overnight his life had ceased to be his own to shape according to his own ambition and talent. That left him frustrated and increasingly irascible. His reaction was to spend as much time as he could get away with far from the 'suffocating' restrictions of Palace life and protocol.

That in turn led to inevitable rumours and in early 1957, after Philip had spent four months cruising the Atlantic and Pacific oceans in the Royal Yacht *Britannia*, the Queen's Private Secretary Sir Michael Adeane felt it necessary to break the royal code of official silence that had hitherto applied in such situations to issue a terse statement from Buckingham Palace. It read: 'It is quite untrue that there is a rift between the Queen and the Duke of Edinburgh.'

The British press accepted Adeane's statement at face value. Thirty-five years later relentless press attention would force the Prince and Princess of Wales to confront the painful but inescapable fact of their incompatibility and their marriage collapsed because of it. The Queen and Prince Philip, however, were given the respite they needed and their marriage survived. It was Philip's last attempt to kick over the traces; by the time Andrew was born in 1960 passions had mellowed and the marital situation was holding steady on an even keel. That meant a corresponding change in both the Queen's and her husband's approach to parenthood.

Philip, older by then and less driven to find compensation for his disappointments, was less demanding of Andrew and Edward than he had been of Charles, while the Queen had acquired the confidence of experience which enabled her to adopt a more relaxed and personal approach to motherhood. It showed with Andrew. It showed even more with Edward. Andrew would always be his mother's particular favourite but it was Edward who was allowed to crawl around on the floor of her study while she worked on her state papers.

Indeed, so intent was she on spending more time with her younger children that she brought her weekly meetings with her Prime Minister forward by half an hour so she would be free to bath Edward and put him to bed herself.

There was a limit, however, to how far the Queen and her consort were prepared to go down this path. Change is rarely in monarchy's best interest. There is security in sameness. It is a bulwark against the agitations of social upheaval and the 1960s were a very perturbing time indeed for the *ancien régime*.

Outside the Palace walls a veritable social revolution was taking place. By 1964 it was well underway. In Britain, Sir Alec Douglas-Home, the hereditary 14th Earl of Home, was swept from power by Harold Wilson and a Labour party committed to tearing down the old class barriers and building a socialist utopia in their stead.

In the United States, still traumatised by the assassination of President John F. Kennedy, his successor, Lyndon B. Johnson, was signing the Civil Rights Act, the most sweeping civil rights law in American history which, he said, would 'close the springs of racial hatred'. In South Africa, a young lawyer named Nelson Mandela was sentenced to life for treason for plotting to overthrow the all-white government.

Jawaharlal Nehru, India's Prime Minister since the country became independent from Britain (thereby stripping the Queen's father, George VI, of his title of Emperor) died. In the Soviet Union, Nikita Khrushchev was ousted in a coup by hardliners led by Leonid Brezhnev.

Meanwhile in Britain, for the first time in almost a century, the Royal Family was being made fun of – on television's iconoclastic *That Was The Week That Was*, produced by Ned Sherrin and presented by David Frost.

And the Western world was gripped by the mass hysteria of that most light-hearted of phenomena: Beatlemania. Even

Prince Philip was touched by it. The Beatles, he said, are 'entirely helpful. I really could not care less how much noise people make singing and dancing. I would much rather they make any noise they like singing and dancing. What I object to is people fighting and stealing. It seems to me that these blokes are helping people to enjoy themselves and that is far better than the other thing.'

The gap between the four long-haired pop stars from Liverpool and the Greek-born Prince was nevertheless a yawning one. When the group performed for the Queen at the Royal Variety show, John Lennon looked up at the Royal Box and invited the poor to clap – and the rich to rattle their jewellery. The 'impromptu' remark had in fact been carefully rehearsed in the dressing-room beforehand. A number of expletives were contained in the original draft which gave crude expression to Lennon's less than deferential opinion of the British Establishment which the Royal Family personified. The Beatles' manager, Brian Epstein, never sure what the rebellious genius would do next, was in a tail-spin of worry lest at the last moment Lennon threw caution and career to the wind and delivered the unsanitised version. He did not, of course, preferring cheeky impudence to crude impertinence.

Lennon was not alone, though, in questioning the value of the Royal Family at that time. At a luncheon of the Foreign Press Association thirteen days before Edward was born, Prince Philip was asked: 'Do you think that the monarchy has found its proper place in the Britain of the Sixties?'

Philip replied: 'Here we are in the Sixties. What am I supposed to say? Perhaps you would enlarge on the question.'

The questioner did: 'One sometimes hears criticism in the press that the monarchy has not found its place, although it is, of course, playing a useful role in this country, but has still not found the right approach to the problems of Britain today.'

Philip answered: 'What you are implying is that we are rather old-fashioned. Well, it may easily be true; I don't know.' He continued: 'One of the things about the monarchy and its place – and one of the great weaknesses in a sense – is that it has to be all things to all people. Of course, it cannot do this when it comes to being all things to all people who are traditionalists and all things to all people who are iconoclasts. We therefore find ourselves in a position of compromise, and we might be kicked by both sides. The only thing is that if you are very cunning you get as far away from the extremists as you possibly can because they kick harder.'

Philip had warmed to his theme. 'I entirely agree that we are old-fashioned: the monarchy is an old-fashioned institution,' he concluded.

And that was the way it was going to stay. The Queen's decision to have her husband by her side during the birth notwithstanding, the great ship of royalty continued on its majestic course with barely a sideways glance at the foam of change churning up around it.

Edward was christened wearing a robe of Honiton lace that had been made in 1841 for Queen Victoria's eldest child, Victoria, who married the German emperor and whose son, Kaiser Wilhelm II, led his nation into war with Britain. He slept in the same cream-painted cot his brothers and sister had used and played with the same toys – the Queen, for all her riches, was forever looking for ways of making small savings, in the endearing if incorrect belief that if she counted the pennies the pounds of royal expenditure would somehow manage to look after themselves.

'I am a traditionalist,' the Queen bluntly declared and the habits of her Court reflected that.

The Royal Family, as well as being an institution that functions best in calm conditions, is also a business. Philip called it The Firm and it employed a full-time staff of several hundred people – chefs, housemaids, dressers, coachmen, footmen, valets, pages, nannies, and office staff. Hierarchical and tradition-bound, they were dutiful, loyal and clung steadfastly to the old ways and the Palace continued to be run in the most paternalistic manner.

One newspaper reported that upon the birth of his third son Philip had immediately ordered champagne for all the staff at the Palace. What actually happened was that a bottle of port was sent to each department of the Household so the staff could 'drink a toast with Her Majesty'. Some departments preferred to raffle it rather than drink it and one lucky footman won a bottle the Queen had been given by the President of Portugal.

Three weeks after Edward was born, fifty of the men who worked in the Royal Mews and looked after the Queen's cars, coaches and horses were invited in to see the still-unnamed prince. The first contingent of twenty chauffeurs, blacksmiths and coachmen were ushered in through the trademen's entrance on a Saturday morning and conducted by a footman up to the nursery on the second floor. Colonel John Miller, the Crown Equerry in charge of the Mews, inspected the men before they were allowed up. One was ordered to have a haircut.

Other conventions continued on their timeless way. Philip may have attended the birth but this was no New Man in the making and two days later and without thinking too much about it, Philip flew to Athens to attend the funeral of his cousin, King Paul of the Hellenes. He saw it as his royal duty to be there rather than at the bedside of his wife. The Queen, the doctors assured him, was doing well. She was comfortable in her room. She had a television set and a view of her gardens to keep her interest and she was well looked after by the Palace staff.

As was his young son. The moment Edward was born the royal child-rearing machinery had clicked into gear. The Queen would indeed spend more time with Edward than she did with her elder children and his childhood was marked by an informality which would have been out of place in Charles and Anne's day. But there was still an order, a seemingly immutable routine to life in the nursery. And presiding over everything, as always, were the royal nannies.

Two

Nursery World

When Edward was three months old his mother took him on to the balcony at Buckingham Palace and held him aloft for the heaving crowd below to cheer. It was his debut on the royal stage, the greatest stage in the world which would shape his life and become his career.

It was not to prove the easiest of performances, however. The script had gaping holes in it. The audience would become increasingly hard to please. And right from the start the cast itself was unsure just how they should play their parts.

This symbolic offering up of a young prince to his people was an ancient and atavistic ritual of monarchy but one that scraped against the grain of the Queen's family. Led by her dignified example, they preferred to keep their majesty hidden behind a mantle of understated mystery. For all the splendour of their trappings, there was still an air of personal modesty, of genteel understatement to their public performances. Vulgar display was to be avoided and that applied most particularly to the children.

'We try to keep our children out of the public eye so that they can grow up as normally as possible,' Prince Philip explained.

It was a commendable stance but one which clashed with the public's increasingly voracious appetite for all things royal, as Philip had been forced to acknowledge. Photographs of the baby Andrew had been severely restricted. That had given rise to rumours in the continental press that he was retarded or deformed or both and it was soon patently clear that Andrew, for all his parents' misgivings, had to be put on public display. He duly was – aged sixteen months, when the Queen brought him out on to the balcony at Buckingham Palace after her Official Birthday Parade.

In the end Philip's advice in the matter had proved decisive. Confined by law to the constitutional sidelines, he once described himself as 'a discredited Balkan prince of no particular merit or distinction'. But if he had to defer to the Queen in public, his private influence over his wife was immense. Major decisions, such as where their children were to be educated, were left to him and that in turn gave him considerable authority over the shape of the monarchy itself. And Philip had very clear ideas on that subject. 'If you are going to have a monarchy,' he said, 'you have got to have a family and the family has got to be in the public eye.'

In the media-orientated age which demands distinct and recognisable characters, that inevitably meant an element of product marketing. Philip understood that. Brought up on royalty's outer rim, he had been well placed to observe the theatricality of its centre. He explained: 'Monarchy involves the whole family, which means that different age groups are part of it. There are people who can look, for instance, at the Queen Mother and identify with that generation, or with us, or with our children.'

This was exactly the approach adopted by the great Hollywood moguls who had turned out stars to suit all occasions. And Edward was the youngest star in this royal firmament.

Each of the Queen's children was markedly different in character – differences which were seized upon and played up for all they were worth by the media for a public ever more fascinated by the reigning family. Charles was shy and sensitive, Anne strong and single-minded, Andrew boisterous and mischievous. Now it was Edward's turn to have his personality codified.

'He is the quietest of my children,' the Queen observed.

Her own mother agreed. 'I've never known a child sit so still,' the Queen Mother remarked after she had taken him to his first concert of classical music.

The image was forming – of a boy sweet of feature, engaging of smile, less serious than Charles, more studious than Andrew, certainly not as domineering as Anne. It was an image straight out of Central Casting. But casting a movie and being royal are not the same thing and this script was fraught with potential difficulties for a royal family trying to adjust to the demands of the modern world, for a prince who would one day want to live his life as he alone saw fit. The obvious danger was that if family or prince failed to live up to their image, they would risk the displeasure of their disillusioned public.

No one within the Royal Family saw it in those terms at that time. Denied the benefit of hindsight, their future looked settled. The old routines of royalty were still in force and Edward's childhood, as one observer remarked, had a 'magical' quality of security about it.

This was still a very grand household with an old-fashioned nursery presided over by Nanny who ran it as a private fiefdom, unchallenged and unopposed. Nanny was not required to clean, cook, do the laundry or even lay the table. Those chores were attended to by the nursery footmen, homemaids and nursery-maids.

The nursery occupied a comfortable suite of rooms on the second floor of the Palace. It overlooked the forecourt and gave Edward an excellent view of the Changing of the Guard. The main sitting room had pale green walls and an open fireplace. Edward's clothes were hung over the brass fireguard to dry. There was a large bathroom with a deep old-fashioned bath with chrome taps.

Edward would be woken at eight and would be sitting down, fully dressed, at 8.30 for breakfast: eggs, bacon and sausage with cereal afterwards if he was still hungry. After breakfast he was taken down to the floor below to see the Queen and then along to his father's study to see Prince Philip if he happened to be around. After tea at the end of the day he would be taken to see his parents again. On Tuesdays, the nights Nanny went to her pottery class, the Queen would make the effort to bath him herself. She might then tuck him into bed and read to him. Philip, blessed with more imagination than his wife, preferred to invent his own bedtime stories.

The programme was virtually the same, wherever they happened to be: Buckingham Palace, Windsor Castle, Sandringham or Balmoral.

For all its apparently timeless routine, though, subtle changes had been taking place. Charles had been brought up by Nanny Helen Lightbody, a no-nonsense Scottish woman who had been recommended to the Edinburghs, as they then were, by Princess Elizabeth's aunt-in-law, Princess Marina of Kent. Eileen Parker, the wife of Prince Philip's Private Secretary Michael, remembers her as 'awfully kind and terribly fair'. In the frequent absence of the Queen, she became Charles's surrogate mother and he adored her.

But Nana, as her young charge called her, was too old-fashioned for Philip's liking. She regarded the nursery as her domain and resented his whirlwind visits which more often than not left his son in tears. She disapproved strongly of his sometimes fierce approach to parenting. She took exception to the way he tried to teach Charles to swim, which was to jump into the Buckingham Palace pool himself, then order his terrified son in after him.

Philip, for his part, felt that Nanny Lightbody was mollycoddling his son. A clash was inevitable and it came aboard the Royal Yacht *Britannia*. In September, 1957, Charles went away to school at Cheam. When he came back at the end of his first term, he discovered to his distress that Nanny Lightbody had been 'retired'.

Control of the nursery then passed to Nanny Lightbody's deputy, Mabel Anderson, who had come into royal service in 1948 at the age of twenty-four after answering an advertisement in a nursery magazine and had first been employed as a nursemaid to Charles. She was the daughter of a Liverpool policeman, who had been killed during an air-raid in the Second World War, and the inevitable Scottish mother. Mrs Parker described her as 'prim and proper' but she was also kind and affectionate and handsome in a tall, sturdy way. While she continued to run her nursery in the traditional royal way, which was according to a strict regime, she had the good sense not to challenge Philip openly, knowing that he did not like his orders questioned.

Prince Philip, Nanny Anderson said, 'was a marvellous father ... he always set aside time to read to them or help them put together those little model toys.' He helped Edward build model ships which adorned the young prince's bedroom.

It was Nanny herself, nicknamed 'Mamba' by Andrew, who had the most say in Edward's day to day life. Despite their efforts to make up for lost opportunities, the Queen and her consort were still away a lot. Even when they were in residence, the demands of royalty meant that Edward could only be sure of seeing his mother at those set times every morning and evening. If she was not busy they would take the nursery corgis, Jolly and Socks, for a walk in the Palace gardens. But even then he had to compete for her attention with his brother Andrew.

His relationship with his grandmother, the Queen Mother, was warm but somewhat distant. The attention she gave depended where the infant stood in the family hierarchy. Marina Ogilvy, daughter of Princess Alexandra, recalled: 'There were an awful lot of things that Sarah [Armstrong-Jones] and Edward would do that Helen [daughter of the Duke of Kent], James [Ogilvy] and I were not involved in.' In 1979, for instance, they accompanied the Queen Mother when she was made Lord Warden of the Cinque Ports and drove down the streets of Dover in a carriage. 'I remember them all sitting in a state coach and we felt rather left out.'

The Queen Mother had always doted on Charles, comforting him when he was upset, providing a soft bulwark against his father's masculine demands. She was also very close to Princess Margaret's son, David Linley. She was always 'perfectly nice', as one member of the Household put it, towards Edward, but she did not make any special effort to see him when he was under the care of his mother, as she would with Charles.

If Edward minded he never showed it. Unlike his rowdy brother Andrew, 'Ed', as he was called by the family and the nursery staff, was a most undemanding child who appeared emotionally well-satisfied with the affection Mabel gave him.

The boys were not as close as public imagination would have them. The more noisy Andrew became, the quieter Edward appeared and Andrew would egg him on to do some forbidden prank then sit back to watch the result. Andrew would subject his brother to some minor bullying, stealing food off his plate, treating him to the odd kick when Mabel's back was turned.

One member of the nursery staff likened them to Laurel and Hardy, with Andrew always up to mischief, especially if it involved making a great deal of noise, with Edward as his foil.

Edward would get his own back by making Andrew appear worse than he really was. If the older boy was late for breakfast, he would be certain to find Edward already sitting at the table, tucking into his scrambled eggs as the clock chimed 8.30am, a picture of cherubic innocence. If it had not been for Edward, Andrew would not have appeared quite so undisciplined.

Another difference was in their attitude to horses. The highlight of Edward's young day soon became his riding lesson. He started almost as soon as he could walk on a shetland called Valkyrie, which he shared with Andrew. The arrangement worked well, but only up to a point. Andrew had developed the painful habit of falling off and quickly developed an aversion to riding. Instead he preferred grooming the pony and putting on its tack; Edward, blessed with a good 'seat' and a natural sense of balance, liked sitting on its back. The problem arose when Edward tried to ride the pony away. This would irritate Andrew who would jealously try and lead it back to the stable and take the harness off again.

'They got along fine, but they are just two totally different people,' a member of the Royal Household explained.

Their four-year age gap only emphasised the contrast in their temperaments. But if the boys were not quite as close as the public, brought up on the notion of a royal family that did almost literally everything together, would have them, Edward was probably the least lonely of the Queen's children.

When Charles was born the notion still persisted that a prince of the blood should be separated from his fellows – for his own good and for the good of the royal family generally. Only by being nurtured in isolation could the majesty of his position be maintained, or so the argument went. That was the way the Queen had been brought up. That was the way her son and heir would be educated, certainly in his early, formative years. By tradition, royal children were joined in their classroom by other children of around the same age. The Queen vetoed that. Charles, she ruled, was still too timorous to face the competition of his contemporaries. Even his sister was barred from his schoolroom at the Palace.

The Queen's cousin, the last Tsar of Russia Nicholas II, had followed a similar policy with regard to his own son, the ill-fated Tsarevich Alexei who was butchered by the Bolsheviks, along with the rest of his family, in a basement in Ekaterinburg in 1918. His tutor, Pierre Gillard, observed that a boy educated in such an isolated way:

> is deprived of that basic principle which plays the main role in developing judgement. He will always feel the lack of that knowledge which is obtained independently of study through life itself, by means of free relationships with his peers, exposure to various influences – sometimes contrary to the views by which he is surrounded, and by the possibility of regular contact and direct observation of people and things. In a word he will be deprived of everything that in the course of time develops intellectual horizons and provides essential knowledge. In such circumstances one needs to be an exceptionally capable person to acquire correct views, a normal way of thinking and the ability to express one's will at the opportune moment. An impenetrable barrier separates such a person from real life and makes it impossible to understand what is happening on the other side of the wall, on which people draw false pictures to amuse and occupy the person in question.

Charles would later say that his mother had made a wise decision regarding his education. Others were not so certain. His governess was Miss Catherine Peebles, another Scots woman. She remembered her young pupil as a 'vague child'. Dermot Morrah, the Arundel Herald Extraordinary who wrote an authorised account of Charles's early life went further and described him as 'a child who had only a vague relationship to the external world'.

Edward's education was altogether more easy-going and companionable. He was spared his elder brother's intellectual and educational isolation and all its inherent dangers. He enjoyed the company of a schoolroom full of children of his own age.

The year he was born, 1964, was an unusually fecund one for the Royal Family. On 29 February of this Leap Year, Princess Alexandra had given birth to a son, James Ogilvy ('I didn't want my son to only have a birthday once every four years – it's bad enough having my own birthday on Christmas Day,' she complained). At the end of April the Duchess of Kent gave birth to Lady Helen Windsor and two days later, on 1 May, Princess Margaret give birth to Lady Sarah Armstrong-Jones. (A fifth child named Mark Lascelles was born to the Queen's cousin, the Earl of Harewood, but as the Earl had yet to marry the mother, his secretary 'Bambi' Tuckwell, the boy was denied a place in the royal pantheon.)

James would accompany Edward to prep school. Helen joined him at Gordonstoun. Sarah became his closest childhood friend. In a family which still preferred to look within itself for fellowship, they provided Edward with a handy group of available playmates.

They all spent Christmas together. 'We would arrive at Windsor on Christmas Eve with our parents and, if we were tiny, we were sent upstairs with nanny. The nannies would have everything organised and they'd go out together with their prams in the park.'

The nannies – Mabel Anderson for Edward and Andrew, Verona Sumner for David and Sarah, Olive Rattle for Marina and James, Mary McPherson for Helen and George – did not always get on. The Windsor nursery was too small to accommodate women used to ruling their own fiefdoms. The tension was particularly marked between the fastidious Nanny Anderson and the equally demanding Nanny Sumner and the nursery atmosphere was one of frosty formality as everyone went about their daily routines.

After nursery tea the nannies would dress their charges in their best clothes and take them down to see their parents. Present opening was always after tea on Christmas Eve and each child had his or her name pinned to a white cloth on their own section of a large table which was divided up with red ribbons and piled high with presents.

'It was all quite wonderful – the tree and the crackers with amazing presents inside,' Marina recalled. The nannies, putting their private antagonisms aside for the moment, enjoyed it as much as the children. 'They would all line up and get their gifts from the Queen.'

The best moment for the children came later. 'We used to pedal our bikes furiously up and down the long green corridor which was lined with glass cabinets filled with Ming vases, and other precious objects,' said Marina. 'David was the ring leader and he would get us all into trouble. I remember he once broke a Ming vase!'

It was decided that James and Sarah, along with Princess Tania of Hanover, granddaughter of one of Prince Philip's sisters, plus any children of members of the Household of a suitable age, would join the prince in the schoolroom in the old nursery wing of Buckingham Palace on the second floor above the Balcony. The rooms, which are now Princess Anne's offices, had been used for the education of royal children since the time of Queen Victoria.

The Queen, who had been so determined to allow Charles to develop by himself, had learned from experience and was now anxious for her youngest son to be educated with as many other children as possible.

The initial plan was for Miss Peebles – known as Mispy, as in 'Miss P' – to continue to take charge of the royal education programme. But in 1968, just a few days before she was scheduled to start, she died.

Anne, who had never developed a rapport any deeper than the ordinary teacher-pupil one with the governess, took her death in her commonsensical stride. Charles, on the other hand, was 'inconsolable'. The poignancy of her final circumstances added to his grief. Mispy had retired to her bedroom in the Palace vastness on Friday night and died, alone and unnoticed. Her body was not discovered for another forty-eight hours.

For the next two months Edward was under the educational wing of Adele Grigg, the governess who worked for the Queen's Lady-in-Waiting, Lady Susan Hussey. Every morning he was driven from the Palace the few short miles to the Husseys' Chelsea house, so becoming the first royal child not to start his education at home. As soon as the Queen engaged Lavinia Keppel just before Christmas, Edward returned to the Palace cloister.

Miss Keppel was a well-regarded choice, though her employment had aroused some inevitable comment amongst the Household for Lavinia was a relation of Alice Keppel, mistress of King Edward VII (and great-grandmother of Camilla Parker Bowles who came to fulfil a similar role for the King's great-great-grandson, Prince Charles).

Unlike Mispy, who had no formal training, Lavinia was a qualified teacher who had once taught at the fashionable Lady Eden's preparatory school in Kensington. She followed a more modern, less formal approach to education than the one favoured by her predecessor, although she continued to follow the basic pattern set down by Catherine Peebles. The day began with prayers and a Bible story; and while the emphasis was still very much on the basic requirements of reading, writing and arithmetic, it always included physical education of some kind.

In the afternoon there were the occasional outings to the London museums. The party of royal children went unrecognised, for since the balcony appearance and the publication of the Beaton photographs very little had been seen of the young prince, even less of Lady Sarah, and absolutely nothing of James Ogilvy. In the absence of anything to latch on to, interest had died away. That was about to change – partly by chance, but more pertinently, by design. For the Royal Family were about to expose themselves to public scrutiny as never before.

In the autumn of 1968 *Paris Match*, the French photo magazine, published a series of family snaps of Edward as a new-born baby, propped up in bed with his mother, his brother Andrew on the counterpane beside her. In the picture taken by Anne, Philip and Charles are kneeling on the floor beside them; in the one taken by Philip it is Anne and Charles who are at the bedside. (Anne's is much the better photograph.) They were delightful, informal – and stolen.

It was not until a year later that it was discovered that a free marketeer in the commercial processing laboratory where the film had been sent for developing was making an extra set of prints to sell to the continental press. This loophole in royal security was immediately closed. By then, however, the photographs had been seen by millions. *Life* magazine in America bought them. In Britain the *Daily Express*, under the guise of providing its readers with a service, had plastered the picture Anne had taken across its broadsheet front page.

'Their very informality cannot but add to the public affection for the Queen as a person,' the accompanying blurb cooed.

Then, to cover its moral back, the editorial stated: 'While it was never the Queen's intention that these informal photographs should have been circulated, their world-wide publication outside of Britain has created an anomaly – which can only be resolved by letting the British people see them.'

It concluded: 'They are probably the most delightful pictures of the Royal Family ever taken. The Daily Express publishes them, confident that it is only fitting that the British people should share a picture series that will catch the interest of the world.'

It did just that – and the Royal Family was appalled. It was a violation of their privacy, a gross intrusion into their family life. There was also the Sovereign's dignity to consider: it was believed by many inside the Palace that photographs of the Queen in bed would detract from her majesty.

Two decades later when similar photographs of the Duchess of York's daughter Princess Beatrice were published in the *Sun*, the Queen proved that there was nothing to stop her resorting to law. She sued and the *Sun* paid an undisclosed sum to charity for committing a 'flagrant breach of copyright'. In 1968, however, the Royal Family was not prepared to exercise its legal muscle, preferring to hide behind the legal illusion that for some unspecified reason it could not 'answer back'. There was sound sense to this approach. The involvement of Edward VII, when Prince of Wales, in a number of salacious court cases had done nothing for the prestige of the Crown. By keeping well away from any similar embroilments, his descendents were better able to keep regal face.

In part, though, this was also policy drawn up out of fear. The bedrock of deference upon which the Royal Family had rested for most of the twentieth century was being replaced by the kind of fickle adulation more appropriate to the entertainment industry. The publication of the Edward photographs was symptomatic of that trend. The public was now starting to claim the right to know anything and everything they wanted about their reigning Sovereign and her kin. Aware of this change in attitude but unsure how best to react to it, this was not an intrusion the Royal Family cared for. When Philip talked about having a family 'in the public eye', he meant at times and in circumstances of its choosing. The Firm was used to stage-managing public interest; it was understandably disconcerted by the way the audience was starting to direct the show.

It was to bring the situation under control, and at the same time to emphasise her constitutional relevance, that the Queen took the momentous decision to allow television cameras to look into her life.

The idea was the brainchild of William Heseltine, the Australian who had joined the Palace staff in 1960 on the recommendation of his Prime Minister, Sir Robert Menzies, and who in 1968 became the Queen's press secretary.

Before his appointment the Palace had maintained a less-is-better approach to public relations. When, for instance, George V's Private Secretary, Lord Stamfordham, suggested that he should try and look a little more cheerful on public occasions, the King replied: 'We sailors never smile on duty.'

Heseltine argued forcefully that smiles, along with walk-abouts and 'photo opportunities' had become essential tools of the royal trade in the modern, media-dominated age when the very notion of monarchy was under increasingly critical examination. A sympathetic, carefully-made documentary, he insisted, could only work in the family's favour. The 105-minute film was called *Royal Family* and, according to Heseltine, it 'enlarged and subtly changed the public's ideas of what the Queen and her family are really like'.

It certainly did that, though not in the way Heseltine might have hoped. The idea came in part from the television programme about the White House arranged when President John F. Kennedy and his wife Jackie were in residence. The American presidency, however, is by constitutional definition a self-renewing institution which every four or, at the latest, every eight years offers up a new First Family, to be dissected and fawned over in equal measure.

The Royal Family, on the other hand, is based on continuity. There is no finality to what it does; it must bear the consequences of its mistakes for years and sometimes decades afterwards and the decision to go ahead with *Royal Family* was bound to have a far-reaching effect. It had an immediate impact on the popularity of the Queen and the Family and the reaction was positive. But by going for the PR option, the Royal Family was surrendering itself to the vagaries of public taste. If they really thought that the programme would contain public interest, they miscalculated badly. It did precisely the opposite. It has been called 'the most fantastic piece of eavesdropping of all time' and it spawned a multi-million-pound business, employing thousands of people – some honest and well informed, many no more than journalistic medicine men trading a charlatan's potion of innuendo and lies. And no amount of stonewalling, official denials and charm offensives could get the business back on a sensible course.

In 1986 William Heseltine, soon to be a knight, was elevated to the post of Private Secretary, tacit acknowledgement, as *The Times* pointed out, that public relations had 'moved from the fringe to the centre of the Crown's function'.

Royal Family, meanwhile, went on to earn several million pounds in today's money in world-wide sales. By another reckoning, many believe that it cost the Royal Family control over its destiny.

It certainly had a profound effect on Edward.

Filming on the joint BBC-ITN project began in July 1968 and carried through to April 1969. For weeks on end an eight-man camera crew provided an animated background to his childhood. The crew were suitably well-bred – the assistant soundman was a Bonham-Carter. It was none the less an adventurous change for a boy who up until then had been cosseted in royalty's ivory tower, only allowed to mix with obsequious employees or carefully vetted contemporaries all of whom belonged to the 'right' background of Court and Family.

Richard Cawston, the award-winning head of BBC Television documentary programmes who made *Royal Family* recalled

Prince Edward's great interest in what the crew was doing. It was shared by his brother.

Said Cawston: 'Prince Andrew's first question when I started on the film was "How do you like being a film director?"

'When I explained to him a bit and showed him some of the gadgets, he looked at me impishly and said: "I'd like to be one myself." '

As it turned out, it was Edward who chose to make the media, and the competitive world of television production in particular, his adult business. It would be overstating the case to argue that this early exposure to showbusiness in its widest sense provided Edward with the inspiration for his future career. At the same time, the coincidence is too obvious to overlook – by the time he turned five years old, twenty per cent of his life had been spent with a television camera at his shoulder.

He had watched the early playbacks and that had helped to shape his sense of self-awareness. That in turn had taught him self-control. In that memorable scene filmed at Sandringham when the string on Charles's cello broke and whipped his neck, Edward was about to cry, then remembered the television cameras and thought better of it. He was on his way to discovering what every actor feels; that in playing a part, be it on stage or before a television camera, he is able to give a definition to his life which may be denied him in reality.

It was a performance that undoubtedly captured the imagination of the estimated 28 million who watched the programme's first screening on BBC in June 1969. They saw Edward throwing snowballs, going on picnics and playing with puppies, helping to decorate the Christmas tree and buying sweets at the village shop out of his pocket money.

They saw the Queen point at a picture in an old photograph album and enquire, 'Who's that?'

'Queen Victoria?' Edward asked.

'No,' the Queen replied. 'Queen Mary. That's Gan-gan.' It was living history of the most syrupy yet endearing kind. Jack Gould, writing in the *New York Times*, noted: 'In scenes of Queen Elizabeth II at the dinner table with Prince Philip, Prince Charles and Princess Anne, or on a family picnic with Prince Edward and Prince Andrew, one sees an identifiable family unit reflecting a diversity of personalities and interest. The human equation comes through.'

The *Daily Telegraph*, more succinctly, observed: 'Prince Edward, as unselfconscious as any five-year-old, is inclined to steal the show.'

It is a poignant comment on his young life that this was the only show that Edward *was* allowed to steal for some time to come.

Three

Boyhood

AT THE AGE of eleven Edward took the starring role of Mole in his school's production of *Toad of Toad Hall*. The experience remains fresh in his memory.

'In fact, the only lines I can remember of any play at all are those first lines I had to speak on stage – since then I have forgotten everything else,' he recalled.

They were: 'Scrape and scratch and scrabble and scrooge.'

His voice became animated at the recollection. For a moment the decades peeled away and he was a young boy again, back on stage at his preparatory school. 'I was below stage, below a trap door and all the audience saw was a completely empty stage and all they heard was, "Scrape and scratch and scrabble and scrooge."

'Then suddenly up I pop, and there I was, right in the middle of the stage!'

The play was produced by Chris Black, a young South African on the teaching staff of Heatherdown preparatory school near Ascot where Edward had been sent at the age of eight, clutching a tiny white teddy bear.

It was Edward's first proper theatrical production and he loved it. His headmaster, James Edwards, recalled: 'He was the first actor on stage and there was a round of applause to greet him.'

Jill Holland, who was the 27-year-old assistant matron in Edward's house at the time, recalled: 'His outfit was made of black velvet – he was black all over.' On his head he wore a balaclava helmet. The little face peering out was painted to resemble the subterranean hero of Kenneth Grahame's anthropomorphic paeon to Edwardian England.

The audience was certainly captive but none the less appeared genuinely to enjoy it. The other important parts were taken by Nicholas Tate as Toad, Andrew Wills as Badger and Alexander Cameron as Rat and together they brought a schoolboy zest to the production which had them rolling in the aisles – in one case quite literally. Said Edwards: 'I remember Wills's younger brother was sitting on the aisle in the third row. He was about nine and he laughed so much he fell off his chair and lay in the aisle absolutely convulsed. The Queen's face!' On this occasion the Queen *was* amused.

Also in the audience was Princess Alexandra's daughter, Marina Ogilvy, whose brother James was also a pupil at the school. She too remembered enjoying the play and her cousin Edward's performance. He was spirited and confident and so very different from the shy youngster who had arrived at the school three years before in September 1972.

As Jill Holland recalled: 'He was homesick to begin with. He found it a bit daunting.' He went to bed at night clutching his little white teddy very tightly.

Charles had found the transition from the security of home to the altogether more austere surroundings of boarding school desperately difficult. Painfully shy, he found it hard to make friends (shyness, he would later observe, drawing on his own unhappy experience, 'is often a disability . . . it isn't only those who are confined to a wheelchair who are disabled'). His greatest friend was also a teddy bear but there the similarity ended. For Charles, the unhappiness of those first few weeks at prep school was a harbinger for the rest of his schooldays; for Edward it was no more than the reorientation experienced by all boys sent away from home at an early age. He was certainly better equipped to deal with it than his open-hearted but sad elder brother had been. He had been well-prepared; he had been to the school several times before with Mabel Anderson to watch his brother play rugby and cricket. The Queen had seen to that. It was part of her plan.

Following that period of early learning in the schoolroom at Buckingham Palace, he was sent to Gibbs, a pre-preparatory school in Kensington. He was joined there by James Ogilvy who, without his infant knowledge, had been assigned the role of Edward's shadow and would then accompany him to Heatherdown. It was, everyone agreed, to the advantage of both to have a ready-made playmate to help them along the path of their education. Something similar had been attempted with Charles but the arrangement had been a less than outstanding success – Norton Knatchbull, Earl Mountbatten's grandson and heir presumptive who was given the assignment of looking after Charles at Gordonstoun was a year older and a class ahead and was understandably more interested in getting on with his own life than playing nursemaid to his gawky cousin.

This time around the arrangement fared much better. Edward and Ogilvy were the same age and facing the same problems at the same time. They got on well together and they enjoyed the same things. Like Edward, Ogilvy also took an interest in dramatics, although it was Edward, whose talent others have always been quick to notice, who took the leading role in the end of term play at Gibbs. It was a thirty-minute production entitled *Lost Property*, and Edward played the part of Tom, the son of humble parents who discovers he can grant the wishes of the other village folk by wearing his magic school cap.

Would that such sorcery had been available a few months later when Edward, son of the most elevated of parents, was driven up the Heatherdown drive which was overgrown with rhododendrons. He was deposited at the red-brick Victorian house and given into the care of James Edwards and his Anglo-Russian wife, Barbara. Gibbs had been a day school and each night Edward had returned to the Palace that was his home (when the teacher had asked everyone to draw a picture of the house they lived in, Edward had drawn a castle). But now his infancy was at its end and the comforts of home, nanny and nursery were about to be put behind him. He was eight years old, and according to the custom of Britain's upper classes, he was sent away to school.

The first day can be a traumatic one. The Queen remembered Charles 'shuddering' with fear on the journey to his prep school. Anne was similarly afflicted; the car that delivered her to her first school had to stop to allow her to be physically sick. But

Edward, like his brother Andrew, was more used to the companionship of people his own age and was not stricken by quite the same terrors. His mother told him to be brave and he was.

It was a still nervous little boy who climbed into bed with his teddy on that first night. For all its apparent severity, the system provides an organised outlet for boyish energies and most pupils come to like their prep schools and look back with the fondest of recollections on their days there. Time lends its own enchantment to memories of pillow fights in the dormitories and midnight feasts and adventures in woods and along river banks and Edward talks affectionately of his five years at Heatherdown. But that was later; he had to settle in first and, as Jill Holland recalled, that took several weeks.

'Edward was very reserved when he first came,' she said.

His bedroom which he shared with two other boys was in a special new-boys' house called Heatherlea, a hundred yards away from the main school. His uniform was black blazer with red piping and, as an extra touch, white piping on the button hole. They wore long flannel trousers in winter, shorts in summer, corduroys and fishneck sweaters in their spare time. Said Edwards: 'The boys had their own rugs and teddies; they were very much encouraged to have things to remind them of home.' The prince's rug was in a red tartan on one side and grey on the other. Edward was always very neat. Jill Holland remembered: 'During the term it was always on its red side. At half-term he would fold the blanket to its grey side rather like a flag.'

James Ogilvy was a new boy with him. Another cousin there was the Duke of Kent's son, the Earl of St Andrews. It was to his brother Andrew that he first turned, though. 'He would spend his break time and his free time watching Prince Andrew's every move playing football,' Jill said. Edward, she recalled, 'stood with his hands firmly behind his back'.

It may have been hero worship. More likely it was a little boy, away from home for the first time, seeking out the reassurance of the familiar. But whichever, it did not last long. As Edwards pointed out: 'They obviously saw each other and chatted together but Andrew was four years older and four years at prep school makes a big difference.'

Edward quickly found his own feet. He was, the headmaster observed, a very independent boy who was capable of looking after himself and expected no special privileges. 'He didn't need anybody,' Edwards said. 'He paddled his own canoe.' If he was ever homesick after those first few days, he did not show it.

Teachers remember him as being on the quiet side, but tougher than he looked; a good rugger player who did not dominate his schoolmates but was not inhibited in making friends, as his brother Charles had been.

He was not outstanding academically but he coped well enough. It was soon apparent that he had an artistic eye but he was also his father's son and developed a particular liking for science. Frank Wilson, who ran the new-boys' house, was also the science master and every term he appointed two lab boys whom he could trust to prepare special experiments. One term Edward was awarded the responsibility and was allowed to put on a science show on sports day. He chose to give a demonstration of the instant freezing powers of liquid oxygen. Edwards remembered: 'I can see Edward now, in his long white coat and looking like a cricket umpire, dipping a strawberry into the liquid oxygen on the end of a long piece of string and taking it out and putting it on the desk and hitting it with a hammer and then it splintered!'

Andrew's sports days were not always so successful. Marina Ogilvy remembers an obstacle race in which each contestant had to wriggle through the rungs of a ladder. 'Andrew was a bit too fat and got stuck and his detective had to pull him out,' she recalled. Edward joined in the laughter at his brother's expense.

The atmosphere, Marina recalled, was 'really nice. I'll never forget the smell of the place – pencil sharpenings, sausages and boys.'

It was a perfectly normal childhood of the kind enjoyed by thousands of other boys from well-to-do families. The fact that he was royal was always a shadow in the background, however. At the Queen's express wish the masters called him Prince Edward while the other boys were all addressed by their surnames. And while the others would be allowed out on prescribed days, Edward would periodically be whisked away, to appear shortly afterwards on television at some state occasion or other. Princess Anne's wedding to Captain Mark Phillips was one such event. Edward was a page and his headmaster gave him some last minute instruction while he was waiting for the car to come and collect him.

'He was very excited,' Edwards recalled. 'He was walking up and down the dormitory passage practising the pace he ought to go down the aisle at. I was standing watching him and saying, "A bit faster – no, that's a bit slow!"'

The other boys took Edward and his royal relations in their stride and turned their names into nicknames. They were known as Pran, Stan, Og and Pred. Pran stood for Prince Andrew; Stan was short for St Andrews; James Ogilvy was Og; and Edward was Pred, as in Prince Ed.

'The other boys must have known who he was, but I honestly don't think they thought of him as different,' Edwards said.

If they did not, the prince himself soon came to realise that he was not the same as other boys; that he was always on show, always being scrutinised. It was a gradual dawning and it affected his behaviour. 'Edward was always more "royal" than his brother,' noted the headmaster's wife, Barbara, whom the boys called Ra Ra. 'He was very conscious of doing exactly the right thing. If he was presented with a whole lot of knives and forks, for instance, he would sit there and watch very carefully to see which one you picked up before he would do it.'

It was part of the intricate process of growing up royal in order to *be* royal and the Queen took a personal interest in his progress. Once so aloof, she had now become involved in those most mundane of motherly concerns – was her son doing well, was he fitting in, did he have friends? The enforced isolation from such ordinary considerations which had been the mark of her own childhood and had been carried through into the early education of her eldest son had been discarded. More; she became one of those mothers who always insist on coming to see her sons perform, no matter how trivial or seemingly unimportant the event.

Said James: 'She came to every show, sports day, play and

carol service that we had. You could guarantee if there was a show on she would be there.'

According to the records, the Queen missed only one, when Edward was playing the part of Saul in *The Boy David* – and then only because she was on a state visit to Australia. The Queen Mother came in her stead. 'Over nine years that is marvellous family support,' said Edwards.

It was Philip, when still the dynamic young naval officer, who had taken it upon himself to map out the overall strategy for their children's education, but it was now the Queen who had taken charge of the tactical application. With Charles and Anne, the Queen had been a distant figure, unable to shed her majesty, always remote. In those early days of parenthood it was Philip who was the more tactile of the two. He could be brusque and severe, particularly to Charles who was frightened of his father, but if he was in residence he would never sit down to dinner without first going up to the nursery to say goodnight. When the Queen and her consort were going out on an official engagement, Miss Peebles or Nanny Anderson would take the children to a window overlooking the garden entrance to wave goodbye. Before she got into the car, the Queen, resplendent in evening gown and tiara, would look up at the two small faces pressed against the window-pane and give a discreet little wave. Philip, on the other hand, would always blow a kiss.

The Sovereign's regal mantle was not allowed to slip, even at bath time. When the Queen walked in everyone had to stand. The Queen would then sit down on a straight-backed chair and watch her offspring at play.

Experience had done much to leaven the Queen's attitude. Only twenty-five when she inherited the throne, she had been overwhelmed by the responsibility and, under the stress of her office, had lost touch with her maternal priorities. By the time Edward made his appearance, however, she had reigned for over a decade. She was confident in her position and determined to make the most of what would certainly be her last venture into motherhood.

She could still be an intimidating presence. She was still the awesomely remote woman in whose presence world leaders, generals and lions of industry instinctively genuflect. When she ventured into the nursery she was quite likely to be accompanied by her page and a footman. There were other left-overs from the old routine. It was only after they had breakfasted, for example, that Andrew and later Edward were allowed downstairs to see their mother who, if they were in London, they were unlikely to encounter again until they were ushered into her presence in the evening. But if the outward formula was still the same, the atmosphere was much more relaxed. 'For the first time she was able to really enjoy her children,' one of her staff recalled.

Edwards remembered: 'Prince Philip appeared but not as much as the Queen. She determined and controlled their early schooling. I discussed their school reports with her rather than him.'

It was the Queen who had opted for Heatherdown because it was close to Windsor Castle and because so many of her friends and relations would send their sons there and she took pleasure in the practical minutiae of first Andrew's and then Edward's school life. Nanny Anderson would collect them at half-term, the end of term and on those two Sundays in between when they were allowed out, but it was almost always the Queen who brought them back, in the green Vauxhall station-wagon she drove herself. (Only on formal occasions such as sports day did she arrive in a chauffeur-driven limousine.) And when she got there, she liked nothing better than to pop into the headmaster's study for a cup of tea and and an informal chat. There was no ceremony. On one occasion when the police lodge at Windsor had failed to ring through with the tip-off that she was on her way, she announced her arrival by poking her head round the door and enquiring of the stunned headmaster who was in the middle of sampling some particularly fine Cheddar cheese with Princess Alexandra: 'Am I allowed in?'

It was not just the confidence to do what she wanted that the Queen had gained from her years on the Throne. She had also become well-practised in dealing with Prime Ministers of the calibre of Sir Winston Churchill and world statesmen as prickly as France's Charles de Gaulle and that had given her a rare understanding of people and personalities. She now applied that experience to her own children.

'She knew their faults and their shortcomings – she really did know them terribly well,' said James. 'Some parents who give their children over to nannies sometimes hardly know their children at all. But she did.' She took a close and persistent interest in their behaviour. One thing she absolutely insisted on was good manners and it showed.

'They both had beautiful manners,' Edwards recalled. It came with what seemed like an in-built sense of decorum. 'They were always so clean and tidy. They would come in out of a great storm with their hair still looking tidy. And their shirts seemed to stay tucked in more than the average boy – very odd. Edward was one of those children who seemed to be able to control life.'

He was also robust of health and hardly saw the inside of the sick bay in the five years he was at Heatherdown. 'He was extremely tough,' said James. But not over-boisterous – that inherent sense of what was right and permissible seemed to hold Edward back from the worst excesses of boyhood.

'Andrew was quite different,' Mrs Edwards said. 'He would hammer at the bathroom door and say, "Can I come in?" I'd reply, "No, I'm washing my hair," and he would answer, "Oh, come on, let me in!" Edward would never do that.'

It was also Andrew, who in manhood gained the reputation of royal Romeo, who first made friends with James Edwards's stepdaughter, Alexandra. (Alexandra would later marry gardener and author George Plumptre whose previous dates included Lady Diana Spencer, the future Princess of Wales.) He taught her to stick her tongue out; indeed, so rumbustious was their play at times that she once punched him in the face and made his nose bleed.

Edward's relationship with Alexandra was an altogether more gentle one; the pair practised butterfly kisses together. He could be a bit of a flirt at times, as Mrs Edwards noted, but when she read to the boys their bedtime story, it was Andrew who would cuddle up next to her and lean his bodyweight against her, while Edward preferred to sit a short distance away. Said Mrs Edwards: 'Andrew was like a labrador puppy – muddy paws everywhere. Edward was far more dignified.'

But if Andrew was rowdier, he too stopped short of the sort of ill-discipline that in those days resulted in corporal punishment. The penalty at Heatherdown was a spanking on the backside with the back of a hairbrush. It was never administered to either Andrew or Edward; there was never any need.

If Edward ever looked like overstepping the mark, his detective, the Scottish-born Andrew Merrylees, was on hand to steer him back on course – quietly, with the most subtle of hints. He stood over six feet tall, was well-built, good looking and spoke with a pronounced Scottish burr. It is easy to picture this bluff policeman, who was assigned to look after the prince when Edward was eight years old and stayed at his side for the next eighteen years, as a substitute father figure. Those who observed the relationship at close quarters saw it more as the 'young laird and his trusted ghillie', those Highland attendants who are allowed to advise and correct their charges and do so without overstepping the mark into familiarity. He was very fond of Edward but always respectful and if he did have to correct him, he did so in the most tactful of ways.

Heatherdown had grown accustomed to royal detectives. 'The boys treated them just like another master,' said Edwards. The detectives, in their turn, settled well into the easy routine of prep school life; Andrew's first detective married the school's assistant housekeeper. ('That was frightfully irritating for me because the Palace could produce another detective, but I had to find a new housekeeper!' Edwards jested.) His successor, Bob Roberts, was a keen cricketer who coached the First Eleven. Andrew Merrylees was a good rugby player who helped with the training and was responsible for weaning Edward off soccer (a game, the prince would later say, only suitable for 'playing on village greens') and on to his own sport.

He was less of a help on the ski slopes of St Anton, at least in the beginning. Edward was not the only one on the nursery slopes that first year. So was Merrylees; he too had never skied before.

Edward was nine when he first ventured on to the pistes of Austria. He was part of the school party James and his wife took out every winter. Edward, more in Anne's than Charles's athletic mould, learnt quickly and soon became a proficient skier. As indeed did Merrylees who, in his thirty-two years as a policeman never rose above the rank of Police Constable but had an enjoyable career none the less. Edward, with his detective always in attendance, so enjoyed his skiing holiday with the Edwardses that he continued to join the Heatherdown party throughout his time at Gordonstoun and on into his Cambridge years.

After the kidnap attempt on Princess Anne in the Mall in 1974 there was talk that those ski holidays might have to be cancelled for security reasons. Closer cooperation with the Austrian police was deemed vital. Merrylees suggested that the ski guides, who had the greatest knowledge of the slopes, might offer better protection.

'I asked how many people we could call on in an emergency and he replied, "About 2,000!"' James said. With that kind of free security force, it was decided that St Anton was about as safe a place as any and the holidays were allowed to continue.

Edward and his party always took a private instructor who led them down the lesser-frequented routes and eventually, once Merrylees' skills were up to it, into the deep, off-piste powder snow. None of the other tourists had any idea who was in their midst – in all the years they went there, neither Andrew nor Edward were ever captured by the photographers.

To ensure their anonymity, both boys travelled under assumed names. Prince Andrew became 'Andrew Pope' because, the headmaster explained, 'there was someone called Pope who had once tried to set fire to Windsor Castle, so I though it was appropriate.'

Continuing with the ecclesiastical theme, though a notch or two down the clerical pecking order scale, Prince Edward was booked in as 'Edward Bishop'.

The headmaster had taken no such precautions with his other well-connected pupils and one year, upon arriving at Heathrow, they were accosted by the airport photographer.

Edwards recalled: 'He came running up, cameras around his neck, and asked: "Are you travelling with Lord Mountbatten?" I said in a sense, yes. He asked: "Is he here? Can you point him out?"

'I had the Mountbatten boys in the party with us – George, the Marquis of Milford Haven, and his younger brother Lord Ivar Mountbatten and they were over bv the bookstall. I hadn't thought to put Lord Ivar Mountbatten under an assumed name and the photographer had seen it on the flight list and thought it was Lord Mountbatten of Burma. He asked me to point Lord Mountbatten out to him and I pointed towards the bookstall. The photographer said, "I can't see him." I said: "He's the chap there, reading a comic!"

'The photographer said "I don't understand." I said: "He's Lord Mountbatten, Lord *Ivar* Mountbatten." He said something about what a wasted journey it had been and I said I was terribly sorry, that it was one of those things. And I had two small boys standing on either side of me, who were absolutely convulsed with laughter.'

They were 'Andrew Pope' and 'Ed Bishop'. The photographer ambled off without giving them so much as a second glance. This was one royal picture story Fleet Street missed. It was not the only one.

When Edward went salmon fishing at the age of eleven in the River Dee with one of the Balmoral ghillies, a photographer suddenly appeared on the bank to record the event. For the rest, though, and despite the increase in interest in the Royal Family, he enjoyed a boyhood remarkably untroubled by press attention. Whereas Charles only had to kick a ball for it to be 'news', Edward was able to enjoy his sport without an audience of journalists scribbling on the touchline.

There was no doubting who he was, though. His Heatherdown contemporary Jonathan Holmes-Smith recalled one rugby match. Edward was playing hooker. 'There was a ruck going on, the ball flew up, and I ran towards it. A little blond boy was lying on his back clutching it and as I ran at him, I got him in the neck with my knee. He started crying his eyes out. The game stopped, everyone gathered around and when he was all right, they all clapped him for being brave and said, "Well played the Prince!" I hadn't realised until then it was Edward.'

Edward eventually made the cricket Eleven and the First Fifteen at rugby and enjoyed himself.

'They were happy times,' Jill Holland remembered.

Edward also did well in other areas. He worked his way up through the school's prefect hierarchy from dormitory captain to house captain, then school captain and finally joint senior school captain. He was also well able to pass his Common

Entrance which would have seen him into any of Britain's top public schools. This was one area in which Prince Philip's writ still applied, however.

Over 65 per cent of Heatherdown's boys went on at thirteen to nearby Eton. Both the Queen and her Private Secretary, Sir Martin (later Lord) Charteris, the future Provost of Eton, felt that Britain's most famous public school might best suit the young Edward. The Queen Mother certainly thought so. Philip would have none of that. He took the view that what had been good enough for him was good enough for his sons. He explained: 'This is something better understood in this country than almost anywhere else – that people very frequently do what their fathers have done. People say, "Oh, he has gone because his father went," and there is no further argument.'

Underlying that seemingly straightforward explanation were substrata of resentment and frustration. Philip, the impoverished scion of the deposed royal house of Greece, had never been fully accepted by the British Establishment which regarded him – and not without reason – as a pushy interloper with disturbingly radical ideas for streamlining and modernising the monarchy.

Philip, for his part, held the old-fashioned power structure of British society in barely disguised contempt. Forced to make his own way in life, he believed that people should be judged on what they achieved rather than on who they were. He regarded the old-fashioned public schools, which Eton epitomised, with suspicion. To him they smacked of unearned and all too often unwarranted privilege – the breeding ground for the elitist old boys' network of which he was not a member. He believed that Gordonstoun – newly established and innovative in method with its accent on individual development and community service rather than team sports and Classics – provided a more rounded education.

Philip had been one of the first thirty pupils at the school Kurt Hahn had established in 1934 on the windswept coast of the Moray Firth. Charles had followed him there and Andrew after him. Now it was Edward's turn.

Four

Private Life Public School

EDWARD HAD AS normal a time at Gordonstoun as a British prince could have. He hated it to begin with, grew to like it, came to thoroughly enjoy it and by the end was glad to leave.

'A school is a school,' he sagaciously pointed out, 'and I don't agree with the statement that schooldays are the happiest days of your life.' It was, he concluded, only one chapter in his life. It was none the less a most important one, as events would prove.

His Gordonstoun 'training' gave him the confidence to pursue his own convictions and that would have a dramatic effect on his later life. He learnt how to mix with people from different backgrounds and developed his love of the theatre.

He was not particularly enthused by all of the Gordonstoun challenges, however, and that too would have significant consequences.

Like his elder brother, the Prince of Wales, he rose to be Guardian, as the Gordonstoun head boy is called, but there the similarity ends. Edward was reasonably popular, made friends, enjoyed his sport, learnt how to get on with girls and had his interest in the stage encouraged. Charles detested the place. He was miserable and lonely and bullied.

Initially Edward also had his problems settling in. He was staying at Balmoral in the days leading up to the start of his first term. When the time came for him to leave, he plaintively said, to the Queen Mother 'Oh dear, the holidays are over, I don't really want to go to school.' She replied, affectionately but in a tone that denied a tearful response: 'Darling, all good things come to an end.'

A member of the Royal Household recalled: 'He really did not like it at first.' But that was just about the extent of it. There was absolutely no truth in the story that he had to be dragged screaming to the car waiting to take him there. His concerns were really no worse than those faced by almost every other young teenager sent away into the intimidating, cold and competitive surroundings of a British public school. Prince Andrew and Princess Anne had been through it. So of course had Prince Charles, the first of the Queen's children to be sent away to school. The other two had quickly settled in. Charles, however, was one of those unfortunate boys who never quite managed to become fully assimilated. He was set upon throughout his time there. His life at the school, he wrote, was 'absolute hell . . . especially at night'.

The school Edward encountered was a very different place from the one the Prince of Wales had known. Charles left in 1967. Edward did not arrive until ten years later and by then the school was fully co-educational with equal numbers of girls and boys. Other, more subtle, but no less important changes had also taken place and they were to do with attitude.

Gordonstoun had been founded by the German-born educationalist Kurt Hahn on the idea verging on an ideal that, as the school motto had it, *Plus est en vous*, 'There is more in you.' James Thomas, Edward's housemaster at Duffus House, explained: 'The object is to identify the strengths and the weaknesses of the people who come here and accentuate the strengths and point out the weaknesses so that they can learn to deal with them.'

Like any system, it is only as good as the people administering it and, with a few notable exceptions, the quality of some of the key staff at Gordonstoun in Charles's time was not all it should have been. The boys, too, were quite unlike anyone Charles had encountered before. Situated in what, before the age of cheap air travel, was an out of the way part of Scotland, it had become, as one disillusioned master observed, a reform school for 'the laird's idiot son'. A notable number of the pupils had failed to gain the Common Entrance pass level necessary to gain a place in most other schools. Many were hearty to the point of boorishness. And while the school certainly had its good points, most particularly in its emphasis on community service, it was none the less rough and crude and ill-equipped for dealing with the heir to the throne. Both Prince Charles and the school found his presence there hard going.

Hahn, a Jew driven out of Germany by the Nazis, attached great importance to the need to 'teach the protection of the weak, the recognition of the rights of the less fortunate and the worth of the simple human life'.

Life was certainly simple enough. Windmill Lodge where Charles was 'incarcerated', as he put it, was little more than a glorified Portakabin. The floors of the dormitories and common rooms were either bare boards or covered with cheap linoleum. Curtains were an occasional afterthought; the windows were left open most nights, even if it was snowing outside. After a night being lashed by the elements, a morning run was a way of warming up.

There was not much 'protection of the weak' readily to hand, however. Boys were left to fend for themselves and Charles, a kind and sensitive youngster who, as an infant, had apologised to his stuffed toys when he knocked them over, had yet to learn how to stand up for himself. After lights out the other boys in his dormitory would mount raiding parties across the room to hit the heir to the throne with their slippers as he lay cowering in his bed, too frightened to sleep. He wrote: 'It's such a HOLE this place! . . . People in this House are unbelievable. They have hardly any manners worth mentioning and have the foulest natures of any people I know.'

Only in matters pertaining to sex, it seemed, were Hahn's philosophical notions put into effective practice. The founder of Gordonstoun never married and had a distaste bordering on fear of anything sexual. Convinced that the West was becoming a 'sick civilisation', much of Hahn's programme was designed 'to kindle on the threshold of puberty non-poisonous passions which act as guardians during the dangerous years'.

What that meant in practice was that boys and girls were kept strictly segregated. During Charles's time, one of the kitchen maids came to a private sex-for-cash arrangement with one of the senior boys; a couple of years after Charles left one leading sixth-former left the school earlier than he had planned after being caught in bed with two more of the maids. A few of the more adventurous boys found girlfriends in Elgin, a twenty-mile round bicycle ride away. (As well as the effort there was also the risk; as part of the rules introduced to protect Prince Charles, Elgin had been placed out of bounds and any boy found there without permission faced being gated and, for a second offence, expulsion.) Such transgressions were very much the exception, however, and none of them involved the Prince of Wales. For the majority of the school's 400 boys and for Charles in particular, girls were a mysterious, unknown quantity.

The next decade wrought an enormous transformation. Charles's headmaster, Robert Chew, retired the year after the prince left and took a lot of his old-fashioned ideas with him. Hahn himself died in 1974. As a consequence of the publicity Charles's presence there had inevitably attracted, Gordonstoun ceased to be an educational backwater and started to attract pupils from a wider range of backgrounds, including many from overseas. Improvements in communication and travel made it easier for parents and pupils to get to Morayshire. New and much better facilities were built, including a chapel, gymnasium and swimming pool. New masters came in, fired with an enthusiasm to get back to the principles that Hahn had originally espoused, but tailored to meet changing social expectations. (The military, for instance, is no longer the career option it was in Charles's youth; the Empire it was raised to defend has vanished.) The food was improved beyond measure; where before it had consisted of the likes of haggis, black pudding and the occasional slices of desiccated lamb, it now comprised a nutritious and well-prepared selection of hot and cold dishes served in the newly-constructed refectory. Sport was no longer the organised activity it had been; the choice was extended beyond rugby to include soccer, squash and, provided you could get a quorum together, just about any other activity that appealed. As Edward himself observed: 'I don't think Gordonstoun's as tough as it used to be.'

Some things did remain the same, though. The pupils were still required to do a compulsory morning run which, at Duffus, took Edward out of the back door, eighty yards down the drive to a big tree and then back again. That was followed by a traditional cold shower (but only after a hot one; the rigours of the Gordonstoun regime were not always as spartan as legend would have it, even in Charles's day).

What had changed was the general ambience and that was primarily due to the most noteworthy change of all – the introduction of girls. As Thomas put it, it gave the school 'balance'. 'With girls being here it is easier to put on a play, for instance,' he said. 'If you have got boys only, you have either got to liaise with local schools and bring girls in or use staff or you have got to dress boys up as girls which is diabolical – I don't think one would dream of doing that now.'

There were other advantages. Boys and girls were now able to meet and get to know each other in a natural way, something that the Prince of Wales had never been able to do. For some this was an opportunity not to be missed. Edward's cousin, George, who had became the fourth Marquis of Milford Haven in 1970 at the age of eight upon the death of his father, had preceded him there from Heatherdown. A handsome fellow with a goodly share of the Mountbatten looks and charm, he had a number of girlfriends whom he entertained in the Services Centre where the school fire engine was garaged.

Milford Haven would later marry Sarah, the Millfield-educated daughter of George Walker, the Billingsgate fish porter turned international business tycoon. Others found what they were looking for at Gordonstoun. 'We have got half a dozen pairs who met at school who are now married,' said Thomas.

As in so much else, Edward was much more circumspect. Of all the Queen's children, he was most like his mother in the way he had learnt to keep his emotions under control in the most royal of ways. His prep school headmaster, James Edwards, remarked on it. So did James Thomas.

'Edward took himself quite seriously,' Thomas observed. 'That is neither good nor bad; it's just that some people do, some people don't.' Given that, it was not surprising, as Thomas noted, that he 'took the fact that he was a member of the Royal Family quite seriously'.

There were reports that, following Milford Haven's example, he formed a relationship with one of the prettiest girls in the school. His contemporary, John Staunton, who became a tree surgeon, recalled: 'All the boys lusted after her, but Edward was the one she bestowed her favours on.'

In fact Edward was one of the better behaved of Gordonstoun's pupils. Said Thomas: 'If he was going to get into scrapes he was going to make sure people didn't know about them because he would feel he was letting the side down.' Quite what Edward meant by 'side' is not clear. It could have been himself, or the Royal Family or, as Thomas interpreted it, 'his position towards the community'. It was probably a combination of all of those things and it sometimes led him to take a too officious view of the behaviour of others.

According to Staunton, 'Edward was always a rather formal chap at school. You could never expect Edward to look the other way if he caught you breaking school rules.' When he chanced upon a group of boys smoking and drinking in the woods, Edward, who was not then a prefect, shouted, 'Get back to your house captains – I'm reporting you for this!'

Thomas says: 'People who did not know him would have probably seen him as a bit strait-laced which he was not – he had a jolly good sense of humour. But he could come across as perhaps taking his responsibilities too seriously.'

Thomas joined the staff of Gordonstoun as a chemistry teacher shortly after Charles arrived. Nicknamed Bloater (it took him a few weeks before he got his body into rugged shape) he succeeded Robert Whitby as housemaster of Windmill Lodge, the Prince of Wales's old house. When Gordonstoun went co-educational in 1972, Windmill became a girls' house and Thomas took his boys over to Duffus, at the western edge of the 300-acre Gordonstoun estate.

As a result of the move, the boys were living in very cramped conditions when Edward arrived in the autumn of 1977. At Eton he would have had his own bedsitting room. In Duffus he slept with twenty-five other boys in a dormitory no bigger than the nursery sitting room at Buckingham Palace. Beds were squeezed in head to foot; some of the boys slept in bunks. So tight was accommodation that at one point boys were using one of the bedrooms in the housemaster's flat as a study.

The Queen and Prince Philip had not interfered in the choice of house; that had been left at the discretion of the headmaster,

John Kempe. When the Queen inspected her youngest son's new home on his first day there, she made no comment.

The prince suffered a few uncomfortable moments that first term. 'In any place where you have got four or five hundred boys and girls, then you are going to get a proportionate chance that there is going to be one or two who are prone to bully – that has been a fact of life since they were writing on cave walls,' said Thomas.

It was nothing like what Charles had to endure, however. But then nor was Edward as vulnerable. 'He was a very gregarious youngster who got on well with pretty well everyone,' Thomas recalled. He was also smart enough to know how to extricate himself from potentially difficult situations – a trick Charles didn't master until many years later, and then only after he had acquired a phalanx of equerries and courtiers and servants and bodyguards to protect his *amour propre*.

'Edward had a facility of being able to say, "If this goes on in this sort of way, there is going to be a hassle, so I'll go and do something else,"' Thomas said. It was a trait that made the housemaster's job a lot easier, as did the presence of Andrew Merrylees. The detective was under orders to keep a low profile and not interfere but, as at Heatherdown, he took an interest in the rugby, played the occasional game of squash and was always there in the background, keeping a watchful eye on his young charge, ready to report anything untoward to the housemaster. He never did. The only notable mishap that first year, indeed throughout his time there, was when Edward had to be rushed to the hospital in Inverness by his detective with an eye problem which turned out to be a piece of fluff that had worked its way behind the eyeball.

One feature of life at Duffus was the regular coffee evenings known as 'brews' which Thomas and his wife held in either the common room or their own flat. 'The boys would come and sit on the floor and we would talk, about anything.' One of the things they talked about was drugs.

When Prince Charles took a sip of cherry brandy whilst away on a Gordonstoun sailing expedition to Scotland's Western Isles, the story made front page news. What a faraway, innocent transgression that was in comparison with the mind-bending excesses of the Seventies. Even Gordonstoun in its remoteness could not avoid the spreading drug culture. Alcohol and cigarettes, the illegal indulgences of a previous generation of schoolboys and which in their time had carried not a government health warning but the threat of expulsion, were now regarded as infinitely preferable to some of the other substances that were becoming ever more widely available.

'There was no question that they [drugs] were closing in and it was to fight the good fight that we warned them, again and again, and kept warning them,' Thomas said. Sometimes to no avail. In 1978 five boys and one girl were expelled for possessing cannabis. It was not the first such incident; it would certainly not be the last. But this time one of the miscreants was fifteen-year-old Constantine Niarchos, son of the Greek tanker billionaire, Stavros, and attracted an inevitable amount of attention.

That scandal did not touch Edward, however. Nor for that matter did any other. It was quite usual for boys and girls at some time during their school career to sneak off into the woods with a few friends and a bottle of vodka (always vodka; Gordonstoun schoolchildren still clung to the old wives' tale that if they got drunk on vodka it did not show). The punishment for a first offence had been the threat of expulsion which would certainly have been enacted on the second. It had since been downgraded to a long walk during which the felon was supposed to contemplate the error of his ways, followed by rustication if the offence was repeated.

Edward was never rusticated; indeed, no one has any definite recollection of him being sent on any long walk which was Gordonstoun's traditional form of penance. Not even his brother Charles, the least rebellious of schoolboys, managed to emerge with such an unblemished record.

'Everybody thinks I was a proper little goody-goody, but they don't really know, do they?' Edward later said. When asked if he got into any scrapes, he replied: 'Not many, but that's always the sign of a good criminal, isn't it? Just because I wasn't on punishment doesn't mean I was on the straight and narrow.'

If he did transgress, it was never very far; that self-defined sense of his royal position always held him in check. Said Thomas: 'It would be potty to sit here with my hand on heart and say I am sure he was totally, one hundred per cent well-behaved the whole time, but compared to many he was certainly not a problem, not at all, because he took a responsible attitude to why he was there, which in some ways was amazing because he was just a young chap.'

That sense of individual obligation was something Gordonstoun sought to encourage in everyone and in Edward they clearly had a willing pupil. Despite his disclaimer about school not being the happiest time, he rose to the school's challenge and appeared to thrive on it.

But whatever he was doing, he was never less than a prince. Visiting dignitaries called him Your Royal Highness and then, Sir. In the manner of both Charles and Andrew, he was called Prince Edward by the masters. His position was not a crutch, however; his sense of his own royalty was more a matter of inner commitment than outward form and his contemporaries called him either Edward or, if they were in his house or knew him well, Ed. It was a display of the egalitarianism which Gordonstoun had traditionally encouraged; as Thomas observed, 'The less important in the social strata you appeared to be, the more familiar you were allowed to be with the prince.'

This air of comparative informality carried through into the vacations. Although it was school that shaped and regulated the major part of the year, it was the holidays which provided the highpoints for all the pupils and Edward had more than most to look forward to. There was sailing at Cowes and cruising on the Royal Yacht *Britannia* around the Western Isles; riding at Windsor; shooting at Balmoral and Sandringham; fishing at Balmoral; swimming in the pools at Windsor and Buckingham Palace; skiing in Austria; haymaking at Gatcombe Park, his sister's estate in Gloucestershire. He learnt to sail and water-ski and to drive in four-wheel-drive vehicles at Sandringham and Balmoral and in the go karts he and Andrew were given.

He always started off his holidays at Buckingham Palace. This gave him the opportunity to catch up on the latest films. James Bond was his particular favourite. With Lady Sarah Spencer, who at the time was romancing Prince Charles (and whose sister, Diana, would later marry him), he would go to whichever West End cinema happened to be screening the latest 007 movie.

In all their trips (and Edward saw every Bond film) they were not recognised once.

Other unremarked visits were paid to WH Smith in Sloane Square, Peter Jones and the General Trading Company. Unlike most of his relations, Edward was always a keen reader. As a youngster he had avidly followed the adventures of Asterix, the cartoon Gaul who fought the Romans. Later, his interests came to embrace thrillers. He also developed a love of pop music and Abba in particular – something which soon drove his young cousins to distraction.

Princess Alexandra's daughter, Marina, recalled Christmases at Windsor when Edward 'would turn one of the drawing rooms into a nightclub. He always wanted to be the disc jockey so he could put on his records and we'd all have to dance – it was quite funny really. But we soon got so sick of Edward's music that we brought tapes of our own.'

His attempts at organising dinner dances were not much more successful. Said Marina: 'After dinner in the dining room he put some music on. It was all very awkward. There were only eight people there and we were all supposed to dance and the atmosphere was terrible – all teenage awkwardness.'

Edward's middle-of-the-road taste in entertainment was very much the legacy of Nanny Anderson, a keen fan of Radio 2 and *Daily Telegraph* crossword puzzles. She left Buckingham Palace in early 1978 and moved to Gatcombe to help Princess Anne with her first child, but her influence lingered on. 'Mabel has formed the monarchy,' one of the Household observed, only half in jest.

She had certainly been the most consistent influence in Edward's life. The Queen, for all her determination to see as much of her second family as possible, still had her state duties to perform. They took her away for a considerable part of the year and the teenage Edward often found himself the only member of the Royal Family in residence at Buckingham Palace. It did not seem to bother him. That sense of self-containment which had always been a part of his character was becoming more pronounced as he grew older. One of the Household who knew him best observed: 'There is a difference between being solitary and being lonely and Edward never ever gave the impression of being lonely. He was quite capable of entertaining himself.'

That is not to say that he did not enjoy the company of others. He was very attached to his cousin, Lady Sarah Armstrong-Jones; she was his closest friend and they spent as much time as possible together (but only in the holidays; neither Sarah's mother, Princess Margaret, nor her father, the photographer Earl of Snowdon, were prepared to test Gordonstoun's theories of co-education, preferring to send her and her brother David to the more 'arty' Bedales). It was Sarah who accompanied him on his shopping expeditions to Sloane Square.

He very much enjoyed the company of Anne and derived a lot of pleasure from helping out on the Gatcombe farm. Edward was not as expert a rider as the princess who had represented Britain in the Olympic Games, but he was a good horseman none the less, and brother and sister rode together most mornings.

He also enjoyed a close rapport with Prince Philip. At first glance Edward, whose youthful looks, as everyone remarked, were almost feminine in their delicacy, had seemed the very antithesis of his hearty, gruff father. But Edward was not as delicate as he looked – and nor was Philip as harsh.

'Prince Philip was always great fun,' recalled Marina who always spent part of Christmas with the Queen and her family. 'He would snap at his children as any father does, but he certainly wasn't cold. And he'd never not have time for them. He was one of those people who got annoyed if you didn't concentrate; if he was trying to teach you something he wanted you to concentrate. Like with me, for instance; he gave me a lot of time driving a couple of ponies and if I started giggling, he got very annoyed. That could be quite scary, but if you got around that, there was a lot of charm underneath.'

When it came to shooting, Philip found a willing pupil in Edward. A keen shot himself, he had started to teach Edward the skills of marksmanship at an early age. 'He began by shooting rabbits when he was quite tiny – about seven or eight,' Marina said.

Andrew had only the vaguest interest in field sports. For him it was little more than a matter of royal form – field sports are part of the rural routine of royal life. Edward, on the other hand, became a genuine enthusiast. Adam Wise, his former Private Secretary, said: 'He always amazed me with his knowledge of things that flew. We'd be out on some Scottish moor and a strange V-shaped thing would pass overhead far too far away for me to see, and he would tell you what it was and where it had come from.'

A high point of his stays at Sandringham was getting up before first light to go duck shooting with his father on the marshes of the Norfolk coast. Unhampered by the trappings of royalty and quite alone, father and son would crawl for hours amongst the tall reeds.

It was not only the wild-fowl that caught Edward's young eye out on the coast. In summer Edward and other members of the Royal Family would frequently spend the day at Holkham, part of which was a designated nudist beach. The naked sunbathers came under the closest of royal scrutiny. As Marina Ogilvy recalled: 'We all used to have a good look through our binoculars. It was very funny – and the Queen Mother's remarks were always the naughtiest!'

Not every holiday was given over entirely to youthful pleasure. When he was fourteen he was diagnosed as having too many teeth for his jaw and he had to have two removed. It was a painful operation which was performed by a private dentist in London's medical heartland. The teeth were extracted one a day over 48 hours. He then wore for a year the metal brace which slowly and very painfully closed the gaps and drew his remaining teeth together again. His mouth bled profusely and he found it difficult to eat for several days after the operation but he suffered without complaint.

Prince Philip and the Queen did not usually reward their children. On this occasion, however, they had the teeth mounted in gold settings and made into chain-linked cuff-links which they presented to him – in recognition, they explained, of his 'pluck'.

It is worth nothing that it was his detective and a member of staff, not his parents, who took him along to the dentist and brought him home afterwards. Old habits of royalty die hard and when he was back from school, Edward quickly found himself falling back into its rhythms. He would be woken just before eight by a footman who would have polished his shoes to the brightness of glass and laid his clothes out for him on a chair in the corner of his bedroom which at Buckingham Palace had a turquoise carpet and white walls. The day would then settle into a routine unchanged since childhood. There would be the 8.30 breakfast, a morning visit to his parents if they happened to be around. And in the evening, if he was in the company of his mother the Queen, he had to abide by the ancient strictures of the Court. Marina Ogilvy remembered when, as a teenager, she tried to leave the room to go to bed before the Queen had retired, only to be ordered to mind her manners and get back into the room again. For the Windsors, immured by their privilege and traditions, life had a timeless quality about it.

The competitive edge of the world outside had started to make its incisions into this cosy environment, however. The Royal Family, which before had never been required to compete in anything, indeed had been firmly discouraged from pitting itself and thereby committing its status against *hoi polloi*, was increasingly being measured against the general criteria. That applied particularly in education. The popular press called the prince Educated Eddie, but he had to work hard to keep that nickname and in the Easter holiday before he took his 'O' levels, a young undergraduate was hired to give Edward and his cousin, David Linley, some vital private tutoring.

The extra effort proved worthwhile; Edward obtained nine 'O' levels, a family record, and moved smoothly on to study 'A' levels. 'Workwise, he was pretty much an all-rounder,' said James Thomas, who briefly taught him chemistry. 'He got a good clutch of 'O' levels and had no trouble getting into the Sixth Form. In some ways that all-round ability made it more difficult for him to choose his subjects because he was quite good at a number.' He eventually settled on History, English literature, and Politics and Economics.

But if it was now vital, because of the attention his grades attracted, for Edward to do well in exams, it was certainly not a case of all work and no play for the most academically-inclined of the Queen's children. Quite the contrary. He enjoyed squash and hockey, played some golf and was an especially keen rugby

The Duke of Edinburgh and Princess Marina Duchess of Kent look on as Prince Edward makes his first public appearance on the Buckingham Palace balcony after Trooping the Colour in June 1964.

The Queen and the infant Prince Edward in the Blue Drawing Room at Buckingham Palace on 22nd May 1964. During the session photographer Cecil Beaton noted that the baby's adult behavior 'pleased the Queen, who was in a happy, contended and calm mood. She not only smiled to my instructions but with amusement at the activities and fast developing character of the new-born'.

Prince Edward clutches the white gloved hand of his nanny Mabel Anderson at Kings Cross station on their way to Balmoral for the summer holidays.

Royal cousins, James Ogilvy, Lady Sarah Armstrong-Jones and Prince Edward on an afternoon outing from the Buckingham Palace schoolroom to BBC TV's *Blue Peter* studios where they play with two seven week old cubs.

Left: In 1968 during the filming of the television show, *Royal Family* Prince Charles was poised to play his cello when, much to Prince Edward's fright, the string broke and hit Charles around the neck. Edward was about to cry with fright, but he remembered the TV cameras and smiled.

Below: From an early age Prince Edward's enthusiasm for the Royal Marines was fuelled by trips to the Royal Tournament. Here the Queen leads Edward and his cousin Lady Sarah Armstrong-Jones into the Royal box for the spectacular.

Prince Andrew holds his younger brother Prince Edward's hands to keep him steady for the camera in the Buckingham Palace gardens in the autumn of 1965

incess Anne and Prince Edward, smartly dressed for the occassion, enjoy a carriage ride at the indsor Horse Show in May 1969.

The Royal Family photographed by the Queen's cousin, Patrick Litchfield, in the gardens of Balmoral Castle in August 1972 to commemorate the Queen and the Duke of Edinburgh's silver wedding.

Prince Philip takes a fatherly interest in his son's skills as a photographer during the Badminton horse trials in 1976.

HEATHERDOWN

presents

TOAD
of
Toad Hall

MARCH, 1975

Above: Ratty and Mole (Prince Edward) outside Badger's front door in the wild wood.

March 1975, eleven year old ince Edward stars as Mole in his ep school production of *Toad of ad Hall*. He still remembers his ening lines, 'scratch, scrabble and rooge' as he popped out of a trap or dressed in black velvet. *Left to ght:* Badger played by Richard Wills, ole played by Prince Edward and t played by Alexander Cameron.

TOAD OF TOAD HALL

by A. A. Milne

A play from Kenneth Grahame's Book "The Wind in the Willows"

Music by C. C. H. BLACK

cast

MOLE	Prince Edward
RAT	Alexander Cameron
BADGER	Richard Wills
TOAD	Rupert Tate
ALFRED	Luke Lillingston and Benjamin Carter
CHIEF WEASEL	Philip Wells
CHIEF FERRET	John Colman
CHIEF STOAT	George St. Andrews
MRS. TURKEY	Richard Pilkington
MRS. DUCK	Roger Evans
USHER	Oliver Steel
POLICEMAN	Charles Harman
JUDGE	Andrew Howland
BRAVE WEASEL	Richard Johnson
PHOEBE	Shaun Browne
WASHERWOMAN	Philip Mallinckrodt
MAMA RABBIT	Patrick McLaren
HAROLD RABBIT	David Cameron
LUCY RABBIT	Nicholas Cunningham
BARGEWOMAN	Anthony Ainsworth

Wild Wooders

James Ogilvy, Alexander Bailey, James Palmer, Stephen Doyle, James Griffith, John Christie, Christopher Wilmot-Sitwell, Thomas Colborne-Malpas.

Field Mice

Antony Griffith, Kevin Bailey, Simon Andreae, George Vestey, Giles Goschen.

Squirrels

James Turner, Richard Cumming-Bruce, Patrick Knollys, Andrew Smith-Maxwell.

Produced by MR CHRISTOPHER BLACK

Our thanks are due to all who have helped in this production, especially:

Miss Christine Larter	*SCENERY*
Mr. David Gray	*STAGE MANAGER*
Miss Verena Russell-Clarke Miss Jill Holland	*COSTUMES*

Part of the 1977 Heatherdown school photograph showing headmaster James Edwards with Prin
Edward sitting directly behind his wife, Belinda.

Duffus House, Gordonstoun in 1981 with housemaster James Thomas and his wife in the centre. Prince Edward is fourth from the left second row from the top.

player who made his way through the teams before making it into the school's First Fifteen in his final year. Charles had hated the rugby. He was bad at it and more often than not ended up being ground into the Scottish mud by opponents who considered it a mark of dubious honour to say that they had clobbered the heir to the throne. The more sporty Edward, on the other hand, enjoyed the excitement of the game and was a good enough player to look after himself. Only later did he encounter the misdirected (and illegal) aggression that had made his elder brother's outings on to the rugger field such a painful experience.

One thing the two brothers did have in common was acting. Said Thomas: 'The thing that interested Edward over all was the drama.' An interest whetted at Heatherdown was honed at Gordonstoun and it became his consuming passion.

Edward himself recalled: 'I became involved in various productions there. There were a lot of very good actors and potential actors at Gordonstoun at the time. We had one or two sons of actors.' They included Jason Connery, son of Edward's cinematic hero, Sean, and Peter Finch's son, Charles. 'Up to then Gordonstoun had always produced massive school plays which were either a Jacobean tragedy or a Shakespeare play, or something which required vast numbers. The mould was slightly broken when I was there. It began to break down that different houses would put on different plays, so we were able to put on smaller productions. The students began to do what they wanted to do. More plays started getting put on and they were of a very different nature to what had gone on before.'

Edward played Paris in the school's production of Shakespeare's *Romeo and Juliet*. In his first year he took the lead in the smaller, house revue of Peter Shaffer's *Black Comedy* in which the lighting is reversed, coming on when it should be off and going off when it should be on. The Queen and Prince Philip came to watch him in that.

Prince Charles, accompanied by the then Lady Diana Spencer to whom he had just become engaged, came to see him in the Feydeau farce, *Hotel Paradiso*, which Edward produced as well as starred in. It was an open-air production staged under the walls of the school chapel. The weather had been fine for the previous nights' performances but it started to rain, as Edward had predicted it was bound to, when his brother and future sister-in-law arrived. Thomas recalled: 'The stage became very slippy and everyone was slipping and sliding and the audience was laughing in all the wrong places.'

It was Charles's first visit to the school since he had left to go up to university. It was Diana's one and only visit to the school which she would later refuse to allow her own sons to attend. Back then, however, the couple were in the first enthusiastic flush of their relationship and both Charles and Diana appeared to enjoy the evening, crouched under umbrellas, watching the young Edward skidding across the stage.

When he appeared in Noel Coward's *Hay Fever* it was again the Queen and Philip's turn to make the three-hour car journey across the Grampians from Balmoral. They had reserved seats; Edward wrote labels and stuck them on the backs of two chairs in the front row. They read 'Mum' and 'Dad'.

Hay Fever was performed in the Services Centre. Just as the performance started, the lights began to play up. In a loud whisper that could be heard several rows away, Philip remarked to the Queen: 'I think they are doing *Black Comedy* again.' The remark produced a ripple of laughter from the audience.

'It was,' said Thomas, 'all very good natured and light-hearted.'

Jason Connery directed Edward in one of the school productions. He said: 'He never minds being told what to do. He listens hard so he can learn fast.'

Edward's enthusiasm for the stage carried through into the holidays when he was forever organising entertainments for his family, writing and starring in his own one-act, usually one-man plays. 'One of his plays was about a man in a potting shed,' Marina remembered. 'It was quite childish, some of it, but there was a lot of humour there as well.'

The whole family, including cousins and aunts, would gather to see him perform. The potential for embarrassment was enormous but everyone appears to have enjoyed the princely shows. Marina said: 'The acting was very good. It wasn't cringe-making at all.'

Charles had also excelled at acting when he was at Gordonstoun. Isolated and unhappy in the role he found himself cast in at the school by dint of birth and personality, he only appeared to come alive when he was able to pretend to be someone else. Edward's enjoyment was more straightforward. As a child he had been entranced, as all children are, by the magic of make-believe and it gave him great pleasure to be able to weave the spell himself.

His Gordonstoun drama coach, John Lofthouse, put it simply. Edward, he said, 'lived for acting'.

The trouble was that his enthusiasm for the theatre, when combined with his other interests, was making for a worryingly overcrowded schedule. As well as his commitment to acting, there were his sport and his involvement with the Air Training Corps. He took an Air Cadet Proficiency Gliding Course at RAF Benson, home base of the Queen's Flight, in 1980; took an intensive course at the Basic Flying Training School at Cranwell; earned his private pilot's licence shortly after his eighteenth birthday; and was head of Gordonstoun's ATC during his last year.

It was, Thomas conceded, a very demanding schedule and his academic work inevitably suffered. When he only managed to scrape a mediocre C Grade in his English A-level and even less impressive Ds in History and Politics and Economics, yet still managed to gain a place at Cambridge University, a by now inevitable storm of criticism was generated.

Said Thomas: 'His A-level grades were not particularly good. He got middle grades and he got unjustifiably taken to the cleaners by the media for that. But there are very few people who would have been able to cope with all he took on and still come out smiling.'

But if the results were not all that they might have been, they were what were expected and it had been Thomas himself who had encouraged the prince to take on all those extra-curricular activities which were bound to have an adverse effect on his academic progress. The housemaster explained: 'We talked about how he should spend his last year – whether he should be nose-down into the books and make that an absolute priority so that he got three top grade As. He was a bright boy, interested, articulate and if he had spent as much time doing academic work as many other people do he could well have got three grade As. But I saw our job as making him or helping him to be ready for the next stage of his life in terms of the fact that he was going to have to meet a lot of people, he was going to have to do a lot of different things, so he needed to be balanced, self-disciplined, well-organised and articulate and I don't think it would have served him well for us to have said, "You have got to get three 'A' levels at all costs at grade A."

'Obviously he had to do as well as he could but I felt he should also take advantage of the leadership potential and possibilities of being in charge of the Combined Cadet Forces, of the sporting opportunity for being in the top rugby teams, and the other broadening cultural opportunities like the plays.

'So my advice to Edward was "You should take every opportunity that the school has to offer because of the life you are eventually going to lead."' It was advice that Edward took.

To add to his distractions, he also became head of House and then head of School in that final year. He was deemed a success. Michael Mavor the headmaster said: 'He is a good all-rounder and had a very nice manner with the boys. As head boy he watched over the whole atmosphere, seeing the boys were happy and dealing with minor matters of discipline.'

It would have been unusual if he had not risen to those positions of authority. Prince Philip had been Guardian. So had Charles. Even Andrew, more bumptious and less disciplined than the others, had become head of House. In the case of Charles, there was a lingering suspicion that he only got the job because of who he was – and then only by staying on for an extra year by which time most of his rivals for the post had left. Thomas was in no doubt, however, that Edward, with his well-developed sense of responsibility, had the leadership necessary to be head boy of Duffus House. 'The biggest difficulty,' he said, 'was that you did not show any favour but without going the other way and making it harder for him.'

The headmaster had been inclined to make Edward Guardian at the beginning of that year but his housemaster was against it and it was Thomas's view which prevailed. 'It would have been an error because he needed to grow into it by being head of the house first,' Thomas said.

Some boys, upon being elevated to a position of authority over their contemporaries, become afflicted with the poacher turned gamekeeper syndrome, behaving like officious junior officers, enforcing the housemaster's orders without question. But although Edward certainly took his duties seriously, he was not the most compliant of prefects and differences of opinion between head boy and housemaster and later Guardian and headmaster were not uncommon. Thomas rcalled: 'If I thought it was his job to do something and he thought it wasn't his job, then in certain circumstances with some people you could say "Come on George it's your job, get on with it," but with Edward you had to be slightly more circumspect. You had to say, "Come on Eddie it is your job because, because, because" and if he was happy with the because, because, then he would do it.'

It was rare for a boy to query the demarcations of house rules. Thomas put it down to Edward's position as the Royal Family's 'tail-end Charlie – I suspect that being the youngest son there would have been an element of being specially looked after.'

Summing up, Thomas said: 'He wanted to know what was expected and that the things that were expected were reasonable and that people could reasonably be expected to do them, which is fair enough, and it is to be encouraged really.'

Another thing Thomas noticed was that Edward took no great pleasure in yomping across the moors of Scotland on school expeditions. 'He went on expeditions because everybody did it but he was not a great expedition enthusiast,' the housemaster said.

They were attitudes and outlooks that went into the making of the prince. They were not necessarily the ideal characteristics for a young man planning to make his career in the Royal Marines.

Five

Home and Away

EDWARD LEFT SCHOOL at the age of eighteen. By the law of his mother's land he was now of age with an adult's legal right to make his own decisions. It would be a few years yet, however, before he found the courage to do with his life as he saw fit. Back in the summer of 1982 he was still subject to the time-honoured traditions of the Royal Family.

'There was a pattern and New Zealand was a part of it,' he told me. 'I knew I was going to university, I knew I had secured my place with the Royal Marines, I knew what I was going to be doing over the next four to five years. It didn't really cross my mind particularly to think of anything beyond that.'

As the son of the Sovereign, he was expected to go along uncomplainingly with the flow. That meant a spell in one of the Dominions. Charles had gone to Australia, Andrew to Canada. That left New Zealand. He was excited at going, although in truth he would probably have been just as happy to have stayed at home.

Like his mother before him, Edward had been a self-contained child. His interests were rooted in the countryside and he was content with himself in its company. He liked riding with his mother and shooting with his father, picnicking on the beach at Holkham and sailing and water skiing at Cowes with his cousins, Lady Sarah Armstrong-Jones and Marina Ogilvy. But he was just as content when he was pottering about on his own.

He had been an easy-to-handle teenager. He was not interested in heavy rock music (Abba being more to his musical taste) or girlie pin-ups (in the matriarchal family he was born into, women were there to be honoured and obeyed). His taste in films and television was middle of the road: James Bond films, Morecambe and Wise, and *It Ain't 'alf Hot, Mum*, the comedy about the army in the last days of the Raj.

Unlike his brother, Andrew, whose inquisitive nature got him into regular scrapes with Palace staff, Edward rarely ventured behind the 'green baize door' into the staff quarters. When the north-east section of Windsor Castle was partly destroyed by fire in 1992, Andrew's intimate knowledge of the secret passages and hidden entrances and back stairways proved of great assistance in the struggle to remove paintings and furniture before they were consumed in the blaze. Although the Castle was Edward's favourite royal home, he was not able to help; he did not even know where the linen room was.

Relations between the brothers as they grew into manhood were friendly but distant. 'I never saw any jealousy between Andrew and Edward, even though Ed was such a beauty,' said Marina Ogilvy.

A member of the Household observed: 'Andrew and Edward are just two different people. There wasn't any animosity between them but they were definitely not close.'

The Prince of Wales was an even more remote figure. Charles had taken great pleasure in romping with his youngest brother when he was a baby and it was for Andrew and Edward, who was four at the time, that he wrote *The Old Man of Lochnagar*, the story of a mythical figure who dwelled on the 3,786-foot high mountain on the Balmoral estate. 'Charles and Edward were very alike,' Marina said. The sixteen-year age gap was simply too great to bridge, however. They were almost a generation apart – in attitudes as well as age.

It was with Anne that Edward forged his closest bond. She was like an indulgent aunt to him. It was Anne who wrote him long, chatty letters when he was at school, who entertained him in the holidays and generally gave him the affection which still did not flow naturally from their mother. She called him Nig-Nog and he always spent a good part of the summer at her Gloucestershire estate, Gatcombe Park, where he had his own room, his own pony (it was an Arab mare which had been presented to the Queen during a tour of the Middle East) and his own car, a yellow Ford rented for the holidays in which he practised his driving around the estate.

'He's not like her, but they are the closest,' observed Adam Wise.

'His best pal' at this time according to Marina, was his cousin, Lady Sarah Armstrong-Jones, daughter of Princess Margaret and the Earl of Snowdon, who loved to escape from the confines of Kensington Palace and her parents' sophisticated friends and be in the country with horses. It was all so pleasant at Gatcombe. They rode every morning. During the harvest they would assist loading a trailer which had been nicknamed The Queen Mary (after the ocean liner, not Edward's redoubtable great-grandmother). They were expected to make their own beds, something the Queen has never done. There would also be days out at local horse trials when Anne would provide the picnic lunch or somtimes prepare fried egg and bacon on the horse box stove. Edward would help; it was the start of his interest in cooking.

'There was nothing nasty about Edward,' said Marina. 'He used to take me to see the puppies at Sandringham or Queen Mary's Dolls House at Windsor. Asking an elder male cousin to show you a bloody dolls house was a liberty, but Edward didn't mind. He was very patient.'

It was safe and cosy but it could not continue for ever. Manhood beckoned, whether Edward liked it or not. And sometimes he did not. As a child he had been able to fly out of airports or mingle unnoticed, at the age of thirteen, with the other spectators at a recording of *It's a Knockout*. Now he was acquiring a public face. There were official photographs and official engagements and his picture started appearing in magazines.

Like all teenagers, he started taking an interest in his appearance, and particularly in his hair. He kept a small comb in the top pocket of his jacket and would anxiously examine his prematurely thinning patch in the mirror. But though he was naturally neat and tidy, he most definitely did not have the innate sense of style of his great-uncle, the Duke of Windsor. He had always worn without complaint his eldest brother's cast-offs, down to his shirts and pyjamas. (On one occasion, when Prince Charles's old dinner jacket was being pressed in readiness for its new owner, his valet Stephen Barry discovered an old-fashioned ten-shilling note in the pocket.) His sartorial conservatism bordered on indifference. When his eighteenth birthday photographs revealed that his unfashionably pressed cords had been let down, Edward could not understand why anyone should care.

That infuriated his cousins, Sarah and Marina, who were forever trying to persuade him to swap his check shirts and tweed jackets for velvet coats and flares.

'One Christmas we tried buying him a pair of jeans and a shirt. We kept telling him, "You'll look groovy Ed," ' Marina recalled. Ed was not interested. 'His dress sense was appalling. So was Andrew's. They both wore very boring clothes and horrible shirts all the time.'

Even if he refused to dress the part, he was still a prince of the blood and that gave him a certain glamour. People started writing to him as if he were a pop star and asking him what his favourite colour was and his favourite recipe. On his eighteenth birthday he was pictured on the front cover of *Dog World* with his labrador, Francis. 'The dog got more mail than I did,' he joked.

Edward had enough mail of his own to be getting on with. 'I remember one hideous moment when an American teenage magazine ran a feature on the teenage Princes of Europe,' recalled Adam Wise. Edward was included alongside such other royal luminaries as Prince Albert of Monaco and Prince Felipe of Spain. 'It showed a photograph and gave a little biographical sketch and said, "You can write to him at Buckingham Palace." The letters eventually started arriving and there were so many they had to be carted off in tea-chests.'

Edward the schoolboy was metamorphosing into Edward the prince and with the attention came the royal commitments. They included a spell in New Zealand and in September, 1982, he was dispatched to the other side of the world to take up the position of junior master at Collegiate School on the west coast of the North Island. Situated in the garden town of Wanganui, it is a fee-paying school constituted on the lines of a traditional British public school, and is affiliated with Gordonstoun.

Edward did not find the transition from schoolboy to schoolmaster an easy one.

'Wanganui is part of the town and it's an all-boys school and a school is still a school whatever you are doing,' Edward noted. 'Here I'm working with the staff and not quite on the same level as the senior boys. It's very difficult when you're almost the same age, yet taking on a slightly different role.'

As a junior master in Selwyn House, his responsibilities included teaching English grammar and literature to a third form. (One of his pupils was John Tanner who in 1991, while a student at Oxford, confessed to the murder of his missing girlfriend, Rachel McLean whose remains were found under the floorboards of her lodgings.)

He also helped with the physical education and took the boys on regular cross-country runs.

'Any more and it starts becoming a job,' he said, adding ruefully, 'I don't think I'm cut out to be a teacher.'

He tried to be philosophical about it. It was, he said, 'part of my educational process. After all, we go on learning 'til the point of death. You can never, ever know everything.'

To fill in the time, he volunteered for all the school expeditions which included camping on the edge of 9,000-foot Mount Ruapehu in an igloo which he helped build with ice blocks.

'I wouldn't do it again immediately, but it was an experience,' was his verdict.

He lived in his own self-contained flat, had two local policemen assigned for his protection and kept in touch with world affairs via the BBC World Service.

London also kept in touch with him. One morning a reporter from the *Daily Mirror* telephoned him and got straight through. Edward, still very much the British prince, was outraged. 'Just what the hell do you think you're doing?' he shouted. 'You've got a right nerve. What on earth gives you the right to call me.'

The reporter explained that he merely wanted to know how he was enjoying his first term as a schoolmaster. 'Well, your curiosity has just killed you . . . in a metaphorical sense. This time I won't do what I could do to you.'

The reporter asked what that might be. 'Something rude will happen to you.'

It was the petulant outburst of an adolescent prince. It was a harbinger of worse to come. As it happened, though, it contributed a valuable piece to the jigsaw of his experience. 'Blimey, people couldn't just call me at home,' he observed. But Edward was not at home. New Zealand was the most British of Britain's former colonies but the British class structure had failed to take root in those far-off islands and the descendants of the original settlers had a healthy disregard for divisions of background.

His pupils showed him a certain old-fashioned courtesy befitting his position. Two of them, Tom Abraham and Duncan Shand, who undertook 'fagging' duties for him, felt he was just like any junior master. They were rather surprised, though, that he never asked them to clean his shoes. They did not realise how particular the prince is about his shoes. They were his one concession to vanity and he liked to have them burnished to a glassy finish, a job he had learned to do himself as well as any nursery footman.

Edward, in turn, was equally surprised by some of the behaviour of the locals. Brought up at the pinnacle of the British class structure, he was impressed and not a little amazed by the egalitarianism of the New Zealanders. As he explained to me: 'I had the opportunity to visit the local high school where, like us, all the boys turned out to play cricket in immaculate whites. I asked them as a matter of interest, "Why is it that you all turn out in whites for cricket?"' Putting on a New Zealand accent, Edward mimicked the high school headmaster's reply, '"It's very simple. If the boys at Collegiate turn out in whites, we turn out in whites. That's 'cos they're no different from us."

'I thought how damn refreshing, how very refreshing, because if that happened in this country, in Britain, the attitude would be one of "spoilt little rich kids". That's the point. But what he was saying was, "We're no different, we want to be up there and smartly dressed too."'

It would be some years yet before Edward would try to apply those principles to his own life. At that juncture he was still very much the product of his royal background. If that had its restrictions, it also had its privileges. They included a week's visit to Antarctica and what could fairly be described without hyperbole as the trip of a lifetime. Over the six days he was there he covered more territory and saw more of its wonders than those legendary explorers, Scott and Shackleton, saw in all the years they tramped the frozen continent.

Armed with an early video camera, which was his hobby and pointed the way to his eventual career, he flew there aboard a C-130 Hercules transport plane of the Royal New Zealand Air Force on 8 December, 1983. Over the next six days he was taken on toboggan and husky-drawn sledge and helicopter tours of the huts Captain Scott had sheltered in on his 1902 expedition, and the base camp he marched off to his death from in 1912. He visited the South Pole itself and stood on the exact spot where, from whichever direction he faced, he was looking north. He checked the experiments into the upper atmosphere which would reveal the hole in the ozone layer. He flew over some of the world's most spectacular mountain scenery, toured the Wright Valley which one of his party described as 'smaller but more magnificent than the Grand Canyon' and saw the Airdevronsix Icefall, a gigantic frozen Niagara Falls that spills down 2,000 feet from the Polar Plateau at a speed of only a few feet a year. He visited a 280-million-year-old fossilised forest and Lake Vanda where, 240 feet below its lid of ice, the water is a pleasant 24°C. He watched Weddell seals frolicking in a hole in the ice and inspected the nesting grounds of the Adelie penguins.

He went to Dry Valley, the driest place on earth. Its annual snowfall is the equivalent of just 5 mm of water which either evaporates or is blown away by the wind, leaving the valley snow-free and ice-free and drier than the Sahara.

On day five he joined the Antarctic Ski Club, the most exclusive in the world. The conditions were perfect as he shooshed down the slopes of the Scott Base skifield – packed powder snow, sunny skies, no wind, the temperature a very agreeable 2°C and no queues. It was better than anything even St Anton had to offer.

The whole trip, Edward said, 'was probably the most memorable week of my life, a unique chance to see the most extraordinary continent on our earth and an experience I will never forget.'

The rest of his stay in the Antipodes was not as eventful. He was made an honorary member of the Ngati-Tupoho and Ngati-Apa Maori subtribes, and proudly wore their ceremonial cloak of Kiwi feathers when he greeted his brother and new sister-in-law, Diana, during their ten-day trip to the island.

He got on well with the locals. He had even made his mark as an author. In collaboration with the school chaplain, the head of the English department and a couple of the pupils he wrote a thinly disguised account of life at a New Zealand boarding school under the name of Fenton-Ryder. Entitled *Full Marks (for Trying)*, it sold 12,000 copies at £6 each, a remarkable figure for New Zealand.

But, for all the attention and the moments of excitement, he had to confess that he found teaching – which was, after all, the reason he was there – 'quite dull'. Two terms teaching at Collegiate was more than enough. He had reached the watershed of adulthood. It was time to get on with life.

Six

The Student Prince

UNIVERSITY WAS THE best of times for Edward. It was solitude after the clamour of public school, sophistication after years of heartiness, freedom after restraint. It was luncheons in panelled halls, dinners by candle-light, beer in the boat club and tea in rooms that smelt of burnt crumpets and yesterday's milk. And there were women to be courted.

His time at Cambridge, Prince Edward said, was the best three years of his life.

In comparison to the excesses of others, his student days were comparatively sober and restrained. He did not drink too much or lapse into lust or take drugs and he was proud to say he never went out in a punt. He never developed the savoir-faire of John Betjeman's silk dressing-gown aesthete waiting for his lavender-scented bath. And he was certainly no Harold Acton, who wanted 'to rush into the fields and slap raw meat with lilies'. But for the first time he was able to enjoy himself in his own way, in his own time and that was important to him.

'I was very much my own boss, running my life the way I wanted to do it,' he said.

He was, he explained, off 'the beaten track' of his life which, up to then, had been carefully controlled and ordered. He had never really been allowed to do anything for himself before. Someone had always been on hand to sort out his problems and make his decisions for him.

He had gone along with that. As an adolescent he was a conformist, content to wear Charles's hand-me-down clothes. And when he did get something of his own, like a new pair of jeans, it was often his valet who went out and bought them for him. As a teenager he asked his mother for new jeans explaining that his old ones were too short and too tight. In shades of A. A. Milne's poem 'The King's Breakfast', the Queen asked her page to ask Prince Edward's valet if it was really necessary. On being informed that the Prince really *did* need a new pair of jeans, the Queen then got back to Edward and told him they would be forthcoming. 'Great news! The Queen says I can have a new pair of jeans!' Edward exclaimed.

Student life was very different. It demanded of him something he had never needed before: self-reliance. Not in the out-of-doors, Outward Bound sense, but in the ordinary, mundane day-to-day business of life – getting up, getting breakfast, deciding what to wear, where to have lunch, what to eat, what to do in the evening. He was not the only undergraduate forced to make those decisions for himself for the first time, but no undergraduate, however pampered, had been as cosseted as Edward had been throughout his young life.

It was something he was acutely aware of and he spoke with feeling of the wide gap between university and home life. At university he was no longer the youngest, the quietest, the cleverest or in line to the throne. He was simply an undergraduate. And if he was never going to be quite like everyone else, he was still able to get on and enjoy himself in a non-royal way. To his peers he was simply Ed.

Before he went up to university he had said how he disliked being royal, how it set him apart, how lonely it was and how inadequate he felt. But during his three years at Cambridge he came to accept his status as a prince of the realm and be proud of it.

'It is really how people accept you as a personality that is the important thing,' he said. 'I actually enjoy being what I am, basically because I have just got used to it.

'I had my friends – the friends that I mixed with and they treated me exactly the same as anyone else – that's what I was used to. But then at university I became very aware of whatever that strange thing is about the monarchy. Because of the things I was doing at university I came into contact with the general public more than I had ever before and I became aware of the impact I had. If I went somewhere with a group of people they became aware of it too. They began to see it in action at a sort of grass roots level.'

The city of Cambridge was proud of its royal connection. His grandfather, King George VI had been there, his brother Prince Charles had been there and they were proud to have Prince Edward there too. And that, he discovered, had its advantages. When, for instance, he tried to rent a taxi for a Rag Week stunt using his detective's name, Richard Griffin, he failed. But when he presented himself in person at the offices of the local newspaper, they agreed to provide a cab in return for some exclusive pictures. The following year they furnished Edward with custard pies for another stunt and charity profits raised a record breaking £23,000.

It was confirmation of the puissance of his birthright. 'I have been treated as an undergraduate,' he said shortly before he left Cambridge, 'and I have lived as normal a life as possible under the circumstances. I may be a human being – but I certainly wouldn't describe myself as normal. That can never be the case.'

When Edward had first expressed an interest in following in the footsteps of his brother, Charles, and his uncle-by-marriage, the Earl of Snowdon and going to Cambridge, it was arranged for him to visit half-a-dozen of the university's colleges. Because of its reputation and location, Jesus College came high up on his list, along with St Catherine's, Corpus and Trinity.

On 6 February, 1981, a day when the wind swept through the Cambridge Backs, buffeting everything in its path, he arrived at Jesus College to meet the Master, Sir Alan Cottrell.

A man of urbane charm and culture and former Chief Scientific Advisor to the Government, Cottrell decided it would be more interesting for the young Prince to be entertained by students than sit with him in the Master's Lodge sipping sherry. He therefore arranged for three undergraduates from the college to show Edward around before taking him for lunch in Hall, once the refectory of a nunnery.

It was a favourable beginning and the teenage Edward, fresh from the harsher environs of Gordonstoun, was impressed with what poet Samuel Taylor Coleridge called 'the friendly cloisters' of Jesus College. Its situation certainly helped. When Charles arrived at Trinity College in October 1967 hundreds of people were out on the streets to greet him and his car was mobbed. And throughout his time there he was ogled by passers-by as they strolled the narrow streets of the centre of Cambridge between the Bridge of Sighs and King's Chapel, crossing through the Great Court of Trinity College where his rooms were situated. 'In Cambridge I feel as though I am in a Zoo,' Charles wrote at the time. 'There are people wandering about everywhere staring at everything that moves and if it happens to be me they seem to gaze and point even more.' His most vivid memory of his first day, he later recalled, was of the burly college porters 'dragging shut those magnificent wooden gates to prevent the crowd from following in. It was like a scene from the French Revolution.'

Charles had warned his younger brother of the problems he had had to cope with and urged him to take them into consideration. Certainly Jesus was more *ancien régime*, set in its own expansive grounds – an inheritance from its beginning as the Priory of St Radegund, founded in the 1130s – which took it off the main tourist route and that was important. It was, however, the way Cottrell had arranged that first visit that finally swung the prince's decision in Jesus's favour.

Cottrell recalls: 'He saw several other colleges, but chose us. I never asked him why, but know that some of the other Masters just took him into the Master's Lodge and interviewed him, whereas when he was with us he spent his time with the undergraduates. That is how it all began . . . We obviously made a good impression.'

While the prince was being entertained by the trio of undergraduates, Cottrell and his wife Jean were giving luncheon to his Private Secretary, Adam Wise in the Master's Lodge. When Wise wrote to thank Cottrell a couple of days later, he said how much Edward had enjoyed his visit and explained he 'now had much to consider and discuss with his headmaster'.

It was Cambridge, not Gordonstoun, however, which now had the commanding say over his educational future and after interviews with the admissions tutor, Bruce Sparks, with the Master Sir Alan Cottrell and discussions with the college council, Edward was duly offered a place at Jesus, alma mater of such intellectual luminaries as Thomas Cranmer, the Archbishop of Canterbury martyred in the sixteenth century by

Bloody Mary; Samuel Taylor Coleridge who absconded from college to join the 15th Dragoons and that most distinguished of broadcasters, Alistair Cooke. Edward, his senior tutor, Gavin Mackenzie, confirmed, did not take the Cambridge entrance examination, but got into one of the world's greatest universities on the strength of his 'A' levels and 'S' levels.

'He applied in the normal way, was interviewed in the normal way and was given a conditional offer dependent on his 'A' level grades, which he met, and got his place,' Mackenzie said firmly.

Edward's marks had hardly been of the highest order, however. When Edward VII's ill-fated first-born son, Prince Albert Victor, who found it a struggle even to read properly, went up to Cambridge he was, as his official biographer noted, afforded 'the privilege of escaping university examinations, a privilege properly accorded to his high rank'. Edward VII's great-great-grandson was given no such regal dispensation. He had taken the examinations his long-dead cousin had been so deferentially spared – and then found himself accused of string-pulling and employing undue influence.

It was pointed out that if everyone with Edward's marks had been awarded a place, Cambridge would have had an extra 10,000 students that year. Cottrell acknowledged the criticism. 'We set a basic requirement, which he passed,' he said, 'but there was a bitter feeling amongst some of the undergraduates because competition to get into Cambridge is extremely stiff and it is not just a matter of passing the basic entrance requirements, but doing jolly well. But nevertheless he was entitled to come and we offered him a place.' Edward's name was posted on the Jesus College noticeboard as a freshman for the October 1983 entrance.

According to Mackenzie, the majority of students were 'very enthusiastic' about Edward's arrival. There was still a sense of considerable unease, however, amongst a number of undergraduates and they presented Mackenzie with a 'beer-stained petition', objecting to the arrival of the prince who, they said, was being given privileged treatment and might not fit in at a College which ranked second highest in the table of Tripos results in 1982.

Cottrell was unsympathetic. He refused to see the petition,

expressing his displeasure at the publicity the protestors had aroused about what was in his view a private college matter.

'The newspapers said they were protesting but they were not,' Mackenzie recalled. 'They were seeking reassurance that he'd come in as a normal candidate, which I was able to give.'

Nicholas Holgate, deputy president of Cambridge Student's Union at the time, agreed it was easy to criticise his admission, but said, 'It would be equally easy to make fun of Cambridge University if it had turned away a member of the Royal Family. It is a moot point that being a member of the Royal Family could become a qualification – like being able to play the clarinet well.'

Faced with such a frosty response on the one, authoritative hand, and droll irony on the other, the objections died away and the undergraduates agreed to 'do the gentlemanly thing' and give the prince the benefit of the doubt. Peter Hemington, the second-year student who organised the petition, declared: 'It is a stand on principle, not a personal vendetta. For his sake, we have to accept him as a normal undergraduate. We will treat him as one of the lads.'

This particular lad also happened to be a 2nd Lieutenant in the Royal Marines. As Charles and Andrew had both observed, princes have only a limited number of career options. By tradition the services are the most acceptable choice and Edward, who at this stage of his life was still very much on the royal conveyor belt, made the decision expected of him. The only real say he had in the matter was in selecting the service.

'He was just another in a queue of kids who were pondering about their future,' said Lieutenant Canning, who interviewed the prince as part of the potential officers assessment course. 'He was also toying with the Royal Air Force at the time, but I found him the sort of chap who would always make up his own mind.'

Edward settled on the Marines after spending two days at Gosport having his potential assessed. 'I'm sure the Admiralty Interview Board were bending over backwards in their assessment of Prince Edward,' says a former Commanding Officer, 'but my understanding is that the AIB performance was quite excellent.' An offer was made, was accepted and it was as a member of the Royal Marines University Cadets Scheme that he arrived at Cambridge University. The Marines were in effect paying for his higher education on the legally-binding understanding that he would repay their investment with five years' service.

'It may well be that had he joined at eighteen he would have found his niche with us,' Colonel Ian Moore said. But it would be another three years before Edward became a fully-fledged Marine. In the meantime, his association with the Corps was restricted to the occasional weekend, holidays, and set exercises like the Commando Training Course he undertook at the training centre at Lympstone which he completed just before he went up.

That, as it turned out, was not enough to sustain his long-term interest. At Edward's impressionable age three years is a long time. He would change: the young man who left the university was very different from the youth who arrived there on 1 October, 1983, to read Archaeology and Anthropology as his brother had before him.

As he drove up to the Master's Lodge he had to face the press waiting for him in the driveway – which at this stage of his life he found more exacting than yomping six miles over Dartmoor. A young nineteen, he was still apt to get a trifle over-excited under scrutiny. (He once frightened off a girl reporter who strayed too close to a shooting party at Sandringham by firing off a few shots only yards from where she stood on a public road and warning her, 'You might get hurt.') On this occasion, however, he kept his nerves under control and went along with the public relations agenda that had been organised for him.

More compliant than Charles, who had refused to wear the college gown as the Palace had urged him to, Edward posed cheerfully with Cottrell and his wife outside the Master's Lodge in an apparently impromptu meeting which had in fact been carefully planned beforehand.

'I got various briefings before he came up from people at the Palace,' Mackenzie recalled. 'We also had a press conference which was extremely well attended. Cottrell and I were in Hall with our bums on the high table drinking coffee and answering lots of questions.'

Instead of the traditional panelled rooms within the old part of the college, Edward's suite at Number 7 North Court was part of the modern undergraduate accommodation designed in 1963 by David Roberts, a local architect. It was red-brick and unromantic and would not have earned the Prince of Wales's seal of architectural approval but the functional rooms each had their own balcony and were accessible via a concrete stairwell with a second exit – essential for security purposes. Edward's study was much like any other undergraduate's – apart, that is, from the telephone, sturdy double locks and accommodation for a detective in an adjoining room.

'I had been slightly apprehensive as to how the security would affect the rest of the college, but it worked extremely well. I allowed the security people to do whatever they wished,' recalls Cottrell. 'I know they had some special curtains which offered some protection and the doors and windows were strengthened, but I didn't ask what else they were doing – I deliberately didn't want to know.'

Edward's two police shadows, Dick Griffin and the perennial Andrew Merrylees were in inevitable attendance. Now it was Griffin's turn to take a practical interest in Edward's sporting activities, just as Merrylees had done at Heatherdown and he was soon refereeing the college football matches. Both detectives, said Mackenzie, 'had to go to all the lectures of course, but it gave us no problems at all'. (It is not recorded if it was a problem for the detectives.)

What did not work so well was the media side. The press, said Mackenzie, 'were a darned nuisance – not so much because they pestered Edward, he was used to it, but they pestered everyone who might have had anything to do with him.'

There were, Cottrell said, a number of attempts to 'set-up' Edward's fellow students while he was in residence. One incident so incensed the Master that he complained to the Press Council. It happened during Edward's first term when Edward was taking part in the college play, *The Crucible*, and the rumour got about that he was having a relationship with leading lady, Corrine Taylor.

She was living in a house by the side of the college which was overlooked by a multi-storey car park. The paparazzi set up their telescopic lenses on the top floor and trained them into her bedroom 'just in case something happened'. Nothing ever did but, said Cottrell, 'I had to bring her back into the college. It was intolerable for the poor girl who was only about twenty. Edward was very annoyed and I complained twice to the Press Council.'

On another occasion an attractive Indian girl who lived on the same stair as Edward came back to her rooms to find reporters sitting on her bed. They cross-examined her – where, they wanted to know, did Edward do his laundry? Again Cottrell lodged an official complaint.

The episode which annoyed Cottrell the most happened before Edward actually arrived at the college. It involved the head porter, John Haycock. Unused to the ways of Fleet Street's royal Rat Pack, the former RAF airman said the 'most silly things' to a group of reporters. When asked, for instance, what he would say if the prince arrived back late in College, he innocently replied, 'Sir, you are a worm!'

The reporters were delighted with the quotes. Cottrell, needless to say, was not.

'The poor man was in a desperate state the next day,' Cottrell remembered, 'but I told him to forget all about it. I told him I wasn't going to pay any attention to it whatsoever.'

He made it quite clear, however, that he would tolerate no such indiscretions on the part of the undergraduates. Lucrative offers were dangled in front of a number of girl students. They were not accepted. The siege spirit of camaraderie had quickly developed and everyone closed ranks around the prince. Which was just as well, for Cottrell had warned that anyone caught selling information would be sent down immediately.

'It was like walking on eggshells,' the Master remembered.

Reporters were not the only people to get excited by the sight of a royal prince. Edward said: 'We get a new influx [of students] each autumn and its, "Spot the Prince" time. But after that they quickly realise that I am almost exactly the same as anyone else. They begin to think "What's so special?" After the novelty wears off, people see you as normal and you can carry on from there. But it takes time to get over the hurdle.'

Some clearly never did. As one contemporary said: 'Every time you go home all your parents want to know is "Have you been to tea with Edward? What's he like? Have you seen his room yet?" It's awful – and I've never met him once.'

Those that did meet Edward liked him very much. It took him a while to settle in, though. Lady Cottrell observed: 'He'd been brought up with people like porters and bedders [Cambridge vernacular for the women who make up the student's beds, wash their dishes and tidy their rooms]. He knew how to relate to them in a pleasant informal way. But he couldn't relate so well to ordinary middle-class people because he had had little opportunity to meet them in his life. He used to spend ages in the Porters Lodge chatting away which I thought was rather sad because although he had quite a few friends he didn't actually mix as well as he might have done.'

Her husband agreed. 'He was a very private person,' Sir Alan said. 'He wouldn't come to me with his problems anyway, but I think a lot of it he kept to himself. He wanted to stand on his own feet. Maybe he could have gone to a bar on Saturday nights and had a few too many beers, but he didn't do things like that. He was very careful. He told me once that he was determined not to do or say anything that would cause embarrassment in public and might get in the press. I thought that, from a young man not yet twenty, it was a sad thing to have to say.'

The prince did not see it that way. He had had his inner eye focused on his royal position and its attendant obligations ever since he was a child; that determination not to put a foot wrong which Cottrell remarked on was simply another manifestation of that notable characteristic. There was certainly no accompanying aura of melancholy. And in the free and increasingly egalitarian atmosphere of university life, his reserve started to break down.

He wrote to Romy Adlington, the model who became his friend, extolling the virtues of university life. He attended lectures, went to libraries, cinemas and restaurants. On occasion he even visited the college launderette (but not too often, if he could avoid it). He was only accompanied by his personal protection officer if he left the college premises.

'If he went to a restaurant one of them was behind him on a bike a few yards away,' Mackenzie recalled. 'But their attitude was that if somebody really wanted to do him harm they weren't going to be able to stop them; they would do the obvious things but would give him as much freedom as they could.'

Those expeditions sometimes drew forth what Edward cheerfully described as the 'theatrical whisper'. As he recounted: 'For example, you will see two people walking towards you and it's really funny as they will try and be subtle about the whole thing. They obviously think I am stone deaf. Just before you get to them there is a sort of theatrical whisper, "That was him." "Was it?" "No . . ." '

The one place where Edward found it literally impossible to turn his back on his royal status was on the rugby field. If he did he was likely to end up on the ground, under a scrum. He was selected to play for the Jesus College 2nd XV. But, just as Prince Charles had discovered at Gordonstoun where he had spent most of his games face down in the mud, the temptation to tackle a royal prince proved too great for some rugger hearties. And a gaggle of some fifty photographers was always on the touchline, poised to record every painful moment, including the time he was knocked out and carried off.

'Rugger is a rough game,' said Cottrell, 'and he got set upon. He was a good rugger player, but a bit lightweight and college rugby players are big hefty chaps and if they fall on you you feel it. He suffered injuries including a torn ligament and, after a bout of glandular fever, he gave it up.'

Edward said: 'I gave up the game because I was getting fed up with being a target.'

The theatre proved altogether more agreeable. It was clearly developing into Edward's abiding interest. It also provided an ideal opportunity for him to mix with people of different race, class and background. Lady Cottrell observed: 'The theatre was a great leveller for him and he had to work alongside all these people. They were a new class of society that he hadn't met before.'

He made his stage debut in his first term playing the judge in *The Crucible*, written by Arthur Miller in the era of Senator Joe McCarthy's anti-Communist witchhunt trials. 'It was an inter-collegiate production with students from other colleges including a young black woman from New Hall. We had sex, race and royalty all in one play,' Mackenzie recalls.

Edward's reviews were encouraging, though that was no less than was expected for someone who had spent his life on a stage of sorts. As he remarked afterwards: 'Life is one big act. You may be nervous but you don't show it.'

He became very involved in CULES – The Cambridge University Light Entertainment Society – which performed not just at the university but at old people's clubs, schools, hospitals and pubs all around the country.

Edward's roles for the Cambridge University Light Entertainment Society covered a considerable range. He was a good mimic – his sketch of Mike Yarwood imitating Prince Charles is one of his best non-public performances – and he enjoyed comedy. He played almost everything from a giant, sitting on the shoulders of his detective, Andrew Merrylees, to a country bumpkin and a drunk. He also performed song and dance routines, which he admitted he found the most demanding. 'It's difficult to concentrate on singing and remembering where to put your feet at the same time but it's great fun.'

For all the fun, Edward soon found that his real interest lay, not in acting, but in stage-management and production. 'The transition came after I started at Cambridge and I was taken ill and didn't want to commit myself to appearing,' he said. He caught glandular fever in December 1983 and, although it was a mild bout, he was told 'to take life very easy – no rugby or drama just passive interest'. He recalled: 'A friend of mine said, "That's fine, I need somebody to stage-manage the production and produce it." So I got involved in the production and management side and discovered what an immensely powerful position stage-manager is.'

His first taste of backstage authority came when he produced *The Tale of Toothache City* which was specifically designed to entertain mentally handicapped children. Edward involved himself in every aspect of the production, from auditioning the actors and painting the scenery, through to driving the minibus to the venues. He said: 'I actually began to find that I really enjoyed putting these things together and trying to turn what was an idea into a reality. I enjoyed trying to find the right team to be able to make it work,' he explained.

The 'team' was very important to Edward. It treated him as an equal, was amused how his royal status generated publicity and gave him companionship. It encouraged him to put his more zany, custard-pie-throwing ideas into practice, including driving a taxi through the streets with two students dancing on the roof – his gimmick to promote Rag Week.

Just before his twenty-first birthday he allowed himself to be roped to a railway line in the path of an on-coming train, re-creating that most clichéd scene from the silent screen, to publicise an hour-long show called *Catch My Foot*. The pictures made every newspaper, the show was sold out and the Queen and Princess Margaret attended a performance and told the cast afterwards how much they had enjoyed it.

On the actual day of his birthday the team thanked him for his efforts and serenaded him at a backstage party which went on into the early hours. On the way home he donned a bowler hat and danced through the streets of Cambridge carrying gifts from the cast. Edward was enjoying himself in his own youthful kingdom.

The entertainment industry is never without its problems, however, even for a prince, and Edward's came at the May Ball he helped to organise. With typical British confusion of the kind which insists on celebrating the Queen's birthday in June when it is actually in April, the May Balls are held in the following month. There are the expensive and formal college dances which last all night and end up with the survivors punting to Granchester for breakfast. There are plays and open-air concerts and all-day, all-night parties which sometimes lead to 'town v gown' conflicts between the sober citizens of Cambridge and the students.

In his last year Edward was entertainments officer at one all-night ball (a double ticket cost £66) featuring magician Paul Daniels, the pop group Mud, and that platform-shoe stomping exponent of glam rock, Gary Glitter. The town folk were quick to take advantage of Edward's involvement, and Council officials armed with noise meters were dispatched to monitor the decibel levels. Nearby residents, Cottrell remembered, 'started ringing up at 8 o'clock on the evening of the ball complaining about the noise. I said "We haven't started yet – it doesn't start until 10 o'clock!" '

The ball committee, having signed a voluntary code of conduct agreeing to cut noise levels, felt obliged to try their best to keep the noise down. It was a hopeless task. Gary Glitter and The Glitter Band, who insisted on playing their music at full blast, proved particularly obdurate. 'We couldn't keep the volume down with Gary Glitter, I'm afraid,' Cottrell said.

One of the committee members went up to sequin-bedecked Gary and said, 'You've got to keep the noise down, it's terrible.'

Back came the curt reply from one of his band: 'F-off!'

The sight of Edward, wearing a trilby and raincoat, shouting into a walkie-talkie and trying to make himself heard over the heavy thump of Glitter who was screaming out, 'I'm the Leader, I'm the Leader, I'm the Leader of the Gang I am,' is remembered with amusement by Cottrell. 'He took it all in his stride and although there were some hard feelings at the time, it all evaporated at the end and nothing happened.'

Helping him enjoy these youthful revels was the small but close group of new friends. The Royal Family traditionally sustains itself and Edward still looked forward to entertaining his mother and father in his room to tea and cakes from Fitzbillies, the famous cake shop on Trumpington Street, but now he could also draw on the fellowship of people from outside the royal circle. They included Quintus Travis and Peter Fraser who, like Edward, were being put through Cambridge by the Marines. Fraser, a Harrogate Grammar School boy whose sporting prowess had helped win him an open exhibition to St John's, became a particular friend. As President of the University boat club he would invite the prince to beery dinners and in turn Edward would invite him to Buckingham Palace and Sandringham.

Like Charles before him, Edward found the proximity to Sandringham and all its home comforts most convenient and he spent many of his weekends at Wood Farm on the edge of the 22,000-acre estate. Like most students he arrived laden down with dirty washing but instead of his mother, there would be a valet or housemaid to do his laundry.

Unlike Charles, Edward did not confine himself to the upper-class huntin', shootin', fishin' fraternity. He had a liking for esoteric sports such as real tennis and enjoyed drinks parties at the elite Pitt Club but, unusually for a member of the Royal Family, he was happy to draw his friends from a broader background. Many of those bonds still hold today and he remains close to such Cambridge contemporaries as barrister Andrew Sutcliffe, financier Mark Foster Brown, and publisher

Damien Riley-Smith who all work with him on the Special Projects Group of the Duke of Edinburgh's Award.

His cousin, Timothy Knatchbull (whose twin brother Nicholas was killed, along with their grandfather, Lord Mountbatten, by an IRA bomb) also joined him at Wood Farm, as did his particular friends, Andrew Ginger from Exeter and Alice Heap who had attended the nearby Hillsrow Sixth Form College and would later marry and then divorce Andrew.

'The three of them were very close,' Mackenzie recalled.

Romy Adlington remembers the weekends at Wood Farm with affection. The house, she said, had 'a cosy lived-in feel with lots of sporting prints and battered old sofas and armchairs'. There was a cook cum housekeeper, Mrs Hazel, in attendance, but Edward preferred to do the cooking himself.

He said: 'I've only ever done spaghetti bolognese once and it turned out completely and absolutely revolting. I'm not quite sure why. But I could introduce you to a few people who have tested my cooking and come back for more.' His chocolate mousse, he said, was his speciality.

These friends were not the only ones given the opportunity to sample it – and a little more besides.

His interest in women was confirmed in the most practical manner and Cambridge offered him the opportunity to continue his romantic development. Says Sir Alan: 'The legal age of adulthood being lowered to eighteen changed the college policy so that everyone was responsible for themselves and there was nothing to stop Edward entertaining a girl in his room if he wanted to.' However, as in all matters pertaining to his royal reputation, Edward remained very circumspect. 'He was very cautious,' his senior tutor, Gavin Mackenzie, agreed, 'but he did have girlfriends.'

Mackenzie recalled arriving back at the college late one night to find Dick Griffin wandering around outside. Mackenzie asked what he was doing. Griffin replied: 'I've been thrown out!'

The ever-faithful Andrew Merrylees was also prone to finding himself out on the street. Against official regulations but in the best romantic interests of the prince, he would tactfully depart, leaving Edward to entertain his female visitor by himself. Merrylees would not return until the following morning.

Edward enjoyed a long-term but unreported relationship with a girl at New Hall. According to one fellow student, he enjoyed the favours of a number of girls. 'He got away with blue murder,' one Cambridge contemporary said. 'All his girlfriends were pretty but from normal backgrounds. Perhaps they all secretly hoped they were going to become Mrs Windsor.'

Said Mackenzie: 'He had been beautifully trained in how to present himself so he'd never be photographed with a glass of anything. He would hide it – and he was the same with girlfriends.'

No matter how enjoyable the diversions, however, the prime object of university was to acquire an education. When it came to his studies Prince Edward was no different from most students. He enjoyed the independence of being able to choose what lectures to attend but found the practical business of getting down to work more difficult, especially because of the amount of time his theatrical pursuits occupied.

'The theatre didn't take over his work,' Cottrell insists, 'although it was his main interest. He worked hard. As a matter of fact, he is pretty bright.'

It was not until he got to university that the prince the press had nicknamed Educated Eddie started developing his intellectual potential, but work was always in competition with his other activities and that inevitably put a brake on his academic progress.

His first year course in 'arch and anth' – once considerd one of the easier subjects – was, according to his director of studies, Dr Kate Petty, 'far more rigorous' and Edward's workload was substantial.

Lord Renfrew, his professor of archaeology who succeeded Sir Alan as Master of Jesus, remembers him as an average student whom he first met in lecture halls. 'He wasn't a swot. He was very much doing his own thing. The great thing at Cambridge is you can choose the balance between the work you do and the recreations you have and he certainly didn't want to become a professional archaeologist.'

Edward did enjoy the week of his summer holidays spent working with fellow students at an archaeological dig on the site of the ancient Roman city of Viroconium in Shropshire. But before he switched to history, he was more interested in the anthropology part of the course. One of his papers was entitled 'The social structure of modern Britain'. It was an analysis of British society since the Second World War, including the emergence of the Welfare State and the National Health Service, the class structure, poverty and unemployment.

'He did not know much about it until he took the course, but he was interested,' recalled Mackenzie. Edward's senior tutor held opinions and views markedly different from anything the prince had encountered before. However, the two established a close rapport and it was to Mackenzie that Edward would turn later for advice at the moment of his greatest crisis. 'He was a very nice young man with a good sense of humour – self-deprecating which I love and very relaxed,' Mackenzie said.

The first essay set for the prince was on the subject of Karl Marx, the founder of modern Communism who argued the state is an instrument of repression, looked forward to the creation of a classless society in which it is certain the House of Windsor would not have featured, dismissed religion as 'the opium of the masses', called for the dictatorship of the proletariat and urged, 'Workers of all lands, unite! – you have nothing to lose but your chains.'

When I mentioned Marx to the prince some years later, he replied: 'Class is the worst thing in the world Marx ever invented!' Marx's interpretation of the capitalist social structure continued to exercise his thoughts, however. Edward continued: 'We use this word – class – as a means to be able to try and differentiate everybody else, to try and package people and keep them in a particular area. It should not be like that.'

Class in its royal sense did have certain advantages, though. Edward wrote an 18,000-word dissertation on the role of Prince Albert in the modernisation of the British Army. He had a privileged access, which other undergraduates did not, to the Royal Archives and royal correspondence and gained a very good mark for himself.

There were other situations when it helped to be who he was. Just after he had sat his finals Edward decided he wanted to throw a farewell party in the garden of the Master's Lodge. 'The college would not have allowed Edward to have it, but as the Lodge garden was under my private jurisdiction we got round it,' Cottrell said. 'It was a privilege but nobody kicked up a fuss. It was a private party for all his friends and people came from all over the place.'

Over 100 people were invited by Edward and two of his contemporaries from college, Rupert Elliot and Tom Hill. The formal invitation was for breakfast in the Master's garden but instead of printed names the card showed sets of initials with Edward's E.A.R.L. (Edward Anthony Richard Louis) in the centre and the others' on either side. The dress was OTT (over the top) and guests were requested to arrive at 10am. 'It was a beautiful June day and a lot of people came up from London,' Cottrell remembers. 'It was a lovely farewell party.'

Edward's princely position, however, did not stand him in good stead when it came to his examinations and his final results were not all that they might have been. He got a 2.2, the medium result at Cambridge. He might have done better but once again the distractions which were deemed to be as important to his education as the academic work itself had taken their examination toll. As Mackenzie said: 'Edward simply didn't work hard enough!'

Lord Renfrew took a more benign view. 'He got a perfectly respectable degree, but he was able to decide what other things he wanted to do and he put a lot of energy into them.'

Edward shared Mackenzie's interpretation. When his mind was stimulated he would find time to study, sometimes working through the night. But going over the same ground again and again held little interest.

'I certainly didn't get a very good degree,' he admitted. 'It was pretty mediocre. I found revision incredibly tedious.'

The student posters which decorated the white walls of Edward's rooms in North Court bore witness to that. One showed a bored-looking orang-utan over a caption which read: 'The more I study, the more I know. The more I know the more I forget. The more I forget the less I know. So why study?'

And he did not, at least not hard enough to gain the degree his tutors thought him capable of. Even so, the delights of Cambridge – the moonlit Cloister Court, the draughty lecture halls and even swotting for exams – had cast their spell and no one was sorrier than Edward to be leaving.

'These have been three of the best years of my life that I am likely to spend,' he told the *Cambridge Evening News*. 'Everybody says that about school, but I don't think I ever enjoyed school as much as I enjoyed university. There's a wonderful mix of people and I am never likely to mix so informally with such a wide range of people.'

He still waxes lyrical about his time at Cambridge and of the wrench he felt at leaving 'time-honoured Jesus College'. Indeed, so taken was he with university life that he thought seriously of staying on. As he explained: 'The transition from there into the big wide world can be quite daunting, especially if you have not got somewhere to go. At least from school to university you know you are going to university. You know you have got something to go to. But if you have not fixed anything after university, it's a real wrench to break out, which is why a lot of people will then decide to do a PhD and stay there.'

Edward thought of doing that; of researching in libraries and laboratories and attending chapel in an MA gown trimmed with white silk. 'It was very tempting,' he said. 'I remember when I was there I thought very seriously about it. "Wouldn't it be nice to be able to stay up?" '

But Edward did have something to do and somewhere to go. He was a Royal Marine and he was due at Lympstone in Devon for the start of his training.

Privately the prince was already harbouring serious doubts about his career in the Marines. Others shared his misgivings. His tutorials with Mackenzie had extended his intellectual horizons. His acting had helped widen his perceptions. 'Being an actor or taking part in light entertainment involves a little introspection,' said Lord Renfrew. 'You begin to see yourself as others see you and I think he may have asked himself whether the paths he had already chosen were in fact the right ones.'

Edward said: 'Everyone thinks I'm mad, but it's probably the greatest challenge I will ever have to meet.'

He was about to discover, in the hardest way possible, just how tough that challenge could be.

Seven

Royal Marines

IT WAS EARLY New Year. The Christmas holidays were over and Prince Edward was on his way back to the Commando Training Centre at Lympstone in Devon. Britain was in the grip of an Arctic freeze and a heavy mantle of snow was drawn tightly across the land which became ever bleaker the further west he drove.

The weather and the outlook matched his spirits. For weeks he had been pondering his future with a despair bordering on desperation. He was a Young Officer in the Royal Marines but the commitment and certainty he needed in order to complete his training were ebbing away.

A glance out of the window was reminder enough of the hardship ahead – of the endless marches across the moors, of being soaked to the skin and chilled to the bone and hungry and exhausted.

Suddenly even the thought of it was unbearable. He had had enough. He would later tell his commanding officer, 'My car started firing on all cylinders.' He knew, finally, with absolute certainty, that he was not prepared to go on – that, against the advice of his training officer and the pleadings of his family, he was going to resign his commission.

Princess Anne also happened to be at the wheel when she heard of her brother's decision. She was in her Reliant Scimitar on the road from Sandringham to London when she heard the news on her car radio that just ten weeks into his training, Prince Edward was definitely quitting the Royal Marines. So shocked was she by the announcement, she later recalled, she had almost driven her car into a ditch.

The Queen was also flabbergasted. The news came as a surprise to her too. Astonishingly, she had not been informed beforehand.

The reason for Anne's reaction was more specific. She had spent a good part of the weekend just past at Buckingham Palace with her brother, talking to him and trying to convince him that it was his royal obligation to see out his officer training programme and that if he quit now he would regret it for the rest of his life. She had spent the best part of Sunday going over and over the arguments. Backing her up was Prince Andrew, a serving officer in the Royal Navy, who was there with Sarah, his wife of five months. Also there to add his weight to the argument was Anne's husband, Mark Phillips, a former captain in 1st The Queen's Dragoon Guards.

The meeting was held in Andrew's quarters on the second floor of the Palace, overlooking the Mall. They had lunch in the comfortable dining room which had once been the Prince of Wales's study and which he had had decorated in warm reds and brown and beige by the interior designer David Hicks, Earl Mountbatten of Burma's son-in-law. There were no servants around to listen to what was said: the food had been left on hot plates on the mahogany sideboard.

The discussion continued on into the afternoon and through into early evening. When Anne left Edward that Sunday night she was convinced that she had persuaded him to stay on to complete the thirty-five week course. Edward had told her he would. He had promised her that he would give it his best shot and see it through to the end of his training. Anne had driven to Sandringham to inform the Queen and Prince Philip, who had assigned her this most delicate of missions, that she had been successful – that Edward was going to complete the remaining months of his one-year Young Officers' training course.

There is no question that Edward believed what he was saying when he made his promise to his sister in front of his brother, his brother-in-law and Sarah. But then everyone left. Edward was on his own and all the doubts reasserted themselves – doubts that he had been harbouring from that first day in September, 1986 when he had reported to the Marines' Commando Training Centre.

Prince Edward had changed. University, he said, 'suddenly opened up a lot of things in life'. His perspective about his royal role and what he could achieve had altered. The rigours of his first ten weeks in the Marines had accelerated the process of self-analysis. Without the presence of his sister to hold up his morale and remind him of his royal duty, he started looking to his future and he did not like what he saw.

That night he made his decision and it was a momentous one. For the first time in his life this most 'royal' of princes, whose actions up until then had been governed and directed and restricted by *who* he was as much as *what*, was going to do what *he* wanted.

And what he was going to do was to resign, to quit if that was what you wanted to call it, and nothing and no one was going to change his mind.

It was the end – not only of his military career, but also of a dream he had nurtured since he was a little boy.

His family had a long association with this most martial of services: his grandfather, George VI was Captain General of the Royal Marines; his father, Prince Philip, succeeded him; his great-uncle Earl Mountbatten was Colonel Commandant up to the time he was murdered. Royal Private Secretaries and equerries were frequently drawn from a Marine background. He had seen the Marines on countless parades throughout his childhood.

Both Charles and Andrew had undergone Commando training before they joined the Royal Navy and earned the right to wear the coveted Green Beret. Brigadier Robert Tailyour thought that Edward might have wanted to go one better than his brothers and make the Marines his full-time career – to prove, in effect, that he was tougher than they were.

Colonel Ian Moore, his commanding officer at Lympstone, is of the opinion that something as colourful but straightforward as the Marine bands, who accompany the Royal Family wherever they go, may have been the trigger that first stirred his interest in the service.

Whatever the reason – and it was probably a combination of all of them – Edward had certainly had his mind set on the Marines from early on. Adam Wise, his first Private Secretary, recalled: 'He had always wanted to be in or inclined towards the Royal Marines from quite an early age – from about ten.'

Colonel Alan Hooper was the commanding officer when Edward did a week's detachment with 40 Commando in Belize. He had first met the prince at the Royal Tournament some years earlier. He recalled: 'Prince Edward at that stage was about fourteen. When I was introduced to Prince Andrew he looked at my uniform and said to Edward, "That's the one you want to talk to about the Marines." I said, "Really?" and Prince Andrew said, "Yes, he's crazy about it." He wanted to be a Royal Marine for a very long time – that is fact.'

If it really had been the stirring sounds of the Marine band resounding through the courtyard at Buckingham Palace that first captured his imagination, then it was the tales of their *Boys' Own*-style derring-do that fuelled his interest throughout his youth. Like a lot of boys, he was enthralled by the tough, adventurous reputation. Said Colonel Moore: 'He was interested in the Royal Marine history from some early stage.'

The Royal Marines is a fighting unit. As Colonel Moore explained: 'We are a multi-purpose amphibious force that can go anywhere at the drop of a hat.' To fight. The Marines helped cover Britain's withdrawal from Empire, 'landing in Suez, fighting in Malaysia and Aden and the Falklands'. There was only one year – 1968 – since the end of the Second World War when the Marines did not see active service – something, Moore said, 'which we pride ourselves on'.

On the rare occasions when the bullets were not flying, the Marines would seek out other kinds of foe to confront in places like the Arctic circle in Norway in winter which, as Moore said, is a form of active service in itself: 'You don't need an enemy there – the enemy is the weather.'

The Marines regard themselves as the hardest, the most determined fighting force Britain can offer. Only the Paratroopers rival them for toughness and, in the honoured tradition of inter-regimental rivalry, the Marines dismiss the comparison. Major Ewen Southby-Tailyour – who was Edward's Commanding Officer during his introduction to amphibious training on the beaches of North Devon – is regarded by the Prince as 'an incredible character'. The handsome, tough-as-nails commander of 539 Assault Squadron, Southby-Tailyour is a yachtsman of international repute who, from his own first-hand knowledge, provided the Atlantic Task Force with vital charts which contributed to the successful landing on the Falklands. He is also the son of a former Marine Commandant General and cousin of Brigadier Robert Tailyour, who was in charge of all officer training, including Prince Edward's.

According to Southby-Tailyour: 'The Commando training is certainly stronger and tougher than the parachute regiment.' In the Paras, he said, all a trainee had to do was enough press-ups to build up 15-inch biceps and be willing to jump out of an aeroplane. In the Marines, he said, tapping his head, 'It's all done up here. The Royal Marine is trained as a rather more thinking man's infantry.'

There was precious little time for thought in the middle of a blizzard in the middle of night in the middle of winter in the middle of Dartmoor weighed down with seventy pounds of equipment. That was what the men had to go through; it was even tougher for the officers. Lympstone is the only training centre in all the services where officers and men train together. This helps forge the camaraderie, the interdependence which leads Marines of all ranks to describe their corps as a 'family'. Everyone is driven hard but it is the YOs (Young Officers) who are driven hardest of all. Said Colonel Moore: 'The young Marines can see the officers are being made to do challenges which are greater than the ones they are being asked to do. The YOs have to do the thirty-mile march in seven hours and the Marines are allowed eight. The YOs have to be better and the Marines know that.'

What the Marines are looking for in their officers, said Moore, 'are people who are highly competent under pressure – pressure of fatigue, of physical hardship, people who are able to take the knocks. In a nutshell: all-purpose intellect, ability to take knocks, ability to stand on your own two feet and be in close contact with the people you are leading and continue to lead them when the going gets worse. Those are the foremost requirements. But there is also this traditional sense for the officers to behave with decorum and value their Naval tradition which is more than 300 years old.'

This, then, was the elite body of 7,000 fighting men that Edward had elected to join. 'Soldier an' sailor too', as Rudyard Kipling, the poet of Empire, called them – and 'no special chrysanthemums'.

It seemed an unlikely choice for a prince who, in the public's imagination, was the most sensitive of the three royal brothers; a young man who was regarded as more bookish than butch.

In his case appearances were deceptive.

Certainly there were those who queried Edward's choice of career. James Thomas, his Gordonstoun housemaster, harboured quiet reservations. Edward, he observed, was not 'a great enthusiast for the great outdoors' in its Outward Bound form – and nothing was more Outward Bound than the Royal Marines. His prep school headmaster James Edwards wondered if he had the single-mindedness the Marines demand. Alan Cottrell, the Master of Jesus College, stated: 'It [the Marines] wasn't right for him.'

There were even mutterings in the Marine itself from certain officers who were concerned, as they euphemistically put it, that Edward might not be 'quite heterosexual enough' for this most macho of Corps.

But what no one doubted, once they had seen him in action, was his ability to meet the physical demands of the Royal Marines. Every Marine who had dealings with him agreed on that point, including the sergeant who was in charge of physical fitness when Edward first arrived in Devon for his basic training.

Marine Sergeant Taff Simmons was a wiry rugby player who, in the words of his commanding officer, hated everyone and everything especially people who did not play rugby and were not Marines. He did not give a damn about the Royal Family. When he was told that he was to have charge of Prince Edward, he said: 'I'll run that little fucker off his feet – Sir.'

Simmons was as good as his word. Having got to bed sometimes as late as three o'clock in the morning, the trainees would be woken up again at 5am for another day of running, marching, wading, crawling through water-filled tunnels, abseiling down cliffs or canoeing down the River Torridge with blackened faces.

After one particularly arduous day Simmons reported to Ewen Southby-Tailyour, 'Good hand, isn't he, Sir?'

'Who?' Southby-Tailyour asked.

'Fucking Prince, Sir. He's not unfit Sir, is he Sir?'

Edward, through guts and pluck and determination, had earned the grudging admiration of one of the toughest men to wear a sergeant's uniform.

In December, 1985, while he was still a student at Cambridge, Edward did a week's detachment in Belize just to the north of Central America's aptly named Mosquito Coast. Poor and under-developed, Belize was under constant threat of invasion by neighbouring Guatemala which claimed this inhospitable stretch of swamp and jungle-covered real estate as their historical right dating back to the old Spanish empire. To safeguard the territorial integrity of its former colony of British Honduras, Britain kept a detachment of troops there and used the opportunity to train them in jungle warfare.

Edward was assigned to 40 Commando under the command of Colonel Alan Hooper who met him at the airport. It was, Hooper recalled, very much a case of the serving officer greeting Prince Edward, the son of his Sovereign. By the time they got to the camp five minutes drive away, however, their roles had been reversed, with Hooper confirmed in his position as the commanding officer, with Edward very much the junior. 'He took the lead in that,' Hooper said. He was not like his brother, Andrew, who had once condescendingly told a Rear-Admiral, 'You can call me Andy,' to be met with the stern riposte, 'And you can call me Sir.' Edward was keen to fit in, to do his duty and his best – without favour.

Throughout his week there he carried the same equipment, slept in the same rain-sodden trenches, ate the same iron rations, swallowed the same anti-malaria tablets and suffered the same discomfort from the mosquitoes and bugs which were indifferent to the strongest repellents and were capable of finding their way through the most well-placed mosquito nets.

'The feedback was very good indeed,' Hooper said. 'He was not treated any differently from anyone else and he did everything he was required to and actually fitted in well. We were very impressed at how unselfish he was. He tried very hard to do things properly. He wanted no favours.'

It was more usual for university undergraduates like Edward to do this week's field training in the summer holiday. Edward had specifically asked for a winter exercise because, he explained, his summer schedule was already filling up with official engagements. The Marines agreed – and set him a punishing itinerary.

It started with a 24-hour 'tenderfoot' course. Edward warned his CO: 'I am accident-prone.' Hooper replied: 'For God's sake do what you're told to do. If you're told to chop a piece of bamboo in a certain direction don't do it any other way.'

In that day and following night he was taught how to make a basic shelter using a sapling bent over to the ground to make a frame which is then covered with a groundsheet. He was shown how to make a fire and how to make himself comfortable at night (off the ground, in a hammock). Most importantly, he was taught about basic movement in the jungle. Said Hooper: 'You keep to single tracks, you avoid cutting your way through a trail, that uses up too much energy so you bypass any blockage you have on the route. That requires a high degree of navigation. It's done on compass work and pacing with your feet. If you have to divert you use a compass bearing. You have to be very accurate, there are no reference points.'

It can be very disorientating for a novice. The jungle closes in and you quickly lose all sense of time and direction which in turn leads to a dangerous loss of confidence. Hooper explained: 'The whole idea of jungle training is to develop confidence in your ability to navigate and be able to survive in this strange environment.'

As soon as he had mastered these vital rudiments he was dispatched to northern Belize to take part in a major exercise which happened to be going on at the time. He was dressed in jungle camouflage, was carrying his bedding and enough food and ammunition to see him through for twenty-four hours and his face was blackened. He was put into a defensive position in a slit trench which he had to dig himself and which he was required to hold against an enemy which mounted surprise dawn attacks backed up by light armour. The trench was two feet wide and seven feet long and it became Edward's home for the duration of the exercise. It was, said Hooper, 'pretty uncomfortable', particularly for Edward who had only just flown out from a British winter and had not had time to acclimatise to the hot, humid tropical jungle.

But as soon as that exercise came to its end, and with barely time for a shower and a change of kit, he was helicoptered down to the south of the country to go out on foot and river patrol through the jungle which was equally gruelling.

'He had no trial preparation at all – he just went with them,' said Hooper. 'The whole idea of this was to give him the experience of operating in the full gambit of Belize.'

It was a tough indoctrination for any young 21-year-old but especially for someone from Edward's cosseted royal background. None the less, he acquitted himself well. Hooper was impressed. He recalled: 'The feedback from the Marines that I talked to, ordinary Marines who shared the trench with him, was absolutely fine. He fitted in well and the Marines liked having him around. They got on very well with him and he did everything he was required to do. This was a guy who asked no favours; he pulled his weight and that was the thing that impressed people.'

The accident-prone prince had managed to complete his week without mishap. He went up to Hooper and said: 'One relieved commanding officer – I'm still in one piece!'

On the day Hooper met the prince at the airport in Belize he had written in his diary: 'I suspect there is some steel there and doubtless considerable determination.' At the end of Edward's week, Hooper noted in his diary: 'Splendid sense of humour, very alert and well read, with a worldliness beyond his years.'

Someone else was also impressed – Taff Simmons. By coincidence the sergeant was in Belize with a section of landing craft. When Edward went aboard the craft he walked over to Simmons and said, 'Hello Sergeant, remember we last met on the beach in Devon.'

Simmons, the tough, cynical Marine sergeant who did not give a damn about anything or anyone, was an instant convert to the royal cause. In Simmons own words, the two were henceforth 'inseparable friends'. And that, as Ewen Southby-

Tailyour pointed out, was the kind of loyalty only first-class officers inspire. He said: 'If you have got that sort of backing behind you on that sort of level you are not going to fail in the Marines if you want to continue in the service.'

At that stage Edward did. Hooper said: 'The thing that makes people stay in the military is actually the comradeship and going through shared experiences with other people and that is what I was trying to give him a snapshot of in Belize and he had come out of it extremely well. He fitted in with the environment. I thought he would fit in well into the Commando life.'

The only reservation – and at that stage it was a slight one – was his inability to relax completely and become just another Marine. It is a vital part of the Marines' 'ethos' (a word that they use with great frequency) that no one, no matter how tough or fit they might be, can survive the rigours of the training programme without the help of their comrades. Indeed, one of the aims of the programme is to foster and develop precisely that interdependency which makes the Marines such a formidable fighting unit.

'They have all found a barrier at some stage and at some stage somebody's helped. It happens to everyone – it happened to me,' said Hooper.

Robin Eggar, in his book *Commando, Survival of the Fittest*, wrote: 'At some point everyone, however prepared, however physically fit, however motivated, will be brought to a point where they will want to give up. It may be the Atlantic gales whipping through Dartmoor, or the insidious Welsh damp at Sennybridge that creeps into the very marrow of your bones . . . Even the fittest can fall to a niggling injury, a groin or hamstring strain that never has a chance to fully recover, so the pain keeps grinding on and on, tightening with each weary step as if a torturer were applying a thumbscrew turn.'

Edward was well aware of this and by a combination of hard physical exercise and a natural mental toughness, did his best to meet each challenge as it presented itself. He had, everyone agreed, 'absolutely the right approach'. There were moments, though, particularly when he was out on patrol in the south of Belize, when the royal reserve which had always been one of his notable characteristics would prompt his colleagues to point out to him that it was all right to unwind and let more of his feelings show.

Said Hooper: 'He was still feeling this way but that was totally understandable – the guy had come from Cambridge straight from Buckingham Palace and then straight out here. We were throwing all sorts of things at him and the boys were saying, "It's OK, you can do that." '

With the best of wills, however, there was always going to be a limit to just what Edward could do. He never pulled royal rank but he was always going to be royal. With the consummate skill bred into him from childhood, he was able to switch from being a Royal Marine, out on patrol in the jungle, his face blackened, his body covered in insect bites, to royal prince, attending a formal, black-tie dinner with the commander of the British forces in Belize on his last night there.

It was switching back again that was the difficult part.

There had been no detective in attendance when he was out in the jungle. Hooper had pointed out that, with 200 armed Marines surrounding him, he was as safe as he was ever going to be. The moment the manoeuvres finished, however, Merrylees resumed his position at the prince's side. When Edward spent his last day water skiing and snorkling behind the coral reef which runs along the Belize coast, Merrylees, ever the faithful ghillie, went with him.

He was still with him the following September when Edward arrived at Lympstone to begin his full-time YO training. Merrylees had inspected the barracks and put Edward in a sparse, 12-foot by 10-foot whitewashed bedroom at the end of the corridor with himself on one side and one of the senior training officers on the other. He had the locks changed and insisted on keeping the keys himself. There were washrooms and empty sleeping quarters between Edward and the other YOs. An invisible but obvious barrier had been placed between the prince and the rest of his batch of thirty-six – 'between the prince and the paupers', as Eggar, who spent fifteen months with the Marines while researching his book, described the situation.

That made it 'impossible for Edward to integrate with his batch mates'. And if he was unable to integrate properly, it would be extremely difficult for him to establish that interdependence which is at the heart of the Marines' ethos.

It was not easy for Andrew Merrylees, either. The YOs were young and extremely fit. He was middle-aged. He would jog the first few hundred yards and then retire to the ambulance Land-Rover which the regulations now insist be on hand at every training exercise. 'It was not Edward he had to worry about – it was Andrew,' one senior Marine officer jokingly remarked.

But it was 2nd Lieutenant Prince Edward (salary: £7,391 per annum) they should have been worrying about. The first royal ever to serve in the Royal Marines was starting to 'wobble'.

Ewen Southby-Tailyour said that, while he did not regard Edward as a likely Sword of Honour candidate, 'he certainly had the ability mentally and physically to do it and become a perfectly good Royal Marines officer.' That assessment was confirmed by the progress he made in September, October and November when, according to Colonel Moore, he came in the top quarter in his batch of thirty, 'so he was clearly pulling his weight'.

Despite his encouraging marks, all was not as it should be. The bright early promise was starting to fade. The enthusiasm which had led him into the Royal Marines in the first place, which had sustained him through the jungles of Central America and had kept him going on those night exercises on Dartmoor was starting to falter – and as every Marine will testify, without total commitment it is all but impossible for a YO to get through his training. Lympstone cadets are put 'under the most extreme physical and emotional pressure possible'. The strain soon shows and stories started filtering out of Lympstone, some wildly inaccurate, others with a grain of truth to them, but all of them pointing to Edward's increasing disenchantment with the service which was scheduled to be his life for at least the next five years.

'If you can do anything you like with your life why spend wet cold miserable nights on Dartmoor unless you have to. Unless you want to be a Royal Marine 110 per cent you will not get through the training because it is so tough,' said Hooper.

The routine was grinding. The winter weather was appalling. Temperatures frequently dropped to below –10°C. He was up every morning at 5.30. He would work through until late the following night. As well as the physical exertion, there were also classroom lessons to attend. 'You are very short of time all the time and the accumulative effect can be very depressing,' Southby-Tailyour acknowledged.

Colonel Moore concurred. The point is to develop the officers' ability to function in the most difficult and demanding of situations. 'The actuality of YO training comes as quite a shock,' Edward's commanding officer said. 'There is a nightmare quality about it.'

It is at this stage that the support system, that old-fashioned but effective spirit of 'one for all and all for one', comes into play. As the going got tougher, however, Edward found himself increasingly isolated down at his lonely end of the barrack corridor. The gap was turning into a chasm.

He was not quite the loner he has been portrayed as. He was not, as Colonel Moore observed, 'the kind of chap who wears his life on his sleeve, who makes friends easily or casually'. But he did have the companionship of fellow recruits like Quintus Travis and Peter Fraser, both of whom knew him from Cambridge, and, most particularly, Michael Fontaine, who died in an accident three years later while serving with the Special Boat Service.

He would occasionally join his comrades for a drink in the local pub and that was important; in the competitive world of the Marines there is little room for misfits or loners. And his *esprit de corps* was such that when it came to the turn of Cambridge to host the annual university cadet entrants' black-tie dinner, Edward insisted it be held 'at my place' which turned out to be the Throne Room at Buckingham Palace. The wine was as good as might be expected, fine speeches were made, and afterwards Edward showed the diners who included Mike Wilkins, the Commandant General, around the Palace. It was, everyone agreed, a most enjoyable evening.

The rumour factory, however, preferred to dwell on other matters.

There was the Kissing Incident. Edward, it was said, was posing in front of a mirror adjusting his cap when a hard-bitten, battle-hardened sergeant walked by. 'How do I look?' Edward is said to have asked.

'You look lovely, Sir, just lovely,' the burly sergeant is supposed to have replied – and then took Edward in his arms and planted a humiliating kiss on his cheek.

The Royal Marines were dismayed by the credence given to the anecdote which, if true, reflected as badly on the Corps as it did on the Prince. Colonel Moore said: 'I was deeply concerned about that story and sought to deny it. Of course, you can never know exactly what is going on but it strikes me as highly unlikely.'

Colonel Hooper was more emphatic. Yes, he said, the kissing incident had taken place, but it had happened a long time in the past and 'It had nothing at all to do with Prince Edward and should be treated as total fiction.'

The Mud Incident, however, did happen.

Adam Wise pointed out that most Marines get mud rammed down their throats for one reason or another 'but the others have been forgotten and only Edward has been remembered'. He discounts the suggestion that it was the result of bullying. 'Bear in mind that his policeman was always with him and if there was an incident of bullying, anything as bad as that, I think the policeman might well have said something.'

There was a hardline school of thought within the Corps that believed that Edward would have been best advised to have dispensed with his detectives while on Marine training. As Hooper had acutely observed, how much safer was Edward ever going to be than when he was surrounded by armed Marines? One detective was not going to make a blind bit of difference in any crisis that might have arisen out in the bogs of Dartmoor. But on the orders of the Queen's courtiers in consultation with Scotland Yard, either Andrew Merrylees or his colleague, Dick Griffin, were with him at all times, and despite Merrylees's liking for the back of the Land-Rover, they always stayed close enough to see and report any untoward incident. They were careful, though, to stay in the background as much as possible and not to interfere except in an emergency.

The mud incident clearly did not fall into that category but it was a humbling moment for the prince, all the same. As part of their apprenticeship in the demanding business of leadership, the YOs in each batch would take it in turn to issue orders to the others. This was usually done in a low-key way. According to Lieutenant Matt Lodge who was on the same course as the Prince and was quoted in *Commando, Survival of the Fittest*, the moment the baton of authority passed to Edward he became 'like a drill sergeant bellowing at a bunch of raw recruits'. The prince, said Lodge, was 'the classic example of someone who wasn't that sure of himself in a command appointment, so he imposed himself by shouting and being authoritarian'.

The story carries an echo of the officiousness which both his fellow pupils and his housemaster had occasion to observe at Gordonstoun. It was not the best way of handling his colleagues who, once they were all in the green battle fatigues of The Royal Marines, were very much his equals.

One afternoon his batch of off-duty Marines were enjoying a game of touch rugby in the mud banks of the River Exe. Edward, who was off games injured, was standing watching with three others who were also unable to play. Suddenly the batch decided that those clean fellows on the sidelines needed to be muddied up. They duly were – and Edward in particular.

Lodge painted the episode in harsh tones. 'They rammed mud in his ears, in his mouth, right up his nose, poured so much inside his shirt he could have been Mud Pie Man.' It was, he said, the batch's 'revenge' for Edward's treatment of them. 'It was a coded warning to Edward to get in line and treat his equals with the respect they gave each other.'

Colonel Moore, on the other hand, regarded it as 'a skylark, not a vindictive thing. It would have happened to anyone who was standing on the side watching in their clean kit.'

Edward kept his feelings to himself and never voiced any complaint. He was taken aback, though, by what happened next.

After he had extricated himself from the ooze of the Exe and was making his way back to the Officers' Mess, a young recruit recognised him and threw him a salute. Edward was astonished that anyone should still be able to identify him in the state he was in. It was yet another – and most unwelcome reminder – that even when covered in mud from head to squelching toe, he was still a prince. The chasm – between Edward's ambitions and the hard reality of his situation – was yawning ever wider. By the middle of December, when he was still only ten weeks into the training course, Edward came to the momentous conclusion that it was unbridgeable.

Incidents like the muddied salute made him ever more aware that, however hard he tried, there would always be limits to what he was going to be allowed to achieve. Brigadier Robert Tailyour said: 'He thought he would be able to do active service as Prince Andrew had set a precedent with his time in the Falklands although he knew he would never be allowed to go to Northern Ireland.' And that, in a small service like the Marines which has no room for passengers, even royal ones, was certain to cause friction.

Tailyour's cousin, Ewen said: 'In the Navy, the Army and the Air Force there are areas where a royal prince cannot serve, but he can easily pass those by with no stigma whatsoever. But there are no gaps in the Royal Marines career structure through which a royal prince can pass without comment.'

Edward, drawing on the experience of three years at university, was now mature enough to recognise the contradiction inherent in his situation. University had also changed his outlook on life which in turn had taken the edge off his military ambitions. There was nothing unusual in that, according to Edward's Cambridge tutor Gavin Mackenzie who observed: 'These people sign up for a short service commission when they are sixteen or seventeen. It sounds fine – you are paid handsomely when you are at university and you go off and do summer camps. But if you believe that university is supposed to be an educative and broadening cultural experience it's hardly surprising that four years later some youngsters change their minds and feel they don't want to go into the military.'

Adam Wise agreed. 'The way they train their officers works very much better if you take them straight from school. Edward, like a number of other YOs who had gone to university first, objected to being 'treated like schoolboys again'.

Colonel Moore acknowledged that it is sometimes easier to educate someone who has first undergone Marine training than it is to 'discipline the educated. It may well be that had he joined at eighteen he would have found his niche with us. But you change at university.'

Prince Philip, Captain General of the Royal Marines, agreed. After Edward finally quit he wrote that 'it might be an idea for University Cadets to do their basic training before they go to their universities.'

What was obvious with hindsight was not, however, apparent at the time. As Colonel Moore noted, 'He kept his own counsel a lot of the time. He knows how to put a good face on things.' He had been trained to stand alone, keeping his thoughts and his worries bottled up inside. That explains why, when the emotional dam finally did break, the Marines were taken by surprise.

The story that Edward was to leave the Royal Marines broke on Wednesday 7 January, 1987, the day he was due back at Lympstone. By pure coincidence, Peter Fraser had also tendered his resignation. There had not been any secret pact, as some newspapers suggested, but their reasons were very similar.

The Prince had been at Sandringham for the Christmas break which is the time, according to Brigadier Robert Tailyour, when many YOs start to 'wobble – when they lose direction or their candle starts to waver in the wind a bit'. Edward had just completed his hardest exercise to date out on the moors of Devon. It had taken a lot out of him and it had left him wondering why he was subjecting himself to such a physical and mental battering.

To compound his problems, he was still in considerable pain from the injury to his knee and it was severe enough to worry his training officers who were concerned that it would increase the already considerable pressure he was under. It was now that he was at his most vulnerable. 'You go back to the bosom of your family and unless your family are very supportive life can be very difficult,' the Brigadier observed.

It had not been the jolliest of Royal Christmases that year. There was a lot of tension in the air but instead of deflecting Edward's thoughts away from his own problems, it only fermented them.

The marriage between Charles and Diana was starting to come apart at the seams – 'They were at each other's throats the whole time,' one member of the Household recalled – and Princess Anne was not getting on well with Captain Mark Phillips. They separated soon afterwards.

For all Sandringham's apparent size, the guests get on top of each other. Confronted with these domestic difficulties, Edward disappeared under his own pall and spent much of the time, when he was not riding or shooting, by himself out on long walks or sitting in his bedroom. The Family was aware that he was having a fit of the 'wobbles'. He had discussed it with them, at first by way of casual comment, then in more detail and they had taken it up, as if by way of a distraction from their own unhappy concerns. They offered advice, encouragement and stern reminders of where they thought his duty lay.

By then, though, he was also talking to other people, people outside the royal laager. In so doing he was breaking one of the Royal Family's most inviolate canons – the rule of *omerta*, of silence. Prince Philip once opined, 'The children soon discover that it is much safer to unburden yourself to a member of the family, than just a friend.'

Prince Edward, alone amongst members of the senior branch of the Royal Family, had broken free from that siege mentality. It was the beginning of what would quickly prove to be a sea change in his life.

Before he even started at Lympstone he was already hinting to Biddy Hayward, the theatrical producer who would later get him his first foothold in the theatre, that he was having second thoughts about a military career.

'He wasn't a whiner and wasn't just saying "I'm desperately unhappy," ' she recalled. 'He was just saying "I am not sure this is the career for me." '

During the Christmas holidays he had dinner with Romy Adlington, the twenty-year-old model whose company he found so enjoyable. The two sat up until three o'clock in the morning discussing his predicament. 'The Prince told me he didn't want to go back to the Marines' camp,' she said. 'He said that being away for Christmas from the pressures of training had made him realise that he wasn't sure if he wanted a life in the Services.'

The person who enjoyed the prince's greatest confidence, however, was Gavin Mackenzie. Well before he told his family what was on his mind, Edward drove to Cambridge to talk to his former tutor. They met in Mackenzie's book-lined rooms at Jesus College.

The Royal Family, for whom military service has traditionally been the only career option, were most anxious that Edward should continue in the Royal Marines. Mackenzie, the academic with little interest in or empathy with the military ethos, took a dramatically different view. He said: 'I told him to get out!'

By that Wednesday Edward had decided to do precisely that. The Marines were shocked. Their most famous recruit may have been finding it increasingly helpful to talk about himself and his problems with people outside his own immediate family, but they did not include his fellow Marines. Said Colonel Moore: 'We had not realised how much the lamp of his motivation had dimmed and how inwardly despondent he must have got.' Edward had succeeded in keeping his royal mask in place right up to his last week in the Marines. When they heard the news on Wednesday morning, most of the officers and NCOs did not believe it.

When they learnt that the story was true and that Edward had already handed in his letter of resignation, most were genuinely upset. Edward's batch officer, Captain Steve Balm, said: 'You cannot help examining what we have done in the past few months and asking yourself the questions: Did we do something wrong? Could we have done something different?'

Edward's Commanding Officer Major Paul Bancroft said: 'One always feels a deep sense of sadness and indeed failure when a trainee asks to leave . . . it's very unsettling to see Young Officers with huge potential and good prospects asking to leave the Royal Marines, not because they cannot hack the training but because they don't think they want to make a career within the Corps.'

Up to 50 per cent of any batch drop out from the courses at Lympstone and for planning purposes the Marines work on an estimated failure rate of 30 per cent. But although failure was built into the system, Edward was no ordinary recruit who could slip quietly away. A last-ditch attempt was made to try and persuade him to change his mind.

Edward arrived back at Lympstone on that Wednesday, two

days after he was supposed to report for duty (Buckingham Palace had initially tried to explain away his no-show by saying he had 'flu). He went into a two hours' counselling session with Colonel Moore and Major Bancroft. The conversations were 'deep and soul-searching' and at the end of them Edward had promised to reconsider his decision.

That weekend Edward returned to London and now it was the turn of Anne, backed by her brother, Andrew, and her husband, to apply the pressure. It was to no avail. Edward was not for turning. Moore said: 'Either the lamp is glowing or the lamp is dwindling and the fact is that come January 1987 his inner motivation for the job was not there.' Against everyone's wishes but his own he went ahead and quit.

On Monday Edward drove back to Lympstone and told Colonel Moore who told the Commandment General who told the Queen. It was a bleak, bitterly cold morning which mirrored the mood at the Commando Training Centre. Edward collected up his few belongings from his room then went into the Mess where the officers were having morning coffee. He walked around, moving from one group to another, hand out-stretched, shaking hands with everyone. Some of the officers took his hand but allowed their eyes to slide away; others went to the other extreme and wished him their hearty best. Everyone was embarrassed. One senior officer remarked, 'It was like coming out on the wrong side of a battle.' The scene was stilted and dramatic and everybody was glad when it was over and Edward drove away in his silver Rover from Lympstone for the last time.

On Tuesday 13 January, Buckingham Palace issue the following statement:

> After much consideration HRH The Prince Edward has decided to resign from the Royal Marines.
>
> An announcement about his future plans is not expected for some time.
>
> Prince Edward is leaving the Marines with great regret but has decided that he does not wish to make the service his long-term career.

There were accusations that he had wimped out, that he was

not tough enough for the Royal Marines, that he 'wept for hours' after taking the decision to resign. He dismissed those reports as so much speculative nonsense. They were, he insisted, 'pure fiction'.

He still had his family to deal with, however. Edward would later maintain that at no time did he take any flak from anyone. That is not the way the Household remembers it. The Queen's initial shock had quickly turned into the icy-cold regal displeasure which is her most potent weapon. The Queen Mother was even angrier. Both had set, old-fashioned ideas as to the behaviour expected of a member of the Royal Family; to them Edward's decision smacked of dereliction of duty.

For a family whose position depends upon keeping up the most correct of appearances, Edward's walk-out had all the hallmarks of a public relations disaster. The Royal Marines certainly saw it that way. They had seen Edward as a 'golden opportunity' (their phrase) to keep the Marines in the public eye when cuts in defence spending were leading to substantial reductions throughout Britain's armed forces. As it had turned out, he had proved himself to be well up to the job, both physically and mentally. And if he was not, as was often stated, the leading candidate for the Sword of Honour – that was awarded to his friend, Quintus Travis – he would certainly have finished well towards the top of his batch.

Now he was leaving – quitting – without completing any of the courses. Major Southby-Tailyour, expressing the opinion of most Marines, believed that the prince should have seen through his basic Commando training and earned his Green Beret before resigning. 'He should have just stuck it out a bit longer,' he said.

Yet for all the furore generated in the military and royal Establishments, there was a strong ground swell of public sympathy for the prince.

The Times's royal correspondent, Alan Hamilton, wrote: 'Most will applaud his decision to quit rather than chain himself to five years of misery. And most will applaud him for breaking a convention which is perhaps becoming outdated.'

Royal biographer Anthony Holden declared: 'Edward is no wimp. He has merely had the good sense to question the value of a military career *per se*, particularly for someone in his own unique position. He has shown that he wishes to be his own man and thus choose his own career, not have it chosen for him, nor to live his life merely by tradition or precedent.' It had been Edward's own decision entirely to join the Marines, but that does not distract from the fact that most people agreed with Holden. Sir John Junor might thunder – and duly did – that Edward was going to be remembered for the rest of his life for his 'irresolution' but a poll of his own readers in the *Sunday Express* found that 80.7 per cent supported Edward, while only 12 per cent were against him.

Many people pointed out that Edward needed as much courage to quit as to carry on, if not more so. Mackenzie, who may have had as much to do with helping Edward to reach his decision as anybody, said: 'I could not teach Edward anything about physical courage or moral integrity. It might take a bit more of both qualities to resign than to remain.'

One man who recognised just those qualities was Edward's father, Prince Philip, Captain General of the Royal Marines. Given his well-earned reputation for irascibility, it was perhaps inevitable that observers would surmise that Philip had been outraged by Edward's decision; that harsh words had been exchanged between the two; even that Edward had been reduced to tears by his father's anger. It was a potent image and it grew in the telling and retelling.

The truth was quite the opposite. Philip was in fact the most supportive of all the Royal Family. More worldly wise than his wife, he was able to analyse the problem in a rational, objective way, while the Queen saw it only in terms of family duty and royal reputation which, by her logic, were one and the same.

Adam Wise recalled: 'The first person he went to when he really had had enough of the Marines was Prince Philip and he was extremely understanding about the whole thing. He was very reasonable and gave him very sensible advice.'

The counsel he gave was straightforward and practical. As he informed the Marines' Commandant General Sir Michael Wilkins in a private and confidential letter which appeared on the front page of the *Sun* (which the paper maintained was read to them over the telephone by a man who claimed he was speaking from a call box in Exeter) the Family had made every effort to try and persuade Edward to change his mind 'but we all made clear that the final decision was his alone'. Edward, he warned, would face 'a very difficult problem of readjustment'.

Said Wise: 'Prince Philip did not get on his high horse at all and did not get cross about the fact that his son was rejecting the Royal Marines of which he was the Captain General.' Philip, infuriated by trivialities, was showing himself to be clear-headed at this time of major crisis. In one of those public gestures so beloved by the public, father and son were photographed walking together side by side to church at Sandringham the following Sunday.

The Royal Marines were less sanguine. At the Royal Tournament that year the 100-odd members of Yankee Company 45 Commando wore T-shirts which bore, on the front, the message, 'You can turn a frog into a Prince,' and on the back, '. . . but you can't turn a Prince into a Marine.' It was just one of a range of sweatshirts the Marines had printed. Others bore such messages as, 'I have gone where princes fear to tread' and 'NOT by Royal Appointment'.

No action was taken against the Marines for their impertinence. A spokesman said: 'Of course we frown on something of this nature because we are aware of our relationship with the Royal Family. But if a Marine chooses to wear a T-shirt when he is out of service dress there is nothing we can do about it.' To underline the point, he added: 'And besides, a sense of humour is a sense of humour and one of the characteristics of the Marines is that we encourage cheerfulness in the face of adversity.'

But what of Edward? His life was to be fundamentally and irreversibly changed by his decision to leave the Royal Marines. Nor was it a decision that left its mark on him alone. The British monarchy in its modern incarnation is very much a family affair in which the actions of one member have a ripple-through effect on the others. By turning his back on the career conventions of his caste, he would inevitably give impetus to the public's changing perceptions of their reigning Family.

Edward was aware of this. They were factors, he said, which he took into consideration as he was struggling to make up his mind. Together they helped him reach his conclusion. He has not changed his mind. Even in the hard light of hindsight he is certain that he did the right thing. And as he explained to me, if he had to make the decision all over again, he would make the same one.

He said: 'I was totally committed. I don't regret anything. I enjoyed the time I spent in the Royal Marines and I was very glad that I had something I was going to after university. I was able to breach that chasm which a lot of students get to if they have not got something to go to. University has opened up a lot of things in life, but still it's a slightly closeted environment and the transition from there into the big wide world can be quite daunting especially if you haven't got somewhere to go.'

At the same time, though, Cambridge had extended both his intellectual and social horizons to a point beyond what Lympstone had to offer him. When he was at school, he said, 'I knew I was going to university, I knew I had secured my place with the Royal Marines, so I knew what I was going to be doing over the next four to five years. It didn't really cross my mind particularly to think of anything beyond that. If I had gone straight in after Gordonstoun there would have been absolutely nothing else. I would not have considered anything else and I would not have got a wider perspective on life and an increasing awareness of my own role in life.

'But that awareness got me thinking when I was in the Royal Marines. I was doing a University Cadetship which meant that every summer and Christmas break I used to go and do a stint, which was fascinating because it gave me in three years a really good insight into how they worked and it gave me the ability of being able to see what life was going to be like beyond Lympstone.'

Lympstone, he said, 'is a training establishment. It is simply there for training. If you can cope with that you can cope with anything else. But it has really got very little to do with anything else you are going to face throughout the rest of your life in a service.' If you are a prince of the realm, that is. As Edward explained: 'Everything has become a great deal more professional in the ten to fifteen last few years – or that is what we call it. There are much greater commitments to whatever it is that you want to try and do. And it is right across the board in every sphere of jobs and even within the Royal Family. If you look at the statistics, everybody is working considerably harder for less.

'I began to realise that, with an increasing awareness, I knew I was not really going to be able to fit in the Royal Marines as neatly as I liked to think I would. I would always have a policeman there. I could never go out with the rest of the lads into the town because everybody knew [who I was]. It was always obvious you were a Royal Marine in Exeter or that part of Devon because everybody had short haircuts. If I went it was perfectly blatant who that particular team was.

'Maybe I was becoming too aware of myself or maybe people were becoming too aware of who I was but it was getting more and more difficult and I didn't see really the way it was going to work. I was never going to fit very neatly in the way I had envisaged it and that more than anything else decided me.'

He had, he insisted, 'nothing against the Royal Marines *per se* – it would have been the same across the board in any of the services.'

He dismissed the suggestion that he should have carried on and completed his 35-week training course before leaving. 'Everybody said, "Why don't you finish the course." But I would have been wasting everyone's time and I didn't want to do that. I resolved in my own mind that a clean break would be the simplest and the best for them.'

He had inevitable moments of doubt and confusion. He knew there would be a welter of unfavourable publicity. It took a long time, he admitted, before he summoned up the courage to act on his intuition. And when he did he found himself in limbo, his future unclear – just as his father had predicted.

'Everything that had been panning out in front of me ceased,' he said. 'You see the railway tracks were there and I was trundling down them and, OK, I'd gone off here and there and done other things, but basically that is where I was going. Then suddenly I had actually gone right off the tracks. Right off the tracks – I was literally off into the bundu.

'Everybody said, "What is the point of stopping if you don't know what you are going to do?" I said I would prefer to do that than carry on doing something that I knew instinctively was not going to go anywhere.'

The decision to leave the Royal Marines is, he said, unquestionably the most important decision he has ever made. After leaving Lympstone for the last time he drove himself back to Buckingham Palace.

That night, for the first and only time in his life, he got roaring drunk.

Eight

Knockout

It's a Royal Knockout remains a sensitive subject with Prince Edward.

When I mentioned the programme to him I happened to call it 'disastrous'. In a voice edged with irritation, he quickly interposed: 'It wasn't disastrous. How can you call something "disastrous" that raised over a million pounds for charity – and is still raising money?'

Yet, for all the money raised and all Edward's undoubted commitment to raising it, the lingering feeling is one of incredulity blended in equal measure with embarrassment – that members of the Royal Family should have involved themselves in that hour-long exercise in televised kitsch.

Members of the Royal Household continue to blanch at the memory. To them it *was* a disaster: without prompting and notwithstanding the problems that have afflicted the Royal Family in the years since, they still mark it as a major contributory factor in the recent erosion of regal prestige.

Edward went into it aware of the pitfalls. In the week before the programme was shown he admitted: 'I've had doubts about it. One always does when one is trying to put on any sort of show . . . Also, the event has the active involvement of members of the Royal Family in a way that hasn't been done before.'

Armed with the confidence of youth he insisted: 'I don't think the British monarchy will suffer in the process. I hope it will be viewed as being like a breath of fresh air.'

It was not; and his own reputation suffered in the process. It was an unfortunate outcome to something that had started off with the highest of hopes and the best of intentions.

The project, he would later explain, was fermented in a wine bar in London's West End. The original idea, he said, belonged to Tim Hastie-Smith, a friend and contemporary from their days together at Cambridge University.

Without Edward's involvement, however, *The Grand Charity Knockout Tournament*, to give it its official (and rather grandiose) title, would not have got started. It was only through his efforts, organisational abilities and, most importantly, the royal prestige he brought to the project, that it was made at all. If Hastie-Smith was the instigator, then the prince was definitely the catalyst. The initial aim, said Edward, was to raise money for the Duke of Edinburgh Award scheme which was celebrating its thirtieth anniversary in 1986. The first thought was to hold a fund-raising ball. But charity balls, Edward said, 'can be far from fun; so the idea of a mini-knockout between teams drawn from different Award Scheme groups sounded fun.'

The original *It's a Knockout* was a television game invented by the French involving maniacal teams of otherwise ordinary people from towns and villages throughout the country and later Europe, battling with each other on giant whoopee cushions or riding ice-cream cartons over models of Victoria Falls. Edward had been a fan of it since the age of thirteen when he had watched an episode being filmed in Windsor Great Park. At one point he had thought of using it in a toned-down form as a novel attraction at a charity ball. That never happened, but it was resurrected from what Edward called its 'pile of ashes' after the success of the 30th Anniversary Tribute Project for the Duke of Edinburgh's Award. With Hastie-Smith and the show's master of ceremonies, television presenter Stuart Hall, Edward conceived the idea of four teams of international personalities from the fields of sport, music, film and television led by royal captains each representing their own favourite international charities. When John Broome, the owner of the 600-acre site of Alton Towers theme park, and Hugh Williams, the then-head of BBC North West, realised that members of the Royal Family would actually be participating they 'positively drooled'. Before anyone had really had time to sit down and think through all the implications, it had become a co-production between the BBC and Edward's own specially formed company, Knockout Limited.

From the offices of accountants Price Waterhouse under London Bridge, Edward set about patiently tracking down celebrities via the transatlantic telephone, convincing them it was a good idea. 'The first question that crossed my mind when I agreed to participate,' recalled Superman actor Christopher Reeve, 'was just how silly is silly?'

He would find out. 'Little did I know what I was letting myself in for,' Edward himself recalled. 'I remember only too well about half-way through [the preparations], waking up in the middle of the night in a cold sweat having just had a nightmare that we were doing it all over again.'

He was not the only one. As the day drew nearer, tensions mounted. Jayne Fincher, the programme's official photographer recalled, 'I encountered a lot of aggression from the other photographers. I was quite surprised how much ill-feeling there was.' There were also forty-eight celebrity egos waiting to be bruised.

On arrival actress Jayne Seymour insisted she had to have the right dress for dinner and that it must be sent for immediately – from America. Superman Christopher Reeve, having flown in from the States, became fog-bound in London and footballer Gary Lineker missed his plane from Spain. The American contingent which included actors John Travolta and Kevin Kline and the rock singer Meat Loaf were wide-eyed with apprehension as they watched the first demonstration of the games by army volunteers. 'One could see quite clearly that it was slowly dawning on those jet-lagged brains, just how silly they were about to look,' said actor Anthony Andrews. Travolta was particularly bemused and kept saying to anyone who would listen, 'I love English things particularly Jaguars and English chocolate.' With no real conviction, he added, 'This seems so typically English.'

The one thing that most definitely was typically English was the weather which, after a weekend of torrential rain, had reduced the Alton Towers site to a morass of mud.

'I remember only too well standing at the window that Monday morning as the torrential rain continued unabated from the evening before,' Edward recalled. 'It was literally the worst moment of my life as I surveyed the soggy scene.'

There was worse to come, however. The press were banned from the site. They tried to sneak in, only to be ejected again. The mood was blackening. The only access was through an airport-style X-ray machine manned by the BBC's Radio 1 disc jockey Mike Smith who threw out several photographers who arrived in fancy dress with cameras hidden under their costumes.

Recalled Jayne Fincher: 'When the press arrived they were put in a pen outside the security fence. All they could see was the celebrities getting out of their coaches covered by umbrellas. It was raining and it was muddy and they were in a bad mood.'

The *Daily Star* had bought first rights for the photographs. The paper's reporter, however, was not allowed in. His name was Andrew Morton – the same Andrew Morton who would later cause such enormous embarrassment to the Royal Family with his book, *Diana; Her True Story*. 'He got really uppity with me,' said Fincher. 'I told him I couldn't help it and he just had to watch it on the TV screens.'

The programme was recorded on Monday 15 June, 1987. An estimated audience of 18 million people watched when it was broadcast the following Sunday. By then the damage had been done. *The Times* described the event as 'the Royal Family's love of pantomine taken to new heights of carefully controlled silliness'.

The only one to emerge with dignity intact was the Princess Royal. Even when dressed in medieval costume and trainers she appeared composed, like a sternly competitive gym mistress. The Duchess of York was less restrained. Her misplaced enthusiasm and Texas-cheer-leader approach to the event was encapsulated by actress Pamela Stevenson who shrilled that she had invented 'a special new Royal Honour created just for her . . . for services beyond the call of Royal Duty – The Order of The Right Royal Jolly Hockey Sticks'.

This is not the way most people in Britain wished to see their Royal Family behave. 'For the best reasons in the world the younger members of the Royal Family wanted to make the monarchy more approachable, more with it,' explained the Right Reverend Michael Mann, who, as the former Dean of

Windsor, was a confidant of both the Queen and Prince Philip. 'I think the supreme example of that was when they all participated in *It's a Knockout*. It was making it a soap opera.' And that was certainly not how the senior members of the Royal Family saw themselves.

The Queen Mother was most upset. She has a tendency to position herself well above the irritations of everyday life – 'What she doesn't want to see, she doesn't look at,' the Queen's former Private Secretary Lord Charteris once remarked – but she could hardly ignore this. She had witnessed the Abdication and seen the damage that had done to the monarchy. She had dedicated herself to helping her husband, King George VI, rebuild its reputation. She did not want to see her life's work undermined.

The Queen echoed her mother's opinion. Nothing infuriates the Queen more than the members of her family behaving in an unbecoming manner and she did not appreciate the sight of the Duke of York grinning inanely; his wife rushing around waving her arms like a footballer who had just scored a goal; and her youngest son Prince Edward dressed as a joker with a yellow plumed hat which made him look, as *The Times* drolly remarked, like 'one of Shakespeare's lesser jesters.' In the years to come she would feel the same about the behaviour of her other daughter-in-law, Diana, when she held a secret tryst with a newspaper journalist in a London square in 1994. The Queen had always been sympathetic towards Diana throughout her tribulations. She most definitely did not approve of her giving private press briefings in such undignified circumstances.

The Royal Family, despite any appearance to the contrary, is not a soap opera. Its members are not forever popping in to borrow a cup of sugar and discuss the latest marital downturn. For most of the time they go their own way in their own time, even if they happen to be under the same roof. The Royal Family is a large and highly complex business and the Queen often has no idea what its members are doing until they have done it. She once said to me that she read *Majesty* magazine in order to find out what her family had been up to and to keep herself abreast of their comings and goings. If she was aware of *Knockout*, it was only vaguely. By the time it came to her attention, it had taken on a life of its own.

Adam Wise, the prince's Private Secretary at the time, admitted that because it was organised under the auspices of the Duke of Edinburgh's Award, one of the four charities to benefit from the monies raised, he had only the faintest idea what it was about.

'What seemed like an innocent bit of fun for a good cause gathered a momentum of its own,' Wise said. 'I don't think anyone realised until too late. It was a bit of a stupid stunt.'

At the outset Edward had insisted: 'We've deliberately kept a sense of decorum to suit the people involved. It's an atmosphere of heroism and gentility.'

That, according to Wise, was likely to be too tame for the general viewer in the opinion of the programme makers whom he felt made it 'much more vulgar than it need have been'. Edward, still only twenty-three, was new to the manipulative ways of the entertainment industry. His raw inexperience showed even more at the press conference afterwards.

Upon arriving in the press tent, Edward started delivering a speech he had prepared beforehand. This was not what the fifty or so journalists wanted. They had spent fourteen hours hanging around on the wrong side of the 15-foot high security fence which stopped them seeing what they had been sent to report and photograph. It was 8pm, deadlines had come and gone, tempers were frayed. When Edward paused for breath Joan Thirkettle of ITN leaped in to ask if the prince was pleased with the way the day had gone.

Edward snapped, 'I haven't finished yet.' Then, forsaking his notes, he said, 'I know the captains have enjoyed themselves. I only hope you have enjoyed yourselves – have you?' He was greeted with silence. He lost his temper. 'Well, thanks for being so bloody enthusiastic. What have you been doing here all day?'

Thirkettle spoke for everyone when she replied, 'You may well ask.'

Edward went back into the verbal fray. 'Have you been watching it?'

The answer was a very muted yes. 'Well, what did you think of it?' This time the silence was broken by a few laughs.

ıce Edward, with his teeth in a metal brace, chats with Sarah Ferguson's mother, Susie rantes, while they watch Prince Charles play polo at Cowdray Park in July 1979.

ıce Edward with Lady Sarah Spencer messing around with boats at Cowes in August 1979. er the romance between Prince Charles and Lady Sarah finished, Edward remained close to na's elder sister.

Prince Edward photographed in the grounds of Buckingham Palace for his eighteenth birthday with his labrador Frances who generated more fan mail from the photographs than the Prince.

ıce Edward on the sea ice of McMurdo Sound being shown one of the solar panels used in the
w Zealand Antarctic research programme during his one-week visit to the Antarctica in
cember 1982.

ıce Edward at his desk in his room at Jesus College Cambridge where he was a student from
33–1986.

Prince Edward launching a sponsored cycle ride for the Duke of Edinburgh Award. From left: th Deputy Mayor of Cambridge, John Woodhouse, Mark Foster-Brown , Prince Edward, Timothy Knatchbull, The Rev James Owen and the city's Police Commander, Chief Supt Harry Gelsthorne.

Playing rugby at Cambridge became impossible because Prince Edward was the victim of unnecessary attacks and his presence attracted dozens of photographers to the playing fields.

ring his time with the Royal Marines, pictures of Prince Edward training were rarely released. ese few were taken during the Young Officer Training at the Commando Training Centre at npstone.

t on exercise on Woodbury Common, Second Lieutenant Prince Edward is selecting munition from a pouch on his hip.

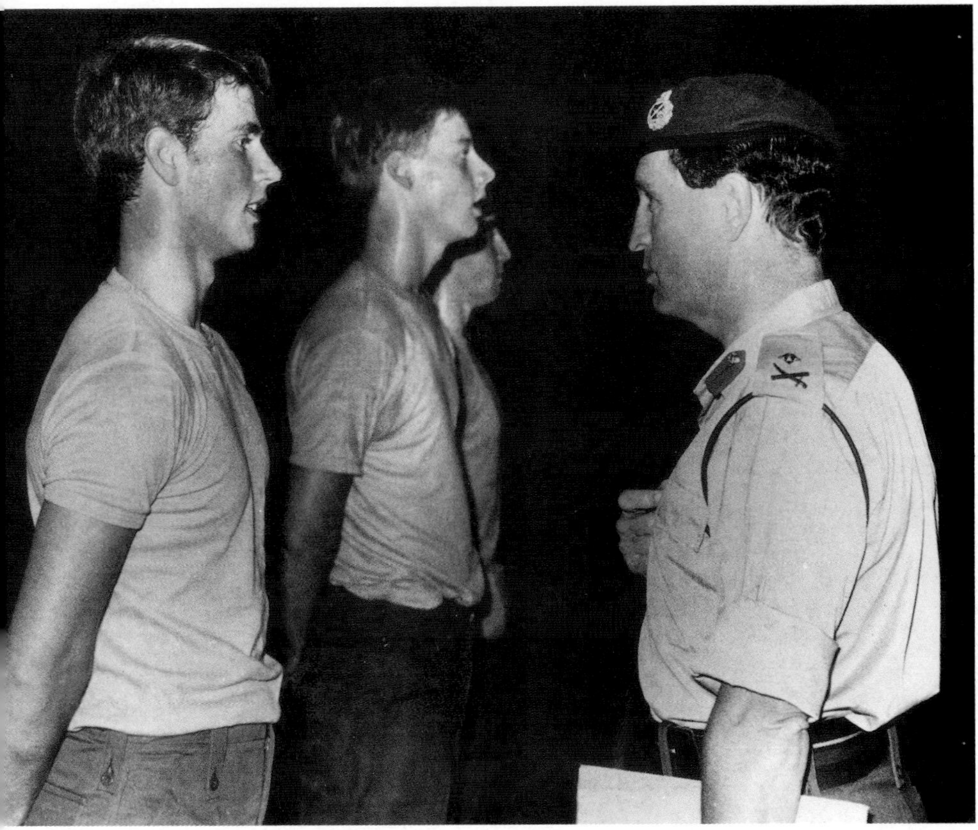

ɔove: Major General Thompson, who commanded the Third Commando Brigade during the ılklands, carrying out inspection of various units at Lympstone. Prince Edward is wearing the ive green trousers and T-shirt used for PE training.

ɛft: Being instructed in the 'Carl Gustav' 84mm rocket launcher. Prince Edward is wearing the ɔung Officer's blue beret with red backing behind the badge.

ɛlow: Prince Edward receiving instructions on a general all-purpose machine gun with a fellow cruit.

During a visit to Ghana for the Duke of Edinburgh's International Award. Prince Edward is the only person in the picture actually watching the ceremony.

Prince Edward and Prince Andrew with presenter Stuart Hall during the filming of *It's a Royal Knockout.*

'Thanks,' Edward said, turning on his heels and walking quickly out.

The petulance of adolescence that had been building up so noticeably over the past five years had cascaded over the edge into tantrum. Edward, always so aware of who he was, had taken his eye off the ball of royalty.

Said Morton: 'He flounced out like a ballerina with a hole in his tights. We were not impressed by that behaviour at all. It is one of those occasions when people like to attack the press. We were just observers at the Royal Family's self-destruction.'

Morton was overstating the case, as he has been known to. There was no doubt, though, that Edward had mishandled the situation. He was tired and tense and the strain of organising everything had finally got the better of him, but the press had not spent the best part of a day hanging around 'for the privilege of being sneered at by a rudely offensive young man', as the *Daily Mail*'s Lynda Lee-Potter remarked. They were there for a story. Edward, by that flash of temper, had given them one. His tantrum made front-page news and inevitably fuelled the controversy surrounding the project.

Edward would later say: 'I thought I had asked a perfectly reasonable question; "Had they enjoyed themselves?" I mean, they could have said no. They could have said anything they liked, but they didn't say a thing. They'd never been particularly enthusiastic about the event in the first place, but I was annoyed I had given them the opportunity to get their knives in.'

On a more defensive note, he said afterwards: 'It was an experiment and a lot of people have learned from it. I don't think it has done an enormous amount of harm and it did an awful lot of good for charity.'

At his gloomiest, however, he recognised the magnitude of what had happened. He said: 'I did make a million for charity but I seem to have lost everything and gained very little.'

Nine

Like Father Like Son

ON PRINCE EDWARD'S bedside table in his Buckingham Palace apartment one book has pride of place. It jostles for space with his Roberts radio, a torch and an alarm clock. People who have seen his bedroom notice it because it is always there.

It is his journal of the Duke of Edinburgh's Award, its handwritten pages bearing testimony to the years he spent achieving his three awards.

The book is a diary of his youth, written in many different hands by those who taught him and those whom he came to respect. He will sometimes glance at it, even now, when he is at a spiritually low ebb. Like an old photograph album, the contents provide comfort and reassurance. It is also a symbolic reminder of the empathy between the prince and his father whose name the scheme bears.

Indeed, his father and the award have been two of the most notable influences on his life. As Edward himself remarked, achieving the final part was actually more important to him than his academic qualifications: 'I think in many ways the Gold Award I got for the Duke of Edinburgh was much more of a challenge, much more of a practical qualification than my degree was.'

'He was genuinely proud of it,' said Michael Hobbs, retired army general and Chairman of the Award since 1988. 'The Gold Award was a major landmark in his life.'

Edward left university in the summer of 1986. His was the first generation since the Second World War to feel the painful grasp of economic change. Suddenly academic qualifications, even a university degree, no longer guaranteed a job. Unemployment became an unwelcome way of life for many graduates. A Duke of Edinburgh Award could not change that, but it could provide the skills to fill the time.

The Duke of Edinburgh started the scheme in 1956 with his friend and protagonist, Everest explorer Sir John Hunt, in an attempt to fill the vacuum created by the ending of military national service. Their aim was to foster 'leadership, self-discipline, enterprise and perseverance'. It was the practical solution to Philip's complaint about the emphasis on the academic to the detriment of voluntary service, cultural activities and sport.

Like so many of Philip's ideas, it draws its inspiration from the Gordonstoun system initiated by Dr Kurt Hahn. But it is not all open-air heartiness. As one Gold Award winner remarked, how else can you improve your cooking, learn to play chess or rear your own pigeons and race them?

'The biggest misconception is that the Award is all about getting cold and wet on Scottish mountainsides,' Edward said. 'You choose your own activities and you're only competing against yourself. All you have to do is stick at things and show some improvement.'

The prince himself spent five years on his Gold Award. He started it while he was still at Gordonstoun and finished it during his last year at Cambridge. He was held back partly because of his other activities and partly because of various rugby injuries. That led him to take up Real Tennis, that early, arcane version of the game they play at Wimbledon.

'I started Real Tennis as part of my Award's Physical Recreation,' Edward said, 'and I started from scratch. Strictly speaking, you only have to play regularly and make progress to qualify, but my coach would only agree to say I had improved when I was playing for the university team – so that was what I had to do.'

At Gold level, the Award requirements, as well as that esotoric ability to handle a Real Tennis racquet, included an expedition and a Residential Project which Edward undertook at RAF Cranwell where he learned to fly a two-seater Bulldog.

For the Skills section Edward started building a sailing

hydrofoil in Gordonstoun's workshops. Although it remained unfinished by the time he left – and is still there today – the point had been made.

For all his protestations, there was no escaping Scotland, however. His Gold Award expedition involved Edward in three nights camping as he walked his way from Blair Atholl to Tomintoul in the Cairngorms.

Although it was May, it was Scotland and it snowed for three days. 'My boots froze,' Edward said, but he enjoyed it if only in retrospect. 'You get a fantastic sense of achievement.'

There was more to Edward's involvement than just a test of initiative and endurance. Adam Wise explained: 'It is important for the Queen's children who are not going to succeed to the throne to have a project that they do extremely well.'

With the example of his father to spur him on, Edward rose to this challenge. When Hahn introduced a personal achievement badge at Gordonstoun Philip won it. Edward was never likely to emulate his athletic father to that extent. That kind of competition holds no interest for him. He was almost as accomplished a rider as his sister, Anne, but had no desire to ride competitively. At Gordonstoun he was taught the value of measuring himself against goals he had set himself. The Duke of Edinburgh Award is an extension of that philosophy. As he pointed out, it is 'tailored to the individual', and with his Gold Award secured, he became increasingly involved in the scheme's organisation. When Prince Philip reached his sixty-fifth year, which was also the thirtieth anniversary of the Award, Edward, while still a Cambridge undergraduate, became directly involved in the fund-raising. Together with a group of friends he planned to surprise his father by raising a thousand pounds for each year since the Duke launched the scheme. They went a lot better and eventually raised nearly half a million. Besides creating an occasion to please his father, Edward's work for the anniversary established an opportunity for him to work in television for the first time since he was the child star of the television series *Royal Family*.

'I started a television series for TV-am called the *Wideawake Club*,' Edward said. 'I put it in motion and fed it into the system – even appearing in a couple of the programmes at the beginning and the end.' He then moved to more serious work with a documentary for the BBC aimed at encouraging more volunteers and adults to get involved with the Award. It ended up as two programmes which were broadcast on two Sundays over the Easter period. 'They were quite successful,' Edward recalled, 'but then I got inundated with hundreds of letters from pensioners asking if I could start an Award scheme for them. We slightly over-pitched that one as they weren't quite the adults we were looking for.'

Edward enjoyed using his organisational skills to put his ideas into practice to generate awareness of the scheme – he wanted people to know it was 'good fun'. He then stepped up alongside his father and became a Trustee of the International Award and Chairman of his own Special Projects Group. Observed Michael Hobbs: 'The two men's talents dovetail together. They don't compete, they complement each other.'

Philip can freeze or melt an atmosphere depending on his mood. If he is irritable or unhappy about something he will make no attempt to hide it. He can on occasion be downright rude. Edward is well aware of the effect his father has and has learnt to subtly move in when he feels that compassion rather than aggression is required.

'Prince Philip's attitude to life was formed by a very tough upbringing,' observed Hobbs. 'He meets discomfort head on and isn't worried by it. He is much less overtly compassionate as a result. He keeps it well hidden.'

Prince Edward, on the other hand, is a product of his generation, and is more at home with young people with disabilities and handicaps than someone of his father's background could ever be. When Edward meets the disabled he will kneel down straight away and patiently wait for a reply while they struggle with their words. Like his sister-in-law, the Princess of Wales and the Duchess of York, Edward is not afraid to show a degree of softness and sensitivity when he is dealing with people that neither Philip, nor his daughter, Anne, care to demonstrate.

The apparent contrast in their personalities tends to show Edward in a downtrodden light and Philip's notorious brusqueness does nothing to dispel the image.

In Australia one year, Philip was due to address 400 businessmen who, in true Australian tradition, were neither sober nor deferential. Shortly before they departed for the banqueting hall a message came through that the Queen required Philip's presence aboard the Royal Yacht. Without a moment's consideration, he turned to his 23-year old son and ordered, 'You do the speech.' Hobbs, in Brisbane with them, recalled the incident. 'I looked at this waif-like figure and thought, "bloody hell!" Four hundred intoxicated Australians, who had been expecting a hard-hitting speech from a man when suddenly up gets this lad whose image was not great. I remember him saying, "Phew!" '

Edward had only a short time to prepare a speech, but refusing assistance and paying no heed to warnings of possible bread roll missiles and references to his sexual proclivity, he insisted he would be all right. Said Hobbs: 'I was very nervous for him and as I predicted when he got up there was a bit of ya-hooing from the edge of the hall and a few shouts of "poofter" and things like that.'

But he did it. And he won his audience round.

'If you're a prince it's a bit like being a bishop – you start with an advantage when you make even the smallest jibe,' says satirist Ned Sherrin, who has met Edward on several occasions. 'Edward is confident that people like his jokes because he is genuinely quite humorous and doesn't suffer from the problem that has dogged other male members of his family – that of thinking he is funnier than he actually is.'

It is humour that comes with practice. 'I have heard his repertoire of jokes quite a number of times, but they are still funny,' said Paul Arengo-Jones, the former Colonel in the Gloucestershire Regiment who is the International Award's Secretary General. Edward writes his own speeches and is not averse to poking fun at himself. 'He turns a switch and plays the part and he plays it very well indeed,' said Arengo-Jones.

Armed with that episcopal advantage and a lot of experience, he can hold an audience for up to five minutes, a minute longer than many professional comedians care to tackle. If any of his one-liners fall flat, he simply presses on, protected by the mantle of his royalty, secure in the knowledge that sooner or later he is certain to raise a laugh. To get it, he sometimes even weaves his family into the plot. At one Awards dinner he chose to mimick his father when he told a story about a visit to a military hospital. He recounted:

> My father visited a military hospital the other day, went to the first bed and asked the squaddie: 'What's wrong with you young man?'
>
> 'Piles,' said the soldier. 'And what are they giving you for it?' asked father.
>
> 'Ointment and a brush,' replied the soldier.
>
> 'And what is your ambition?' asked father. 'To get out of here and become an officer,' the soldier replied.
>
> Father went to the next bed; 'And what's wrong with you young man?'
>
> 'VD,' replied the squaddie. 'And what are they giving you?'
>
> 'Ointment and a brush.'
>
> 'And what's your ambition?'
>
> 'To leave here and go to Sandhurst.'
>
> Father then went to the third soldier. 'What's wrong with you?'
>
> 'Laryngitis,' he replied.
>
> 'And what are they giving you?'
>
> 'Ointment and a brush.'
>
> 'And what's your ambition?'
>
> 'To get the ointment and the brush before those two!'

The joke is not a new one but hearing it delivered by Prince Edward in imitation of Prince Philip gave it an original edge and had the audience laughing. And sharing in the joke would always be Edward's father.

For all their superficial differences, Philip's relationship with his youngest son is based on genuine respect on Edward's part and equally genuine affection on Philip's. The Duke is not a demonstrative man, but in private he will affectionately put his arm around his son's shoulder – he calls him Ed – and give him a kiss.

It was Philip for instance, not the Queen, who came to see

Edward receive his degree on graduation day. And it was Philip and not Edward's mother who showed the most compassion over his decision to quit the Royal Marines. 'There is a tremendously close relationship there,' says Arengo-Jones.

Edward, he says, has studied his father and learnt well, including how to work a cocktail party. Like the Duke on a good day, Edward can move smoothly through a room, sipping a drink, smiling at the appropriate moment, making a humorous remark, before seamlessly moving on. It is an acquired skill, one that did not come easily, and is something the Queen still finds difficult to do after more than four decades on the Throne.

That Edward should study his father is perfectly natural. That Philip should take such an interest in his son is perhaps more unexpected. Philip's relationship with his youngest child is conducted on a level of easy familiarity that he could never manage with his eldest. The distance between Philip and Charles is quite extraordinary. For long periods their only contact is via memo. His relationship with Edward is conducted on a much more informal, friendly level. The two, Arengo-Jones observed, 'are always talking'.

Philip also talks about Edward in a way he never does about Charles. Said Hobbs: 'He tells people he meets at parties about his son's achievements or makes off-hand references to him in speeches, like "God knows what we would have done without Prince Edward's special projects." '

After he quit the Marines Edward found himself with time on his hands for the first time in his life. In a deft parental move the Duke, aware that his son needed something to pull him out of his apathy, asked him to help with the Award while he considered his future.

'People said don't go rushing into something, hang on, take your time because you've got to be sure whatever you do is the right thing,' Edward recalled. 'That is why there was a very long period between leaving the Marines in 1987 and starting with the Useful group in 1988. It was actually pretty busy.'

The work which occupied him for the next nine months and still occupies him today, involves a diverse group of ten men and one woman, who form the scheme's Special Projects Group.

Chaired by Prince Edward, the committee is the 'think tank' whose job it is to devise and run fund-raising events.

Once a month the group meets in one of the empty rooms in Buckingham Palace to hold post-mortems on completed events, review progress on those to come and discuss ideas for the future. These sessions are conducted with much merriment and often last for up to three hours, but although everyone is a volunteer who gives of their time freely, the business in hand is serious; since 1986 the group has raised 2.5 million pounds.

Many of the team are friends from Cambridge. They have included financier Mark Foster Brown, publisher Damien Riley-Smith, barrister Andrew Sutcliffe, and Edward's attractive former escort, Rhian-Anwen Roberts.

Malcolm Cockren is the chairman of Ardent, Edward's television production company. He formally joined the group after the financial success of its first enterprise, *It's a Royal Knockout*. 'We spend as much time as is humanly possible on events, and I'm very proud of our projects,' he said.

There is an air of missionary zeal to their commitment. 'If we don't look after youth today, we'll have nothing to look forward to in the future,' says Cockren.

It was just such a notion that inspired Philip to start the scheme and if father and son are at Buckingham Palace at the same time, they will often have a working breakfast together. They are just as likely to communicate by internal memo, however, distributed in re-used envelopes.

This strange strategy adopted by what is, after all, one of the richest families in the world is encouraged by the Queen, who is so cost-conscious that she sends memos in old envelopes with the last name crossed out in pencil in her own hand. She once requested a more powerful light bulb for her bedside lamp, 'but not until the one I have now is finished'.

If the Royal Family's concern over pennies astonishes observers, so does their use of the memo pad.

'It slightly surprised me that Prince Edward has to write to his father and say, "This is what I really think." And yet they live in the same house,' said Hobbs.

In the popular imagination, the Royal Family are in daily consultation. In fact, they live surprisingly separate lives. They seldom get together during the week, even if they happen to be under the same roof at Buckingham Palace. The Queen in her private apartment often has her dinner alone which she serves herself from a hotplate. Philip, meanwhile, having returned late from an engagement, could be dining on the floor below with his Private Secretary. At the same time Edward could be having a snack by himself in his rooms. It would not occur to them to pick up the internal telephone to organise an impromptu family supper.

That impersonal approach has even been known to apply to family birthdays and anniversaries. It is probably the only way that the Royal Family, who have an anniversary of some kind or other to celebrate almost every day, can maintain their individual space. Such *faux pas* as forgetting to give a present would reduce the members of most other families to tears. Not the royals. They derive a wry amusement from these unexpected breaks in their carefully ordered routine and humour is particularly important to Edward.

'We British have a very robust sense of humour and part of that is to put things down,' Edward observed. It is sometimes too negative for Edward's taste 'It's serious having people constantly hark on about the bad things when there are so many good things going on out there,' he complained. For the most part, though, he is able to see the funny side of things, including the problems generated by his own royal position.

While in The Gambia in 1993, he was invited to attend a ceremonial gathering of tribal chiefs. Protocol demanded that his entourage should be almost as big as the King's and amidst much laughter, Edward enlisted every available person to make up the numbers: his policeman, his Private Secretary, even his valet.

'We sat there for a whole morning in the intense heat, waiting for something to happen and we boiled, and boiled and boiled,' recalled Arengo-Jones.

On one side of Edward sat a minister in full tribal dress, on the other a young minister in Western clothes. Edward was watching the ceremony while the ministers talked behind him and around him and in front of him to the assembled press. 'And it was Edward the media criticised for looking bored,' said

Arengo-Jones. That might once have sent Edward into a temperamental tailspin. This time he turned it into an amusing anecdote.

The Duke of Edinburgh Award is not his only charity commitment – he is involved with some twenty other organisations – but it is the one that commands his special attention. It brought him closer to the father he so admires. It also brought him closer to a young woman named Sophie Rhys-Jones, who over the past two years had come to play an increasingly important part in his life.

At the beginning of 1995 Michael Hobbs formally wrote and asked her if she was interested in being involved with the Award on a freelance basis, helping to promote its public image.

She agreed.

'She is a successful, sensible, well-balanced person,' said Hobbs.

Edward had every cause to agree with that assessment.

Ten

New Prince New Friends New Ideas

On February 14, 1988, Prince Edward started work at Andrew Lloyd Webber's Really Useful Theatre Company and so became the first son of a reigning monarch in all of British history to take a job outside the services.

Lloyd Webber declared: 'I am delighted that Prince Edward is to join the staff.'

In truth, Lloyd Webber had been anything but. In fact, Edward was lucky to have the job. Just a few days before he was due to start, serious objections to his employment were raised. Not, as might be imagined, by the Royal Family or even the Palace old guard of courtiers, but from the composer. The Prince of the Theatre had suddenly had grave doubts about the wisdom of employing a Prince of the Realm. Edward, brought up to expect all doors to open for him because of who he was, had to persuade Lloyd Webber to hire him in spite of who he was.

Even Edward had harboured doubts about his ability to make such a dramatic break from tradition. The theatre had long been his interest 'but I had dismissed it as a profession', he told me. 'I thought it was something I would never be able to do so there was no point even considering it.'

But he did. Despite all the obstacles and against all the objections, this was the job he truly wanted. He worked hard to get it and he was delighted when he did. It would expose him to a fair amount of ridicule, introduce him to the bitchy backstage milieu behind the bright lights, involve him in a ruthless struggle for corporate control and test his loyalties. It would become his career.

The long haul out of the royal enclave and into the brittle, competitive world of the theatre had its innocent beginnings all those years ago at his preparatory school in Berkshire. It was playing Mole in the end of term production of *Toad of Toad Hall* that had first stirred his interest. That had grown at Gordonstoun and at Cambridge. By the time he started in the Royal Marines it had become a consuming ambition.

It was his mother's sixtieth birthday which presented him with the opportunity he had been looking for. As part of the celebrations, Edward decided to put on a special surprise show for her at Windsor Castle. As befitted the occasion, he wrote two years before to Andrew Lloyd Webber, the most successful British composer of his day. Andrew in turn enlisted the assistance of lyricist Tim Rice, with whom he had written such phenomenally successful musicals as *Jesus Christ Superstar* and *Evita*, which alone has earned over a billion pounds in box office receipts. Honoured by the invitation, they gave their services for nothing.

'It was a mini operetta, a humorous piece about cricket, something I had always wanted to write,' recalled cricket-mad Rice.

Entitled *Cricket*, it had its première in the chapel which was later destroyed in the fire of 1992. Afterwards there was a large party but only the immediate family, plus King Hussein of Jordan who is highly regarded by the Queen, and his wife, Queen Noor, were invited to see the show.

A lighthearted tease on the grand people who play cricket and the rather flashier types who prefer racing, it starred Ian Charleston, the *Chariots of Fire* actor. Edward, as well as helping with the production, also had a small walk-on part.

'It was never intended to be a major production and most of the tunes wound up in other shows, but the Queen really enjoyed it,' said Rice.

During the production Edward met Biddy Hayward, Lloyd Webber's one-time secretary who was now an executive director of his Really Useful Theatre Company and the organising force behind his worldwide theatrical interests. Edward telephoned her shortly afterwards and asked if she could organise tickets for *The Phantom of the Opera*, yet another of Lloyd Webber's astonishingly successful musicals. This Biddy duly did and afterwards she and Edward and Michael Crawford, the star of the show, had dinner together in a French restaurant around the corner in the old red light district of Soho.

Biddy recalled: 'On the way to the restaurant we were discussing the military and he said he was not particularly happy there – that it was not for him.'

She attached no import to his comments. It was, none the less, a remarkable admission. Edward was not a man to unburden himself to close friends, never mind near-strangers. It was a significant measure of his disenchantment with his career in the services that he should choose to mention that to someone he had only met a couple of times before, even if, as Biddy said, their empathy with each other was such that they became instant friends.

As it turned out, it was a friendship that was to stand him in good stead. They kept in touch and Hayward was one of the people he turned to after he quit the Royal Marines.

She supported his decision. 'I feel quite passionately that if someone decides, at whatever age, they are in the wrong career, then they must change. It is much easier to carry on with the tide and so much braver to stand up and say, "This is not for me." I respected him enormously for that. I thought he was incredibly brave.'

The decision to leave the Marines had only been arrived at after considerable soul-searching. The one to join the theatre was taken spontaneously. 'I gathered from a jovial remark he made one day that he would like to work in the theatre and I said, "Right, I'll talk about it." And I did.'

Hayward is an intelligent, determined lady who, through her organisational skills and force of personality, was accustomed to getting her way. Meetings were convened and discussions held with Lloyd Webber and Brian Brolly, the company's then managing director. Neither shared their executive director's enthusiasm. Was Edward serious, they wanted to know? What would he do? Was he up to it? If he was, would he be allowed to? And, very much to the point: what did the Really Useful Theatre Company, already so extraordinarily successful, have to gain by employing the Queen's son?

The answer to that last one was simple: his enthusiasm. 'I

knew he really loved the theatre and that is vital, said Hayward. The industry needs people who are passionate about it, who truly believe in quality and standards and the arts.'

Lloyd Webber was persuaded and Edward was invited to an informal luncheon at the company's office. That went well enough for further discussions to be held in the days that followed. An offer was formulated and put to Edward. When he agreed Brolly and Hayward went to Buckingham Palace.

Back in December, 1965, shortly before Prince Charles flew off to boarding school in Australia, the Queen and Prince Philip hosted a small dinner party at Buckingham Palace. The guests included Prime Minister Harold Wilson, the Archbishop of Canberbury, Earl Mountbatten of Burma, the Dean of Windsor, Sir Charles Wilson, chairman of the Committee of University Vice Chancellors, and the Queen's Private Secretary, Sir Michael Adeane. Together they represented the spiritual, military, royal and parliamentary authorities of Great Britain and they were there to decide the future of Prince Charles. Notable by his absence from the discussions was Charles himself. He was to be allowed no say in the matter.

The deliberations carried on well into the night. The following morning Charles was informed of the committee's decision. As Mountbatten explained it: 'Trinity College, like his grandfather. Dartmouth Naval College like his father and grandfather, and then on to sea in the Royal Navy.'

It was safe and predictable and no wonder Charles would later complain, 'You cannot understand what it is like to have your whole life mapped out for you a year in advance. It is so awful to be programmed.'

Edward was changing that. By his own volition, he was taking command of his own life. He had switched the programme. There were no Archbishops or statesmen or Admirals waiting to greet Brolly and Hayward when they arrived at the Palace; no formal dinner under chandeliers with an army of footmen hovering in attendance. It was, as Hayward recalls, 'informal and very pleasant'.

The meeting was held in a ground-floor office. Gathered round a polished mahogany table were the Queen's Private Secretary, who in 1988 was the Australian-born Sir William

Heseltine, Prince Philip's Private Secretary Brian McGrath, the Queen's Press Secretary Robin Janvrin and Edward's Private Secretary Adam Wise. Edward was not there. But then neither were the Queen nor Prince Philip. 'It was all very matter of fact,' Hayward recalled. 'We discussed the ups and downs and then we all parted and said, yes, we would go ahead.'

Both the Queen and Prince Philip had harboured strong reservations about Edward's choice of career. This was simply not what members of the Royal Family were traditionally expected to do. Sons of the Sovereign were expected to serve in the armed forces or retreat to the shires to live out their lives as betweeded country gentlemen. But the old order was breaking down. Old rules and codes were being discarded and in the face of their son's obvious enthusiasm, neither the Queen nor her consort felt they had any real grounds for invoking the royal veto. On 18 January, 1988, Buckingham Palace formally announced that Prince Edward would join the Really Useful Theatre Company, that his decision had the full support of the Queen and the Duke of Edinburgh and that he was to be paid an undisclosed salary (it was, in fact, an initial £10,000 a year) in addition to his annual Civil List allowance of £20,000.

'I am delighted with the prospect of joining the company, to learn more about the theatre professionally,' the Prince said.

Lloyd Webber had endorsed those sentiments – and then promptly had second thoughts, to the extent that two weeks before the official Palace announcement he had tried to cancel the whole deal.

'Andrew suddenly panicked,' Biddy recalled. 'He said, "You know this can't go ahead, this is a bad idea, it's not going to work." '

It was that old concern – of what, if anything, could Edward possibly contribute to the success of the company – rearing its head again. The prince was already patron of the National Youth Theatre and the National Youth Music Theatre and his contribution was well received and most welcome. But that was all on the amateur patronage side. It was employing him on the professional production side which worried Lloyd Webber. Edward was about to discover in the most practical way possible that his royal status, that traditional guarantee of privilege, could actually work against him.

Biddy Hayward insisted: 'It sounds terrible to say, but the fact that he was royal didn't matter to me. If you began to think it through practically and logically you would get into a cupboard and put a brown paper bag over your head because employing the Queen's son doesn't make sense because you are always brought up to believe that the Royal Famiily are somewhere up there. But we have seen an enormous change and that change in attitude is part of it. The fact that he is the Queen's son became an unimportant factor; I was getting to know him better and I liked him as a person.'

Andrew Lloyd Webber, responsible for a multi-million pound industry based on his own talent, could not afford the luxury of such democratic opinions without giving them due and careful consideration. It had not been his idea to offer Edward a job. The proposal had been Edward's own, supported by Biddy Hayward. There was, Lloyd Webber's spokesman Peter Brown explained, an 'ambiguity' to the idea of employing the Queen's son. 'People love to knock Andrew because of his success and the concern on our side of the fence was that we would give people more grounds to take shots at him; that we were laying ourselves open to the criticism that we were brown-nosing.'

Another meeting was arranged, this time over a very English cup of tea in Lloyd Webber's sumptuous home in Belgravia in the expensive heart of London, just five hundred yards away from Buckingham Palace. There was no natural camaraderie between Edward and Lloyd Webber. Both regarded each other with a certain deference, although both were at pains to conceal that and would have been embarrassed if anyone had pointed it out.

Andrew said, 'I have to tell you what I'm really worried about. If I have an opening and the Queen turns up everybody is going to say that she has come because of you, not because it is some charity night.'

Edward replied: 'I accept that, but she would never come just because of me. She would only come because it was a charitable thing.'

Edward was composed and rational but he was arguing for his

future and his commitment showed. Biddy observed: 'He desperately wanted to work in the theatre.' If he was to get the chance, he was going to have to convince Lloyd Webber that his royal position would not compromise his employer in any way. It was a question, said Biddy, of putting the problem of his royal status 'into perspective. He put it in such a calm and sensible way.'

And he was successful. By the end of afternoon tea Lloyd Webber had accepted Edward's arguments. A few days later the announcement was made – and Edward instantly found himself saddled with the label of 'royal tea boy'.

That was Biddy's fault. Edward was hired as a production assistant. When she was asked what those duties included and will he make the tea, she replied, 'Like the rest of us he will have to make the tea and answer the telephones. He will have no special status at all and is starting on the lowest rung of the ladder.'

By attempting to underplay the story, she had inadvertently built it up. As she later admitted, 'It conjured up the image of this poor young man racing around with trays of tea and sweeping the stage.'

Edward playing along with the role he had been cast in. On his first day at work the 'royal tea boy' arrived at the Palace Theatre clutching a packet of PG Tips tea-bags.

'That's what I love about him, the way he takes the negative out of life and turns it into humour rather than allowing it to get him upset and becoming chippy about it,' said Biddy, who had deeply regretted her remark.

In fact, Edward did help make the tea. He was starting at the bottom; he was, the newspapers pointed out, a general dogsbody whose job it was to fetch and carry for the others. But as Hayward said, everyone on occasion would make the tea, 'including me'. And Edward's duties quickly went well beyond trying to remember who took milk and with how many sugars. The Really Useful Theatre Company handled the licences and services of all Lloyd Webber productions around the world. What that meant in effect was that if an impresario wished to mount a production of *The Phantom of the Opera*, for instance, they would work through Really Useful. Control was tight, with

Lloyd Webber, through this theatre division, setting the rules for the costumes, set, lighting and script of every production wherever it was staged, from America to Japan.

The information was stored on computer and the prince was set to work, coordinating box office marketing and advertising, casting and merchandising. He came to oversee a lot of the work on *Cats*, yet another of Lloyd Webber's hits and was in charge of coordinating all the information for the French production of the musical based on T.S. Eliot's poem. He was made responsible for the refurbishment of the London production of *Starlight Express* and went to Vienna for the opening of *The Phantom of the Opera*. He was in New York for the opening of *Aspects of Love* (though that, for reasons of rumour and gay innuendo, was not the trip he most enjoyed).

He was also invited to the casting sessions where he was invited to give his opinions which, according to Hayward 'were worth hearing'.

He visited New York and stayed at the Carlyle, arguably the best hotel in America, not as a member of the Royal Family but as a private citizen. He dined out at the fashionable Upper East Side restaurants. Placido Domingo was at the next table at the Tratorria del Arte opposite Carnegie Hall one night when Edward was eating there with Peter Brown and Biddy Hayward. Recalled Brown, 'Placido saw Edward and kept looking across as if to say, "I know that face." But the penny didn't drop. He sat down. Then he got up again as the penny *did* drop.'

Brown, the most socially adept of men, introduced the prince to the opera singer. 'It was funny, because who would expect to see Prince Edward there?' he said. Very few people. Those born royal do not frequent restaurants. Yet there was Edward, happily sitting in a trendy New York eaterie.

The informality was just as apparent back in London. The Queen has only ever been to one restaurant in her life. The Prince of Wales does not frequent ordinary restaurants. On the very rare occasions he does eat out publicly it is only at exclusive (for which read very expensive) private dining clubs like Mossiman's and Annabel's. The Duchess of York once complained that Prince Andrew had never even been to a pub. Edward, however, was a regular customer at a number of cheap and cheerful Soho establishments.

There was always going to be a limit, however, to how far from his royal station Edward could be allowed to pull. The hard working, vital, commercially driven environment of the Palace Theatre was utterly different from the dusty, old-fashioned work ways of Buckingham Palace but he still worked in the shadow of his royal heritage. He was still required to do his share of royal engagements. He was involved in over twenty charities and they took a share of his time. At night he went home to Buckingham Palace. And because of the constant security threat posed by the IRA to members of the Royal Family, there, lurking in the background, was the ever-faithful figure of Andrew Merrylees, the policeman who was now of an age when all the other detectives seemed very young.

'His detective didn't follow him into the loo,' Hayward noted, 'but he was always around.' Edward, with a lifetime's experience of having a bodyguard, thought nothing of it. 'If you are used to having a child with you then you accommodate to the child's needs. He was used to having the detective so he accommodated to the detective's needs.'

All the detectives were well versed in fading into the background and the other employees of the Really Useful Theatre Company soon stopped paying any attention to them and got on with their jobs. So did the young man they knew as plain Edward Windsor. That was what Biddy and her band of enthusiastic young assistants who worked in the open-plan office at the top of the Palace Theatre called him. That was the name he introduced himself by on the telephone – to the frequent astonishment of the people on the other end of the line.

It was as informal a life as any Sovereign's son had savoured in modern times and Edward thoroughly enjoyed himself. When he first started he would punctiliously refer to his parents as 'the Queen and Prince Philip' in the respectful manner members of the Royal Family are taught to adopt. A few months later he was talking to Biddy about 'my mother and my father' and he took a genuine pleasure when they came to see *Aspects of Love* on which he had worked. He got on well with his fellow workers and with many of the people in the casts of Lloyd Webber's various productions. On a cold winter's day he would go with them for a lunch of egg and chips in a local Soho greasy spoon and join in their laughter when the other diners would look at him and say, 'No, that's not him.' He took in good part their occasional teasing – about his accent, his public school education – and respected the way they never referred to any of the royal scandals that were coming to dominate the front pages of the newspapers. He was involved in something he loved and found the work challenging and interesting. The tone was set by Biddy Hayward who said: 'I believe working has to be fun – I can't bear power struggles.'

But a power struggle, from Edward's perspective, is exactly what erupted in the Really Useful Company after he had been working there for two years. Andrew Lloyd Webber would never have described it as such. It was, after all, his genius that was the foundation of the business and the bottom line was that the company was his to do with as he wanted. Biddy, a caring person, sensitive to human fallibility, had very clear ideas of her own about the way it should be organised and the direction it should move in. She had no compunction about expressing them. Disagreements were inevitable.

Towards the end of 1989 Lloyd Webber, restlessly looking for new outlets for his talents, started hinting that he was considering a move into films and away from stage production which was what kept Hayward employed. At the same time he made the decision to take his group out of public and back into private ownership. Hayward objected. She preferred dealing with a board which arrived at its decisions by consensus. She did not relish the prospect of working for one man, however talented, with the unchallenged power to countermand her every decision.

Said Hayward: 'If I've done a contract for a production (and I've done it) and Andrew rings me up at ten o'clock at night and says, "Cancel, cancel," and he's the hundred per cent owner, what do you do? You cancel. If it's a public company you say, "Andrew, it's a board matter, I'll have to take it up with the board." It allows you a little time to reason it through, find out what's worrying him.'

It was from exactly this kind of board interference, however, that Lloyd Webber wanted to free himself. Relations between the composer and the woman who had started out as his secretary seventeen years earlier deteriorated rapidly. There were a lot of late night, transatlantic telephone calls in which voices were raised and harsh words exchanged.

At the beginning of June, 1990 Biddy Hayward and Andrew Lloyd Webber parted professional company. 'I was fired,' said Hayward. 'I was given four days to get out.'

As a very junior member of a group which the Stock Exchange valued at £150 million, Edward had no part to play in this acrimonious dispute. He had seen very little of Lloyd Webber since that teatime meeting in Belgravia when he had talked himself into the job. The composer did not fraternise with his employees; he spent his working day composing. He visited the office only rarely and when he did he usually dealt through Hayward who in turn would be responsible for passing on any instructions. If Lloyd Webber was the general, Hayward was the colonel. It was to Hayward, therefore, that the team were directly answerable and, as is the case in the military, it was with their colonel that their personal loyalties lay.

Hayward did not mount a coup. Less than two weeks after her dismissal, however, six members of the Really Useful Theatre Company offered their resignations and walked out on Andrew Lloyd Webber to rejoin Biddy Hayward. They were general manager Harold Dagnall, production administrator Trevor Jackson, Robert Eady (box-office), merchandising coordinator Anne Simpson, Clare Vidal-Hall the PA and Edward Windsor.

In a statement issued through Buckingham Palace, Edward said: 'I am particularly grateful to Andrew Lloyd Webber and the Really Useful Theatre Group for their support and encouragement over the last couple of years and especially for giving me the chance to work in the theatre professionally. I hope to use this experience to progress further into production and explore new areas.'

Lloyd Webber was flabbergasted by the walkout. He had had no inkling that it was coming and was 'deeply offended' by what he regarded as the disloyalty of his departing staff. He covered his sense of outrage with PR platitudes: 'Mr Lloyd Webber is very relaxed about it all,' said his spokesman Peter Cunard, a former employer of the Duchess of York. 'He does not think it is worth spending any time over it. He is too busy to talk about it. These things happen in any business and it is a good move for the people concerned and he wishes them well.' There was really no disguising his feeling that he had been badly let down and there was a suspicion, inevitable in the circumstances, that Biddy Hayward was behind the defection.

Much was made at the time of a 'secret' meeting that took place on the night of 20 April at the Scandic Crown hotel near Victoria Station, around the corner from both Buckingham Palace and the theatre where *Starlight Express* was running. Shortly before midnight seven of Lloyd Webber's employees slipped into the nondescript hotel whose clientele was mainly Scandinavian tourists. They went up to the ninth floor where two conference rooms had been booked and ate a light supper. They did not re-emerge until 2am, by which time a motley gaggle of late night photographers, who had been tipped of by one of the hotel staff, were waiting for them.

Why, the press wanted to know, were they there? When Edward and his colleagues refused to comment, the deduction was that they were conspiring together. When first Biddy, then the other six all left Lloyd Webber's employ within six weeks, the conclusion was that that was where a plot had been hatched. According to one melodramatic account, it was Edward himself, in a ruthless bid for power, who was the perpetrator of an underhanded intrigue.

Hayward gave a more mundane account of events. The 'secret' midnight meeting, she insisted, was no such thing. 'It was,' she said, 'a standard production meeting. It was a very effective way of working, we would see the show then discuss any problems with the creative team over dinner. Someone would take minutes to ensure we dealt with everything quickly and efficiently.' That the meeting happened to be held just before she left was, she said, 'coincidence'. Nor, she insisted, was there anything to be read into the fact that her team, including Edward, resolved to follow her so soon afterwards; that, she said, was entirely their own decision.

'They did not hand in their notice straight away,' she said. That they quickly did was not entirely unexpected, however, despite what Andrew may have thought. They had enjoyed working with Biddy and they hardly knew Lloyd Webber. They were naturally concerned about what was going to happen next and who might be brought in to replace Hayward. There was also a feeling that her dismissal had not been well handled and there was sympathy for Biddy who was embroiled in a row about contracts and compensation. There were rumours that more 'redundancies' were to follow. A few days later they held a meeting, discussed their options and decided to hand in their resignations and join their old boss in a new venture.

'I think it was a case of better the devil you know than the devil you don't,' said Hayward. She continued: 'I shall be eternally grateful to those people – it will be on my gravestone, my thanks to those people, not because of anything to do with Andrew (that is irrelevant), but because if those people left I clearly could not have done anything wrong.'

Edward might have been expected to stay on with Lloyd Webber, the most powerful force in British theatre. The prince is a man of intense loyalties, however. He does not form friendships easily but he values the ones he has forged and places great store in them. Biddy was his friend. She was the one who had got him the job. She was the one he lunched with and talked to and worked for. He had been close to tears on the day she left. Andrew, on the other hand, was his employer. He went with Biddy.

That was not the end of his relationship with Lloyd Webber. There was no personal animosity between them; indeed, they were to work together again (although this time it was on a more conventional footing at the National Youth Music Theatre). It was just that in this case, in these particular circumstances, Edward opted for friendship over professional expediency.

It was a risky decision and, as it turned out, he made the wrong choice although, to be fair, that was primarily due to circumstances beyond his control. The theatre is an unpredictable business at the best of times but no one foresaw the international crisis that eventually consumed the new venture.

The company was called the Theatre Division and in the manner of new enterprises, it started out on a wave of optimism. Its first production, starring Nicola Pagett, Christine Kavanagh and Juliet Ormond, was *The Rehearsal* by the French dramatist Jean Anouilh. It opened at the Almeida Theatre in north London and, to the immense satisfaction of everyone concerned, transferred to the West End's Garrick and was nominated for an Olivier Award. Next came *The Same Old Moon* which started off at the Oxford Playhouse before opening at the Globe in London. That was nominated for an *Evening Standard* Award.

Edward had been instrumental in getting *The Same Old Moon* on to the stage. It was he who had recommended it to Hayward after being sent a copy by its Dublin-born writer, Geraldine Aron. Not all of the critical reaction had been favourable, however, and the plays were soon battling for economic survival.

The economic recession was biting and West End audiences were dwindling. A number of prestigious productions closed, including Jeffrey Archer's *Exclusive* and a revival of William Ince's *Bus Stop* with Mick Jagger's wife Jerry Hall in the role Marilyn Monroe had played in the film.

Things were hard for everyone, and for Edward in particular. He was a prince in a business fighting for its survival and there were moments when his status attracted unwanted attention and exaggerated any minor difficulty. It is one of the penalties of being who he is. As Biddy Hayward put it: 'He has advantages – but he also has grave disadvantages.'

As a member of the Royal Family, he was used to being briefed by experts, assimilating what they told him, and then spouting it out again. That irritated some of the people he met who thought he was being too clever for his own good.

His royal background was also reflected in his workrate; he was not used to working under intense pressure and there were occasions, said Hayward, when he did not work fast enough for her liking. When that happened, she had no compunction about telling him so.

His appearance at the opening of *The Same Old Moon* was misconstrued. The entire production team were in the foyer greeting everyone. As a vital member of that team Edward had every right to be there. The Royal Family had its place in the public's preconceptions, however, and his presence on hoi polloi's side of the presentation line sent the wrong signals to some people. 'I assume some people thought we were just a lot of rich kids trying to prove something, being too smart for our own good,' Hayward recalled.

His official engagements were another area in which his 'royalness' interfered with his career. Absences which had been accepted and acceptable when he was working under Lloyd Webber's larger and richer umbrella now became a source of friction. On one occasion Biddy actually lost her temper with him. It happened when he turned up very late for a rehearsal.

'When he finally arrived I said, "Where have you been?" He said, "I'm sorry, I had to do something first and couldn't get to a 'phone." I absolutely let rip and said, "You of all people tell me you couldn't get to a 'phone! Of course you could get to a 'phone!" '

Edward was silent for a moment. Then he said, 'I am very sorry, Biddy.' She accepted his apology and the team, including the chastened prince, got back to business. As far as she was concerned the matter was closed. He was a highly regarded member of the team – 'He had to be good otherwise he would not have lasted the course,' said Hayward – and like everyone else he was to be excused the occasional lapse.

Others were not so understanding, however. In the middle of one technical rehearsal Edward, who was technical administrator, had to leave for Windsor. 'He used to drive me up the wall,' Roger Penhale, *The Same Old Moon*'s stage-manager was quoted as saying. 'At times it seemed as if he was only playing at theatre. He did not always take things as seriously as he might.'

That was only true to the extent that Edward had a fall back position which the others did not. But if his hunger was not the same – the prince was never going to wind up in the dole queue if the business folded – his commitment was just as great. It was a matter of royal pride. He was the most famous tea boy in the world. The others may be out of pocket; Edward would have to meet the cost of failure out of his prestige.

There came the point, though, when no amount of hard work and dedication could save the situation. It arrived when Iraq's Saddam Hussein ordered his army to invade Kuwait. The tourist industry collapsed overnight as the Americans, on whom everyone depended, cancelled their vacations out of fears for their own safety. Hotels emptied and the West End fell silent.

'I have never known the streets of London so empty as they were at that time – it was quite frightening,' Hayward recalled.

Her fears were well founded as one by one the backers for the Theatre Division melted away. It desperately needed investors for the company itself and 'angels' to put up money to finance the shows they wanted to put on. In the end they found neither, though not through want of trying. Recalled Hayward: 'Edward was wonderful. He was not a drama queen in any shape or form. He tried actively to help the company through his contacts. He hassled people to invest.'

It was to no avail. No new backers could be found and plans for a £2 million musical revival of *Billy*, starring Jonathon Morris from the television situation comedy, *Bread*, had to be abandoned. The creditors started moving in and at one stage Edward was manning the pumps, fielding their calls. Six weeks after it opened, *The Same Old Moon* closed.

On 12 July, 1991 the curtain came down on the Theatre Division which collapsed with debts estimated at £600,000.

'We are proud of the quality of our productions,' said Biddy Hayward, 'but despite our efforts both with *The Rehearsal* and *The Same Old Moon*, we were too new and our resources too limited to survive one of the worst economic climates and total lack of tourism in the spring of this year.'

Andrew Lloyd Webber, back from another planet, described the news as 'shattering' and went on to say, 'I wish Biddy could have told me because perhaps I could have whacked some money in.'

At the age of twenty-seven, Edward Windsor was out of work once again.

Eleven

Managing Director, Edward Windsor

IN THE SUMMER of 1994 Ardent Productions submitted its first company report. It revealed nothing out of the ordinary. Ardent is a television production company with offices in a street once famous for its Greek restaurants in the television heartland of London's West End behind the Tottenham Court Road.

Business had been slack over the first thirteen months. It had no turnover in that period; its pre-tax losses amounted to £90,038 and its assets, which were listed as options on proposed future production developments, added up to all of £6,000.

By the high profit, high risk, high failure-rate standards of the television industry, Ardent was only just holding on. But two things stood out.

The first item that caught the attention of an enquiring eye was the name of the principal shareholder. Of the 300,000 ordinary £1 shares, 205,000 are registered in the name of E.A.R.L. Windsor.

The next piece of information to excite interest came under the listing of bank and cash. The figure was £709,418.

There it was, in black-and-white. Prince Edward aka Earl Windsor, was sitting on nearly three-quarters of a million pounds. In cash. It had indeed been a fast climb up from the down days of 1991 when the Theatre Division had turned bottom-up and Edward had found himself out of a job. Then the future had looked particularly bleak for the prince. Now, with his company's bank account awash with funds, it was bright with promise.

It was Edward's own single-mindedness that had pulled him

out of the hole he had been deposited in by events largely beyond his royal control. It had taken a lot of persuasive talk to get his company off the ground. There was a lot of opposition to him staying in the entertainment industry at all. His father, in particular, harboured grave misgivings.

Prince Philip wanted Edward to learn accountancy. At the very least he wanted him to take a management training course.

It was a suggestion that was out of sync with everything Edward had ever expressed an interest in. Unlike his brother, Charles, who needed three attempts to pass 'O' level maths, Edward had always been comfortable with figures. He did not, however, see that as the foundation for a career.

Yet a career was exactly what Edward urgently needed. The old certainties were crumbling. The cotton wool of deference was being rapidly picked away and the Royal Family, up to and including the Sovereign herself, was being asked to pay its way.

Philip, whose perception of the Royal Family's exigencies had been honed by being brought up on royalty's impoverished outer reaches, was simply being protective. When the Queen was a child, her grandmother Queen Mary had sternly enquired of her governess, 'Is Arithmetic really more valuable than History?' It was most unlikely, she said, that Elizabeth would ever have to concern herself with household accounts. That was most decidedly no longer the case. Indeed, there were moments when the most pressing problem facing the Royal Family *was* those very accounts of which the old Queen had been so dismissive. Now even princes had to earn a living and Philip was only trying to ensure that his son had the qualifications necessary to survive in a hungry, increasingly competitive environment.

At the end of 1992 the gale of economic change ripped through the corridors of Buckingham Palace and Edward felt its blast. There was, he said, 'the vote of total lack of confidence and understanding of certain members of the Royal Family's activities, which basically resulted in the Queen being asked to pay tax, and certain members of the Royal Family effectively losing their Civil List allowance.'

Edward was one who lost his allowance from the public purse. It had been set at a sum of £96,000 a year which was supposed to see him through until the year 2000 when it was due to be reviewed. Out of that he had to pay for the upkeep of his royal office which included a valet, his secretary Lisa Bugge, part-time secretary Sarah Warburton, and the salary of his Private Secretary Lt-Colonel Sean O'Dwyer, late of the Irish Guards. Now those expenses had to be met by the Queen from her private income. That was hardly going to break the Windsors' bank, but it did put extra pressure on Edward; in the business of royalty, appearances count for a great deal and he had to be seen to be earning his keep.

He had absolutely no objections to that. His determination to make his own way had marked him out from early childhood. The point had now been reached, however, when what Biddy Hayward called his 'learning curve' which had started with Andrew Lloyd Webber's Really Useful Theatre Company and carried him on through the Theatre Division should be nearing a destination.

Meetings were held, various options were discussed, and the Royal Family's advisers, prompted by Philip's concern, made a number of suggestions. 'There were a lot of people advising him at that time,' recalled Malcolm Cockren.

Twenty years older than the prince, Cockren was an insurance broker who had made the entertainment industry his speciality. He had first met Edward when his company was invited to insure *It's a Royal Knockout*. Cockren had left school at the age of fifteen to make his own way in life. By the age of twenty-one he had his own brokering firm and a client list which included Walt Disney and British Lion. He had branched out into film and television production, with seats on the boards of a number of entertainment-orientated companies both in Britain and the United States. Despite the obvious difference in background and experience the two hit it off – 'I enjoy his company; there is never any shortage of conversation,' Cockren said – and he became 'a sort of adviser' to the prince as the discussion about his future gathered pace. Like the one where it was decided that he would be allowed to join the Really Useful Theatre Company, these meetings were conducted in an informal and friendly atmosphere. They again involved Prince Philip's Private Secretary Brian McGrath; Robin Janvrin who had now been promoted to the position of Assistant Private Secretary to the Queen; and, in place of Adam Wise, the affable and efficient O'Dwyer.

'Certainly accountancy was high on their list of priorities,' said Cockren. 'Legal work' was another idea. And as a sort of career catch-all, Philip came up with the management training proposal.

That was not in the least what Edward had in mind. It was soon abundantly clear to everyone, said Cockren, 'that the only business that really interested the prince was the entertainment industry'.

For a son of the reigning Sovereign to be directly involved in business was a new and worrying notion. Commerce had always been anathema to the Royal Family. It was partly a snobbish thing; the British upper classes, brought up to regard land as the only honourable measure of wealth, traditionally look down on 'trade'. That was not going to influence Philip's judgement. He had always been impatient and, on occasion, rudely dismissive of the Establishment's prejudices as patronising and old-fashioned.

But direct involvement also went against the grain of the impartiality so vital to the good name of the Royal Family and even Philip had to take that into consideration. It is because of this impartiality that they do not vote, although some of them hold strong political opinions (Prince Charles, for instance, was vehemently anti-Thatcher). It is why they prefer to play the role of 'ambassador' for all British industry rather than of salesman for any one company. As Philip acknowledged, 'Any member of the Family who has been anywhere near a commercial activity is always criticised because it is going to give them an unfair advantage.'

Edward, his eye constantly on the ball of his family's reputation, had always had to take the issue of 'commercialisation' into consideration. But then, he said, 'a certain event occurred which basically convinced me that I really wasn't concerned about that any more.'

The event he was referring to was the loss of the Queen's tax immunity and the loss of his Civil List allowance. As far as Edward was concerned, he was now free to pursue his career as he best saw fit. He was smart enough to heed the advice of experts, however, before he committed himself. Cockren recalled: 'I explained the pitfalls to him. We discussed various types of business in which he could become involved and I said there is only one industry I wouldn't become involved in – and that is the theatre business.'

The theatre had been Edward's great love since he was a little boy. Its appeal had been powerful enough for him to discard all other career options. But now it was his own money, in part at least, that was to be on the line and that put a different complexion on the situation. 'My advice to him was not to go into it,' said Cockren.

Edward had already witnessed at first hand the problems that were encountered all too frequently in that emotionally charged, financially unstable industry. In Cockren's opinion, 'It was just too dicey to take another chance.' Edward's interest switched to television.

It would have been feasible for Edward to have taken another job and become a salaried employee as he had been with both Lloyd Webber and Hayward. The prince, however, was ambitious. He had reached the stage when he wanted to strike out on his own. He also had his other commitments to consider. Even though he no longer had the Civil List to call on, he still had his quota of charity work and state duties to fulfil. 'Being realistic there are some commitments that I'm going to have to make which are connected with the Royal Family,' he acknowledged. 'I've cut down on functions a lot but I'll always have those other commitments and interests.'

They had caused a problem before and might well do so again. It would be easier for his duties, Cockren pointed out, if Edward was his own boss and therefore freed of that conflict of interest.

In the end the Queen and Prince Philip gave their consent to their youngest son branching out into hitherto uncharted territory. 'They wanted him to be happy,' explained Cockren. 'They wanted him to be successful.'

To give him the best shot at the latter, the accounting firm of Coopers & Lybrand was employed to put together a business plan. Cockren's initial idea was to set up some sort of trust funding specifically 'to distance him personally from the company should it run into trouble.'

That was not what Edward wanted. This was going to be his company and he wanted people to know that. So he sat down at his word processor and rewrote the business plan to include himself as an investor. 'You've got to put your money where your mouth is,' he said.

Cockren was impressed, not least by Edward's technical skill at the computer. He remarked, 'He has total business acumen; his memory is a great asset and so is his ability with figures.'

Edward was doing what he had told his family he wanted to do which was involve himself in a company right from the beginning, learning as he went along. He did not wish to remain hidden in the background. He wanted to be out there, taking his chances, being judged on what he achieved, not who he was.

'Not everyone in the entertainment business is in love with the Royal Family and there are sometimes clear disadvantages to his title,' Cockren observed. 'He had to convince people in the industry of his ability. He doesn't want anyone to think he is after an advantage and will go to great lengths to make sure people don't feel they are being put in that position.'

It is to emphasise precisely that point that his business cards were printed in the name of Edward Windsor. But that still left the crucial decision: What business? With the theatre out of the equation, Edward's interest switched to television, the medium that, at the age of five, had aroused his first stirrings of interest in the entertainment business.

When he held his first meeting with Cockren on 17 February, 1992, television 'was simply a box in the corner of the room'. He knew nothing about the industry, its intricacies or any of the people involved in it. He did have that facility to learn quickly, however and with Cockren's help he set about gathering together the best advice and expertise he could find.

In this instance being a prince was no handicap. With Cockren's help he pulled together a high profile, highly professional team able to hold their own in the rapacious world of television production. Cockren was chairman. The joint managing director was barrister turned television executive Eben Foggitt. The finance director and company secretary was

Malcolm Eldridge, a member of the Guild of Film and Television Production Accountants. The team was completed by Graeme McDonald, the heavy-hitting ex-head of drama at the BBC, ex-controller of BBC2 and ex-managing director of films and drama at Anglia, who was responsible for such television hits as *Bergerac* and *All Creatures Great and Small*. 'Graeme is a bit of a prize for the Prince,' the former BBC1 controller Jonathan Powell noted.

Edward was joint managing director. He called himself 'team leader', and it was a responsibility he took seriously. After an hour spent working with O'Dwyer on his royal schedule, he usually drove himself to Ardent's offices in his green Rover Vitesse, his detective at his side, arriving there by 9.30. He would then put in a full working day, often not returning to the Palace until supper time.

There were inevitable setbacks and disappointments. A £1 million deal with Nickelodeon, the extra-terrestrial American entertainment channel, fell through. Some schemes evaporated before they came into focus. Others never got beyond a brief, cursory discussion.

There was method in the delay. 'What I didn't want to get involved in was a scenario where Edward was going to be criticised for doing something he believed he was doing for all the right reasons which might end up being a problem for the Royal Family, like the *Knockout* programme,' says Cockren.

Edward agreed. As he acknowledged, an invitation to have lunch with 'Edward Windsor' might set the ball rolling, but the ideas themselves have to be good if they are to succeed.

His search for suitable projects took him to the South of France for the television festival in Cannes. There he did a £100,000 deal with the Australian-born Bruce Gyngell, former chief of TV-am, to produce a documentary series on the Commonwealth. Gyngell, carried away by the garishness of these occasions, introduced Edward around saying, 'Would anyone like to have their photograph taken with the prince?' Edward went along with it. His commitment never wavered. Neither did his caution or sense of responsibility – the hard lessons learned at the Theatre Division were very much to the fore in his thinking: 'I am nervous – it is not just my imcome but other people's survival on the line,' he said.

There was a third consideration – his backers. The prince has £205,000 of his own money committed in the company. But that is on paper, not in the bank. That £709,418 revealed in the company report is primarily drawn from other sources. They remain anonymous.

Those nameless shareholders do not include any member of the Royal Family – the British Royal Family, that is. But Edward Windsor knows a lot of people, including the Sultan of Brunei, the richest man in the world with a fortune estimated at US$25 billion. Edward knows him through his royal connections and through the good offices of the Loewe Bell public relations organisation which represents the Sultan in this country and some of whose executives have on occasion done work for Edward. It is no secret amongst Edward's friends that the Sultan is one of Edward's backers. Officially, however, he remains just another anonymous shareholder.

'I won't comment on our investors,' said Cockren, 'other than to say that, as chairman of Ardent, I am responsible to those shareholders for the conduct of the company. I am very proud of them and I am very proud of what Ardent is achieving.'

By the beginning of 1995 the company had two major drama productions with a production value of over £4 million in serious development. It was ahead of its business plan schedule.

Ardent hopes to be one of the top twelve independent production companies in Britain by the end of this century. It would please Edward's father if it achieves its aim. It would satisfy his backers, however rich they might already be.

Edward's future depends on it.

Twelve

Pretty Women

THERE HAVE BEEN seven women who have occupied prime position in Edward's affections. Despite all the denials and disclaimers, all of them, at one time or another, enjoyed the prince's amorous attentions. There were others but these were the main players. Indeed, half might well have made him a suitable wife. They were Romy Adlington, Eleanor Weightman, Georgia May, Rhian-Anwen Roberts, Ruthie Henshall, Gail Greenough and Princess Martha-Louise of Norway.

His romantic adventures began long before he met any of them, however. Like many young men of the upper classes, Prince Edward lost his virginity to a servant girl. That at any rate is what the Palace staff believe. That was certainly the claim of one comely housemaid who ardently related how, in the summer of 1982, she took her royal duties seriously enough to lay down her virtue for the manly well being of the Queen's youngest son.

It was an encounter which the maid – at twenty-one she was three years Edward's senior – took indiscreet delight in describing in graphic detail. It happened, she said, shortly after Edward had left Gordonstoun and had joined his mother's summer court at Balmoral.

Built by Queen Victoria, the castle sits sternly on the banks of the river Dee, an imposing memorial to the granite-hard moral standards she personified. To the staff who accompanied the Queen on her annual three-month sojourn north, however, Balmoral offered a most welcome change from the strict formality of Buckingham Palace and the winter excursions to the dreary social outpost of Sandringham which they heartily dislike. Balmoral was as much a summer holiday for the Sovereign's downstairs entourage of maids and footmen, butlers, pages and chefs, as it was for the Royal Family itself.

At the Queen's express wish Balmoral is run as informally as is regally possible. Picnics and evening barbecues are the order of the royal day. They take place regularly and regardless of the weather – the Queen Mother, even in her nineties, continued to venture out on to the hills wrapped in a tartan rug to join the others eating the sausages and chops they take an almost childish pleasure in cooking themselves. Once the royal party has departed the staff are free to do as they wish. They swim in the lochs and take long walks through the woods and across the hills. Taking their lead from their royal mistress, they hold a lot of barbecues of their own. They have their own social club which holds regular dances and fancy dress parties in the large log cabins dotted around the estate. And they enjoy their holiday flings – of different kinds, each according to his or her taste, and much to the Queen's fascination.

Indeed, such were the romps that the staff nicknamed the castle, 'Immoral Balmoral'.

A noticeable percentage of the Queen's Household (although by no means all) is homosexual. Unlike her great-great-grandmother, Victoria, who was appalled by the very notion and, in the instance of women, refused to acknowledge even the possibility, the Queen has always taken a most tolerant view of her employees' sexual orientations. She does not express disapproval but instead takes a lively interest in the romantic comings and goings of her staff – in all their assorted manifestations. Trapped since birth in the labyrinth of Court life, she has made it her business to know every nook and cranny of the small world she inhabits – and the interests and proclivities of those who share it with her. 'There is very little that goes on that she does not know about,' one former member of the Household said. In a manner reminiscent of Louis XIV, she collects information and welds it into an instrument of her authority and members of both her staff and family have been disconcerted by her knowledge of matters they thought (and often hoped) would remain closely-guarded secrets.

'A good gossip is a wonderful tonic,' is how the Queen herself ingenuously summarises this exploitation of Palace power.

The talk at the castle that summer, however, was most definitely not to the Queen's liking.

The maid was young and pert with an outgoing manner that had already attracted the attention of a number of the younger footmen whose inclinations lay in that direction. Her interest, however, was directed upstairs – first at Viscount Linley and then, when that came to nothing, towards Prince Edward.

Balmoral, the one stopover on the royal itinerary where the staff are allowed to speak to members of the Royal Family without having to wait until they are first spoken to, was an ideal setting.

One night in August she crept across the castle from the servants' quarters and into the small first-floor bedroom where Edward lay asleep in his single bed.

The following morning she walked into the staff dining room and announced 'as bold as brass', as one footman recalled, that she had taken Edward's virginity.

Only two people can confirm the veracity of that declaration but, believable or not, gossip of this import tears through the castle like one of its notorious winter draughts and by lunchtime everyone in the Household knew her story – including the housekeeper, who severely reprimanded the maid for what she described as her foolish headstrong ways.

Edward just wanted to forget. He was both angered and upset by the affair. He felt used and let down and foolish. If he had made a mistake, it was of the kind made by thousands of other youngsters of the same age. But, as he had always inherently known, he was not as other youngsters. His indiscretions would not be allowed to fade into memory. He was a Prince of the Blood and that meant that everything he did, no matter how commonplace and normal, could be turned into a source of embarrassment to him and the family of which he is so proud and protective.

That hard realisation was to colour his future relations and set the pattern for all his courtships. Experience had been added to instinct.

The members of the Household were not the only people who

would have been interested in what the housemaid had to tell. The Royal Family, however, closely guards its private lives and the Queen does what she can to preserve and safeguard the reputation of her family. In 1983 for instance the then Attorney General Lord Havers applied for an injunction on behalf of the Queen against Palace employee, Michelle Riles. She was trying to sell an account of her time in royal service, which New York literary agent Lucienne Goldberg described as, 'a million dollar property'. The injunction was granted and Michelle Riles duly disappeared into obscurity taking her story with her.

Episodes like this served to reinforce the family's concern for their privacy.

Back in his bachelor days, the Prince of Wales had been advised by Princess Margaret: 'If you don't want to be seen you don't have to be. We have a lot of homes to go to – use them.' It was advice that Charles chose to ignore. He was determined to conduct himself as he best saw fit, unfettered by traditional royal stricture, and he made a point of taking his dates along with him to the opera, to polo, with the inevitable consequence that most of his romances withered under the spotlight of public scrutiny before they had a chance to get properly started.

His example served as a cautionary tale for his younger brother for whom privacy became a consuming concern of almost obsessive proportions. There were no public outings to restaurants or nightclubs or sporting fields. Instead he kept his romantic trysts within the protective walls of Buckingham Palace, Windsor Castle, Balmoral and Wood Farm on the Sandringham estate which had originally been given to Charles as a courting den.

He tried to include other members of his family in his news blackout. When Prince Andrew returned from active service in the South Atlantic and went on holiday on the Caribbean island of Mustique with Koo Stark, he was escorted by a press armada. Edward described the treatment meted out to his brother as 'despicable'.

'He was only a sailor,' Edward complained. 'He'd been at war; he wanted to get away from everything and relax and unwind and get some sun. He missed summer and he had every right to go on holiday. Not only did they hound him over the affair, they actually hounded him to such an extent that he had to stop the holiday. He came back from that holiday more drawn, more tired than he had from three months at war and I think to treat someone who's just come back from serving their country like that is absolutely despicable.'

In the naïve sense, Edward was absolutely right. But royal romances, especially when the girl being romanced had once appeared in a soft-porn film, were headline news. That was the price exacted for the privileges that came with being born royal. Edward refused to see it that way. A late developer and naturally shy, he hated the idea of anyone prying into what he considered his private business. That only re-enforced his sense of being different which made it harder still for him to make any meaningful emotional commitment. He was always on his guard.

This reluctance to unburden himself, at an age when his contemporaries were talking endlessly about themselves, their hopes and their ambitions as they busily defined themselves in their own minds in readiness for adulthood, made it difficult for him to have anything other than superficial relationships with girls. Some girls found this off-putting. Others went along for the royal ride.

In 1986, during his time as a student at Cambridge, Edward commented on the problems of being royal and having a relationship. 'It's not going to affect me at all because my anonymity has gone and I accept that,' he said. 'But you become very conscious of the feeling that if you try to get to know anybody they are going to suffer a stigma for the rest of their lives. I cannot have a normal relationship with just about anybody, but that's the way it goes.'

The failures of the marriages of his beloved sister Anne and then, in rapid and ever more embarrassing succession, Andrew and Charles, made him even more determined to put caution before commitment. Somewhat ingenuously, he believed everyone should go along with him. In December 1993, following reports that he was planning to marry Sophie Rhys-Jones, he went so far as to issue a statement to Britain's newspaper editors which read:

'I am taking this unusual step of writing to you directly in the hopes of stopping your reporters and photographers from destroying that part of my life that I am entitled to regard as private and more importantly, Sophie's life.

'We are not planning to get married – we only met each other in the last few months – but we are good friends. If this situation changes we will let you know in a proper and formal manner.'

At the end he added: 'I am very conscious that other members of my immediate family have been subjected to similar attention and it has not been at all beneficial to their relationships.'

If Edward's pleas fell on deaf ears it was not for lack of trying. Some months later he made another complaint, this time to the Press Council, about 'peeping tom' photographs taken of him and Sophie sharing a kiss in the grounds of Balmoral estate. The pictures were taken from over a kilometre away and the newspapers who ran them were forced to apologise. For such a private person as Edward to have such intimate photographs published was profoundly embarrassing.

His complaints, no matter how justified, did little to enhance his popularity with a media which was becoming ever less deferential. Nor did they achieve what he hoped for, as he himself later acknowledged.

'There was a pause,' he told me, 'and then various commentators started saying things like people in glass-houses shouldn't throw bricks . . . which I never understood because I hadn't thrown any bricks. I had just said, "Stay away, lay off – please." '

They were never going to do that and by asking that they should he inadvertently fuelled exactly the kind of interest he was so anxious to avoid. In a society increasingly sceptical of the motives and behaviour of its leaders and public figures, Edward's oft-repeated demand for privacy created the impression, in some quarters at least, that he had something to hide.

The Queen might have warned him of the danger he was laying himself open to. As a baby Prince Andrew had been kept out of sight and and had been labelled as mentally retarded as a consequence. Was it not to dispel the shadow of similar rumours that she had raised her youngest son aloft on the balcony of Buckingham Palace so that the people could see him and he would be spared the cruel calumnies that rushed to fill the vacuum created by the absence of real information?

Edward, however, chose to eschew his mother's wise example. He went out of his way to shield his romantic life from the public's gaze. His former Private Secretary, Adam Wise, observed: 'Prince Edward, I think it is fair to say, is very keen on keeping those aspects of his life which he regards as private private. I don't think he wishes to share his private life with the rest of the world. He did not see it as anyone else's business who his particular girlfriend of the moment was. He was extremely discreet and so were his girlfriends. They were always good at disguising anything that may have been going on from the press. The care he took to keep his private life private was working.'

But that, as Wise acknowledged, created other problems. Edward, he said, 'was not throwing the right amount of red meat to the lions'. He was rarely seen with a young woman and whispers about Edward's sexuality soon became widespread. Because he did not appear to have any girlfriends, said Wise, 'people said he must be queer. That was pure spite.'

The evidence was circumstantial but no less compelling because of that. He was good looking in an angelic way (everyone, from Cecil Beaton onwards, had remarked on that). He had a well-developed interest in the theatre. And he had been brought up surrounded by homosexuals. (Royal service is poorly paid and riddled with extraordinary rituals of protocol but it does offer the curious attraction of dressing up in courtly clothing which has always appealed to a certain sort of gay man – upstairs as well as downstairs.)

Like his mother, Edward was untroubled by any of this. When one of his staff came and told Edward he was leaving his wife and going to live with another man, the Prince was unperturbed. He said he did not mind what anyone did when they were not working as long as it did not get out of hand with the press. Edward was confident in his own sexuality. As Peter Brown, former president of the Beatles' Apple Corp, best man at John Lennon's wedding to Yoko Ono and for many years Andrew Lloyd Webber's public relations adviser observed: 'He is clearly comfortable in the company of gay people.'

British society, however, takes an exquisite delight at being shocked by the sexual behaviour of its upper classes and the notion of a gay prince was too tantalising to be ignored. The gossip took on a life of its own. Edward, it was whispered in ever-widening circles, was homosexual.

The rumour reached the Royal Marine depot in Devon where it created a stir of apprehension. Homosexuality is not only regarded with distaste by the military, it is also technically illegal. Said a former Royal Marines officer: 'We were slightly worried that he might not have been totally heterosexual.'

The story crossed the Atlantic and entered the realm of the absurd. Rupert Murdoch's mass circulation newspaper the *News of the World* published a claim by fraudster and conman Duane Hoffman that he had seen Edward embracing a young man who Hoffman alleged spent the night in the prince's hotel suite in the autumn of 1986. Hoffman also falsely claimed that the prince had asked for a young man to be sent to his room and then asked for the £500 bill to be sent to the British embassy.

The militant gay rights lobby was determined to claim him as one of their own – a By Appointment royal endorsement would have suited their political purposes and when Edward started work in the theatre he was given the nicknames of Dockland Doris and Babs Windsor. That, as his former boss Biddy Hayward pointed out, was par for the theatrical course: 'There is a trend in the world of theatre and showbusiness whereby people have nicknames,' she said. 'For example, Michael Crawford was often known as Betty and Anthony Andrews as Julie.'

It was none the less most unusual for a member of the Royal Family to be addressed in such a familiar and blatantly sexual way and Edward was concerned and upset by the implication. As Adam Wise observed: 'The politically correct approach is to say: What does it matter? But of course it does and it did very much to him. He was about twenty-three or twenty-four when this sort of thing came up.'

The matter came to a head in the spring of 1990 when Edward took the unique royal step of discussing his sexuality in public. The prince was in New York for the Broadway première of Lloyd Webber's musical, *Aspects of Love*. Just before he flew in, a London gossip columnist had written of the 'touching friendship' that had developed between Edward and Michael Ball, the 27-year-old star of the show.

Ball, who had once been covered in gold paint and packed in a box as a surprise birthday present for Elton John's manager, John Reid, had been dating 46-year-old Cathy McGowan, former presenter of *Ready, Steady, Go!* the quintessential Sixties television pop show, for more than a year before the rumours started. Being an actor familiar with the gay scene he paid little heed to the backbiting. In the charged atmosphere of the first night party in New York's Rockefeller Center, however, matters quickly spun out of hand.

Edward was chatting with a party of friends including Peter Brown who recalled: 'A journalist from a nearby press table came over to him and asked him quite politely how he had enjoyed the show. Edward mouthed the usual theatrical platitudes about how wonderful it was and the reporter, who was unaccredited, left.' That might have been the end of it but a few moments later Edward wandered off on his own. The reporter saw his moment and struck. He stopped the prince and asked him point blank, 'Are you gay?'

Said Brown: 'Edward was so taken aback that he was completely thrown.' Caught unprotected and off-guard, the prince spluttered angrily: 'It's just outrageous to suggest this sort of thing. It's so unfair to me and my family. How would you feel if someone said you were gay? I am not gay but what can I do about it? Why do certain people try to make more of things? I can only repeat – it's very unfair.'

Then, in a reference to a successful libel action his cousin had recently brought, he added: 'I am beginning to think that Viscount Linley might have had the right idea. The press has to be a lot more responsible. I wish I could be left to enjoy the theatre. I love it.'

When the story made headlines the following day, friends of Edward, including his first real girlfriend, Romy Adlington, spoke out in his defence. 'There's no question of the Prince being homosexual. Nothing is further from the truth.' she said. 'He's heterosexual and very manly.'

His friends and colleagues continue to echo her opinion. Michael Ball's understudy, David Gree, dismissed the rumours as 'utter rubbish'. 'He's a real man and if a pretty blonde in a short skirt is around, Edward's the first person to have a good look. He's just one of the lads. He mucks in with everyone and is always surrounded by beautiful girls because he is so charming. Women love him.'

'I've never heard so much utter nonsense in my entire life,' said Biddy Hayward. 'I've seldom come across a young man who appreciates women as much as Edward does. I have never known a gay man believe Edward is gay and I always think that is a good barometer.'

Paul Arengo Jones, secretary of the International Duke of Edinburgh's Award, preferred to rely on a woman's instinct in this delicate matter. 'A lot of people say to me, "Oh, Prince Edward, you've heard about him, haven't you?" We had some appalling stories told to us. So I told my wife Josephine that the first time you meet him, you decide. Afterwards she said, "It's crazy, of course he is not!" '

Jones believed it was Edward's enthusiasm for the theatre that fuelled the rumours. 'If you have friends in the artistic world you have got friends who are that way inclined.' Biddy agreed. 'I think it really came from the fact that there is a terrible assumption that everybody in the theatre is gay,' she said. 'If you leave the army because supposedly you are not capable of flexing your muscles with the rest of them, then I suppose the assumption is that you must be a raging queen which is unutterable rubbish.'

Wise agreed: 'I think the problem was there he was with all the luvvies in the theatrical business, we never hear about his girlfriends, he has deliberately chosen that business, therefore he must be queer. It's false logic really.' He concluded: 'I can firmly say there is no evidence for it whatsoever.' Said Hayward: 'He likes women. He appreciates a pretty face like any other young man.'

The Marines also arrived at that same conclusion. So did his tutors at Cambridge. On several occasions girls were smuggled into his rooms to spend the night with the student prince. Andrew Merrylees turned a blind eye to such escapades. 'There was no doubt in Andrew's mind they were all girls – thank God for that,' said Southby-Tailyour. 'That scotched the rumours.'

Edward chose to make a joke about it all. No young, straight man likes to have his sexuality queried and Edward was no exception. But, as Biddy Hayward observed, 'he has a great sense of humour about how he is perceived – because, I suspect, that is the only way to deal with it and retain your sanity. We had some great laughs. He is able to laugh at himself.'

Certainly his own family had never harboured any doubts. Women have always loved him – from infancy through to adulthood. He never had trouble getting himself a date when he wished for one.

'I think girls were attracted to the idea of the whole thing, as most young ladies would be,' his cousin Marina Ogilvy recalls. 'But he was always very careful. You would never catch him snogging in a corner.'

Like most teenagers, however, that was exactly how Edward began his romantic education. It started in his sixth-form year at Gordonstoun in the company of Shelley Whitborn, a robust girl groom who was employed on his sister's estate in Gloucestershire. Her father sold spare car parts in the Guildford area and Shelley had few ambitions beyond wanting to be either a policewoman or to work with horses. She chose the latter and took a job as a trainee groom working for Mark Phillips's mother, Anne.

A renowned horsewoman in her own right, Anne Phillips also had the reputation for turning out excellent female grooms and Shelley was a product of that expertise. She first came to Edward's attention in the summer of 1980 when she was helping out at nearby Gatcombe Park and was asked to look after his much loved pony, Flame who had fallen dangerously ill.

Edward, who had hardly noticed the homely Shelley until then, was extremely grateful to her. He believed, quite rightly, that she had saved his pony's life. During that summer at Gatcombe they spent hours in each other's company. When he left he started writing to her. They were not love letters, just chatty notes from an adolescent boy to someone he genuinely admired, was grateful to and quickly came to like. Shortly after the wedding of the Prince of Wales to Lady Diana Spencer their friendship moved up a gear.

Three days before the wedding, Princess Anne and her then

husband Mark Phillips threw a party in the gardens of Gatcombe. All the estate workers were invited, including Shelley who wore her best frock.

It was a warm summer evening that might have been designed for a Merchant Ivory film. The long trestle tables covered with linen tablecloths groaned with food and drink and bunting covered the side walls of the house. Anne, acting the local squire, invited some Morris dancers to entertain her guests; Mark Phillips and his mother entered into the festive spirit by leading the dancing on the gravel driveway in front of the house.

Edward's favourite cousin, Lady Sarah Armstrong-Jones, all tangled hair and generous mouth, was there. But she was 'family' and Edward was growing up and it was Shelley who excited his attention. When the disco struck up John Lennon's hit, 'Woman' Edward put down his glass of dry sherry and, much to the winking, nudging amusement of the grooms who were standing around drinking beer and cheap white wine, he walked across and asked Shelley to dance.

Shelley came in for a lot of ribbing the following day. The other staff mockingly bowed to her and called her 'Viscountess Whitborn'. 'This is your big chance,' they joked.

Back in the real world the big chance belonged to Lady Diana Spencer. She was the girl who had really got her prince. Shelley, meanwhile, had to step back into her own life again; she was not able to renew her acquaintance with Edward until after the wedding.

The intervening days were rush and chaos for Edward who, with his brother, Andrew, were the Prince of Wales's two 'supporters', as the Royal Family's best men are called.

There was the christening of his niece, Princess Anne's daughter, Zara, held in Windsor Castle's private chapel which was later destroyed by the calamitous fire of 1992. It was followed by a grand luncheon party where the guests included Prince Charles and Camilla Parker Bowles whose husband, Andrew, was one of the godparents.

There was the pre-wedding ball at Buckingham Palace. It was the largest and most glittering party the Royal Family had hosted in over half a century. So overcrowded with guests was the Palace that Princess Grace had to share a sitting room with

Prince Harald, the Crown Prince of Norway (to the delight of Norway's future king and the intense annoyance of the retired Hollywood queen).

And in between it all, Edward had to fit in his driving test. He took it on the afternoon of Zara's christening and passed first time. It would have annoyed Prince Philip and Andrew Merrylees, who had encouraged Edward to drive around the royal estates as soon as he was big enough to see over the steering wheel, if he had not.

Then there was the wedding itself. He was awoken that morning as usual at 8.00 by his valet, who drew back the curtains so the prince could look out over Green Park where crowds of people had camped out over night. 'Every time you looked out from the front of the Palace or the side of the Palace all you could see were just hundreds and thousands of people,' a member of the Palace staff remembers. 'They were all cheering and there was a constant noise and rumble. It was an electrifying atmosphere.'

Charles, with no inkling of the disaster to come, remembered being 'carried along on a wave of enormous friendliness and enthusiasm. It was remarkable. And I kept telling myself to remember this for as long as I could because it was such a unique experience.'

After the service itself, Edward and Andrew decided to have some fun. They stood at the door of the Ball Supper Room where the wedding breakfast took place with football rattles and took it in turns to announce the guests: 'One King in Exile,' shouted Edward as 'Uncle Tino', King Constantine of Greece entered. 'One King of Norway, One Queen of Denmark . . .'

They teased Diana for getting Charles's name muddled up during the ceremony and when the newly weds departed for their honeymoon, they decorated the carriage with silver helium-filled balloons and hung a 'Just Married' sign written in red lipstick on the back.

In truth, however, Edward was quite relieved when the festivities were at their end and his life could return to what he regarded as normal. He had been most inconvenienced by Diana's presence. She had been installed on his floor and used his staff. Now he was his own boss again and he took immediate advantage of the situation and invited Shelley up to London the next night to see *For Your Eyes Only*. Still the avid Bond fan, he was looking forward to seeing the latest movie and had told Shelley to be at Buckingham Palace in time for the evening performance in Leicester Square.

In order to keep the date with her prince, Shelley asked Captain Phillips if she could borrow one of the estate cars, a Ford Fiesta, to drive herself to Buckingham Palace. Amused by the incongruity of the situation, Phillips agreed, but reminded her not to drink too much and to be back at the stables in time for the early morning ride.

When Shelley arrived at Buckingham Palace, Edward could have been excused if he hardly recognised her. Apart from that night at the Gatcombe party, he had only seen her in riding clothes or jeans. Now she was wearing her best frock. Her face was made-up, her hair was carefully blow-dried.

Awkward and nervous, the two teenagers made polite conversation in Edward's apartment until it was time to leave for the cinema. Afterwards Edward politely showed her back into her borrowed car and saw her off on the road back to Gloucestershire. Apart from a small inner circle of staff and family, no one would have known about the date between the prince and the groom but on the M4 motorway near Theale in Berkshire she lost her concentration and crashed into the back of a trailer carrying a rare Alvis Speed Twenty coupé, which had just been lovingly restored by its owner.

'I suddenly felt an enormous bang at the back,' said the owner, Michael Geoghegan. 'I stopped and saw the Alvis wrecked on the carriageway and smoke pouring from it. I just couldn't believe it.'

Nor could Shelley. Captain Phillip's car was a wreck, she had bumped her head on the steering wheel, was slightly concussed and had hurt her leg. She was also shocked and very dazed when the Thames Valley police arrived.

To make matters worse they did not believe her story. 'She was talking about a party with Prince Edward that she had been to and was saying she was on her way back to Gatcombe Park,' a police spokesman said. 'The patrol car officers were suspicious, but discovered she was telling the truth when they checked the car's owner.'

Having convinced the police she was not inventing her story, Shelley was taken to the Royal Berkshire hospital in Reading where she was joined by her parents. She was later fined £80 for careless driving.

That mishap did not affect her unlikely friendship. If anything it seemed to draw them together. It was as though Edward felt responsible in some way and just before he returned to school in January 1982, Shelley was invited back to Buckingham Palace. This time she travelled up on the train and Edward arranged for her to stay the night. The routine was similar, but instead of seeing a film they stayed in and had supper, served by a footman in Edward's rooms.

Shelley, the groom from Guildford, was impressed and understandly a little overawed. The food was beautifully prepared and the wine delicious. Knowing that she did not have to drive home, Shelley drank liberally to ease her nerves. After dinner they talked into the small hours and, according to Shelley, had a little kiss and cuddle on the sofa before Edward shyly showed her where she was to sleep.

It was in Prince Andrew's bedroom next to his. There was a convenient connecting door and Shelley lay awake for most of the night, convinced that at any moment Edward would come creeping through. But Edward was a young gentleman. Staff might creep into his bedroom but he did not creep into theirs and Shelley's wait was in vain. The prince remained stoutly on his side of the door. In the morning he politely kissed her goodbye and saw she was taken to the station for the journey back to Gatcombe.

That was not the end of their relationship. They continued to write and telephone each other. He enjoyed the company of Shelley and girls like her feeling comfortable in their lack of sophistication. Eventually, however, they drifted apart, as they were bound to – this was one romance that could never develop beyond an adolescent fling. The gap in their respective social statuses was simply too great, as Edward was very well aware. He had, however, been allowed to go out with her – a startling break from royal tradition.

Unlike Charles, who had his dynastic responsibilities to consider, Edward was able to date more or less whom he chose. Nor was he backward about coming forward. Whilst he was in New Zealand he co-starred with 17-year-old Alison Bell in an amateur production of *Charley's Aunt*. 'I remember after the play he came up and gave me a surprise kiss. He has lovely soft lips,' she said, adding, 'He is definitely not shy with girls.'

Unlike Andrew, whose lusts were straight to the point, Edward was always more attracted to personality than to other more obvious allures.

In Romy Adlington he appeared to have got both. She was the 17-year-old model daughter of a Hampshire wine merchant and they met at the Royal Yacht Squadron Ball at Cowes in the summer of 1983. Before she went, her mother Anne, who had made the dress Romy wore, jokingly told her that if any royal asked her to dance she was to say, 'My Mum doesn't want to go down the Mall wearing a hat.'

She made an instant impression on the 20-year-old prince who had just returned from New Zealand. The next day Romy telephoned Anne Adlington and said, 'Mum, get ready to go down the Mall wearing a hat!'

When they met again two nights later at the Royal London Yacht Club Edward spent the entire evening talking to her. He asked her to accompany him to Balmoral.

Romy declined. She had been booked for a series of modelling assignments by her London agents, Models One, who once employed Mick Jagger's wife Jerry Hall, and her mother said it would be unprofessional to cancel them. Edward was nothing if not persistent, however. He wrote to her. He telephoned. He took her to the theatre and afterwards drove her back to Buckingham Palace for a light supper. She stayed the night. 'It was obvious he was not used to having girlfriends spend the night with him,' she said. 'We were both a bit young and inexperienced. But in a way that was quite sweet.'

Edward telephoned afterwards. He was very keen to see her again. 'I was halfway through Sunday lunch with my mother when the 'phone rang,' Romy recalled. It was Edward, again urging her to join him in Scotland. This time she agreed. 'I told him I would love to come,' she said.

Edward's need to conduct himself as clandestinely as a spy gave the trip its own flavour. As he carefully explained to her in a letter, he preferred to travel under an alias (he used his second name of Richard) and she had to wait until a party of other young people were arriving to avoid being detected by what he called the 'pressmen'.

Romy's Balmoral trip set the pattern for Edward's love affairs over the next ten years. Most rich young men of his background would have sent round an airline ticket for her. The Royal Family is notoriously tight with money, however, and Edward made Romy pay for her own flight to Aberdeen. Once there, though, she was engulfed in the cotton wool of royalty. She was met by a chauffeur-driven Range Rover and taken to Balmoral Castle. On arrival she was met by Edward and the Queen on the front doorstep. 'She was just as I imagined her but less formal and more smiley than at public engagements,' Romy recalled.

There is a timeless routine to Balmoral. A maid unpacks the guest's clothes. When Romy left everything was wrapped in different thicknesses of tissue paper, including the Pooh Bear she had taken with her. Black-tie dinners, served at 8.15pm in the candle-lit dining room, hung with portraits of Queen Victoria and her family, are interspaced with those obligatory barbecues at one of the estate's log cabins. Luncheon is usually a picnic, transported to a favoured spot overlooking one of the glens in Prince Philip's Land-Rover and its specially converted picnic trailer. These outings take place regardless of the weather.

'I remember one bitter day when we had all gone shooting,' Romy recalls. 'I was so cold I was blue in the face. The Queen Mother came over to me and offered me a sip of some sloe gin. "This will warm you up from the inside," she said.'

She went on drives with the Queen who 'drove at breakneck speed' around the steep mountain tracks. She shared a sense of humour with Princess Anne whose deadpan expressions made her laugh. Romy bought a pair of union jack boxer shorts on a shopping expedition to Ballatar. Anne, Romy recalled, 'kept saying how smart they were and so patriotic. The shop assistants couldn't tell if she was being serious.'

One morning Romy went for a ride with the Queen on one of Anne's horses. It proved too mettlesome for the model girl from

Micheldever and ran away with her. Out of control, horse and rider galloped past the Queen, the height of bad equestrian etiquette. In her embarrassment, Romy called out to her Sovereign, 'Race you, race you!' The Queen's answer was lost in the wind.

Such mishaps notwithstanding, Romy's visit was judged a success. The Queen liked her. So did Edward and the young couple had spent hours together. He opened up to her in a way he had never done before.

'The transformation in Edward was remarkable,' Romy said afterwards. 'He was a totally different person. He could really unwind. He was able to be a human being rather than someone who was constantly aware of himself. Far from being the tense and stressed boy at public functions he was able to smile and be normal.'

Back in London they continued to see each other. For all Edward's soul searching, when he was with Romy he was able to see the funny side of things and laugh about his worries – one of which, inevitably, was being spotted out on the town with Romy. One evening they hit on the idea of dressing him up in disguise for their dinner date and Romy got a make-up artist friend to create a new face for the prince.

'We built up his nose, greased his hair back, added sideburns and gave him a wonderful moustache, stuck on with glue,' she recalled. 'It looked a bit odd, but not so ridiculous that you would notice straight away.'

They went out to a West End restaurant and were hardly able to stifle their laughter as the waiters looked at them, trying not to stare.

'We thought we had got away with it until the end of the meal,' Romy said, 'But just as coffee was being served Edward leant across the table and his moustache caught fire on the candle. It frazzled away completely, apart from the bit in the middle which made it look like a Hitler moustache.'

If Prince Edward had had his way, their relationship might have developed from there; he was in love. He often went to stay at Mrs Adlington's home and when she set up her own custom balloon business, Edward gave her her first commission. She put the logo, EJSH, which he had personally designed, on to hundreds of balloons for the joint twenty-first birthday party he held with his cousins, Lady Sarah Armstrong-Jones, James Ogilvy and Lady Helen Windsor.

As his feelings intensified, however, so Romy's lessened. They would continue to see each other throughout most of his time at Cambridge and she was a frequent guest at Wood Farm, but almost from the start of her friendship with Prince Edward she had another boyfriend, film director Nick Hooper. Romy kept on seeing Edward, but as a friend, not a lover. It was a painful time for the prince. He even organised a birthday party for Romy, only for her not to turn up. Edward was reduced to telephoning Mrs Adlington and asking, 'Where is she?'

Romy said: 'He was looking for a really committed relationship – more of a commitment than I could give him at the time. I knew he was very upset, but I tried to explain that I wasn't ready to settle down.'

Edward found the rejection hard to deal with and the burden of his royal status weighed heavily on him as never before. Romy remembered: 'Many times he has said that if he had any choice in the matter he would throw in the royal life.'

But that, as he well knew, was an impossibility. For bad as well as good it is his destiny. As he observed, 'I hadn't any choice in the matter.' And besides, he was still at the age when what seems like overriding emotional pain quickly turns into the faintest pang before disappearing altogether. It was only a temporary setback: this was one lovelorn royal patient who was soon on the road to full recovery, with Cambridge providing the ideal convalescence.

Student life allowed Edward a new freedom. It also afforded him the opportunity of extending his social orbit. Romy continued to feature in his life. In a letter dated 9 November, 1983, he was writing to her from Cambridge in his typically chatty style: 'I have some good news and some bad news. The good news is that I'll be able to get Wood Farm on the 18th and stay until Sunday evening. Good being relative to the fact that you will be there. The bad news is that you might have to drive up with my brother!' But he was now more friend than suitor. Other young women apart from Romy were now taking his interest.

One of them, Eleanor Weightman, a history undergraduate at Newnham College, first met Edward in a crowded lecture hall. She was sporty and fun, they became friends and their relationship followed his now familiar pattern. He invited her skiing, they sailed together at Cowes and she joined him on the Royal Family's annual cruise aboard the Royal Yacht *Britannia* round the Western Isles of Scotland. She went to Balmoral (paying for her own air tickets, of course). He watched her play ice-hockey, she stood on the touchline while he was beaten to a pulp playing rugby, and he weekended with her parents at their home in Cheshire. He called her 'Munchkin' after the dwarfs in the Wizard of Oz. Friends described their relationship as 'chummy'. In 1986 she circumspectly said: 'I sometimes pop into his room for tea after I've been rowing. Our friendship is neither new nor romantic. We've known each other for a year and a half and we share a lot of interests.'

Edward certainly appeared to share her interest in ice-hockey, because he once drove to Oxford's city ice rink to watch her play in a late-night match. 'We couldn't understand why he came – except he must like butch sweaty women,' joked Barbara Fenton, the captain of the team.

Munchkin was not butch but Edward was not her only admirer. She even had a jokey sign on her college door, 'Appreciate me now, avoid the rush later', and she turned up for her graduation escorted by a husky American oarsman.

Once again Edward questioned his royal status. 'It must be the quickest way there is of losing friends,' he sadly said. 'They get caught up in all the attention that I get.'

What Edward, consumed with post-adolescent angst, did not yet understand (or was refusing to acknowledge) was that this was exactly what some of the girls enjoyed. The prospect of being photographed with a royal prince was quite enough to spur some young women to develop a relationship. The British, in their self-effacing way, are traditionally most disdainful of this aspect of human nature but it is there all the same, a fundamental part of human psychology, and Edward's ability to sort the wheat of genuine commitment from the chaff of self-promotion would become a measure of his advancing maturity.

The girls who adorned his arm after Romy and Munchkin fell

into three different categories – friends who looked like lovers, friends who became lovers and girls who were not averse to a little publicity. Beautiful blonde Swede, Ulrika Jonsson was one of the latter. Interviewed by a Stockholm newspaper she confessed she had dinner with the prince at Buckingham Palace and he had visited her Maida Vale apartment. 'The hullabaloo that followed the news that we had been out together frightened me a little,' she said innocently. 'Suddenly I realised what it is like to be in the public eye. But the experience has taught me a lot. Edward warned me what it was going to be like.'

Ulrika was a junior secretary at TV-am where she met presenter James Baker who is one of Edward's closest friends. They went to the Henley Regatta Ball – via Windsor Castle where they picked up Edward. The 19-year-old Ulrika said she was more impressed by the 'glorious garden' where she sipped Pimms than the castle. She was standing right behind Prince Edward, however, when they were photographed.

'It is the first time the public saw anything of me,' Ulrika said, 'but my friendship with Edward is something I've been labelled with.' She went on, 'The picture that linked me with Edward was only the second time I'd met him. I was going out with James, him and another person. We got out of the same car, that's all.'

She complained to her mother that she would like to be famous for something she had done, not someone she had known, but she did not do badly out of her brief association with the prince. She rose from being TV-am boss Bruce Gyngell's secretary to the station's weathergirl in just two years. In 1990 she married cameraman John Turnbull – they have a son, Cameron, born four years later – by which time she was the presenter of children's favourite TV show, *Gladiators*. She said she was grateful to Edward for helping her learn how to deal with being a public figure, which that photograph helped her become.

One who was less enthusiastic about the publicity that went with her friendship with the prince was Georgia May. She was first linked with Edward in 1986 when she picked him up at the Royal Yacht Squadron Ball which was becoming something of a happy hunting ground for the prince. Slipping away from her own escort she asked Edward on to the disco floor – much to the surprise of the girl he was already with.

The scene was witnessed by a gossip columnist from the *Daily Express* who had miraculously managed to gatecrash the ball, the most snobbish and elitist even on the Cowes social calendar, and who duly recorded the scene in technicolour detail. 'We just danced and danced – I had a wonderful time,' a breathless Georgia said afterwards.

This was entirely in character. As one of Edward's friends said, 'She's a gutsy, no-nonsense, forthright girl.' It was the start of a tempestuous relationship.

Georgia, who was twenty at the time, was the daughter of David 'Daisy' May, who once skippered for the late newspaper magnate Sir Max Aitken and ran the Berthon Boat Company in Lymington, Hampshire. As such he was a leading light in the Cowes sailing community and had known Edward all his sailing life. At first David and his Belgian-born wife, Catherine were amused by their daughter's sudden fame. But they did warn her that it could get difficult. It duly did.

For all Georgia's forwardness, the romance got off to a slow start. Edward was going through a restless period and she still had a fondness for the Australian and New Zealand sailors she had met at the America's Cup in Western Australia. As he had with Romy, Edward found himself in competition, this time with a New Zealand yachtsman called Ed Danby. This time, however, the princely Ed came out ahead. He got on well with her. They both enjoyed outdoor activities like sailing and riding and the athletic Georgia, who was three years Edward's junior and worked as a financial secretary in London, had the kind of zany, open personality that appealed to Edward.

'They are potty about each other,' a friend said. Georgia, according to the conventions governing such matters, was more cautious. 'Edward,' she said, 'is very humorous and kind. He can be rather shy at first, but once you get to know him he's great company.'

The feeling was mutual by the time Edward invited her to spend New Year with him. This is usually a strictly family affair until after the celebrations so when Edward invited Georgia to join him at Sandringham her presence there sparked off inevitable rumours of an immediate engagement. Her father tried to calm the situation. Georgia, he said, was far too young to marry although 'they had a number of things in common and got on quite well'.

It was at this point that the situation started spinning out of control. Danby was quoted as saying that he was coming to England to marry her and Prince Edward had better step aside. Then her father's flamboyant private life was exposed to some most unwelcome scrutiny when it was disclosed that May, who had been nicknamed Daisy since his early days in competitive sailing when he used a motif of the flower as his emblem on his spinnaker, shared a flat with a man eighteen years his junior.

'All this attention is terrifying me,' Georgia complained and the relationship fizzled out soon afterwards. Edward was upset. This time, though, there was no hand-wringing on his part. He was now well installed with Sir Andrew Lloyd Webber's Really Useful Theatre Company and was ideally positioned to meet attractive young women. Like his great-great-grandfather, King Edward VII, he developed a penchant for actresses and amongst the several Lloyd Webber shows on stage in London there were plenty who were happy to entertain him.

One was Catherine Caldicott, two years Edward's senior and personal assistant to Sarah Brightman, the star of *Phantom of the Opera* who was then married to Lloyd Webber. She was invited to Sandringham for a shooting weekend. Marsha Bland, the tiny dancer with the 'big voice' from *Cats* was another. Marsha failed to get the Sandringham treatment but was a regular supper guest at Buckingham Palace after the show. The daughter of a bus driver from Leeds, she described Edward as 'really nice – he's very enthusiastic and *Cats* is his favourite musical.'

'He's always had girlfriends,' his former boss Biddy Hayward confirmed. 'I think he chooses friends carefully and he cares for them. But I don't think he feels he needs to prove anything so he hasn't needed to be the stud about town with a string of girlfriends. He has looked for girlfriends he wants to like as a person first.'

One of those was actress Ruthie Henshall. They met when she was in the cast of *Cats*, the most successful musical in the history of London's West End. He continued to see her when she was appearing in *Miss Saigon* and starring in *Crazy for You.*

Ruthie would insist, in the fine theatrical manner, that they were just good friends. 'We have a great time together and we have a mutual interest in the theatre. He's a friend and I should think he's allowed to have some friends,' she said. Of her late-night suppers in Buckingham Palace she said: 'When you have friends and you go and visit them it's usually at their house and that's the reason I go to Buckingham Palace when I visit Prince Edward – that's where he lives.'

She admitted, though, 'I will never get rid of that "Prince and the Showgirl" label. The same thing happened to Koo Stark who is still described as the ex-girlfriend of Prince Andrew.' She continued: 'People try to put me in a certain category and because I have never talked about my relationship with Prince Edward, they have had to guess what it was – and they have usually been wrong.'

Not as wrong as all that. A friend of the prince said: 'She taught him a lot of down-to-earth earthiness. She was a spirited South London girl who taught him to have a good time.' It really was too much the prince and the showgirl to progress beyond a good time but the relationship was none the less very important and beneficial to both of them. When Ruthie eventually fell in love with John Gordon-Sinclair, her co-star in the musical *She Loves You*, her mother Gloria remarked, 'Edward woke her up to the fact that nice men are much nicer to be with and I thank him for that.'

Edward's attraction to showgirls, initially fuelled by his love of the theatre, was compounded when he discovered he felt more at ease in their outgoing company than he did with girls from his own social background. The monarchy in all its theatricality, and the stage, with its commitment to the creation of a world of its own imagination, have much in common. The job of being royal, as Edward once observed involves 'a certain amount of acting'. And actresses, trained to give a performance, sometimes find it easier to deport themselves in the presence of members of the Royal Family than do many young county girls.

One such 'county' guest recalled to me how she was sitting

reading the paper one weekend at Sandringham when underneath the bottom of her newspaper she spied a familiar pair of ankles walking across the hallway in front of her. Knowing they belonged to the Queen she kept the newspaper pressed to her face until they had passed – terrified the Queen would stop and speak to her and that she would not know what to say.

By contrast, Koo Stark got along famously with the Queen. The two would sit down on a sofa and chat away together for hours at a time (much to the puzzlement, it must be said, of some of the Queen's staff who took their mistress's status more seriously than she ever did).

For their part, the showbusiness set enjoyed having the prince in their midst. He was a constant source of entertainment and they enjoyed teasing him about how he spoke and his old-fashioned ways but most of the people he worked with genuinely liked him and were unafraid to show it. For an informal twenty-fifth birthday celebration at a restaurant in Covent Garden, Ruthie Henshall, Ria Jones and Marsha Bland, who were all appearing in *Cats* at the time, each sang him a love song – vying with each other for the best performance.

The girls, who had already given a private cabaret performance at the Palace for an official party the week before, loved the competition. Ria Jones sang the Tim Rice composition, 'I Know Him So Well,' Ruthie sang the Garland classic, 'You Made Me Love You', and Marsha sang 'The Man That Got Away' from *A Star is Born*.

Edward was flattered to have three attractive women duelling vocally for his undivided attention. But then that was one of the attractions of working in the theatre: it helped broaden his outlook and in the process he gained in self-confidence. Most importantly, it helped him see his royal background in a wider context than had previously been the case. 'He plays lipservice to it,' Biddy says, 'but he tries to live his own way, which I think is admirable.'

It was from a more conventional background that Edward was expected to pick a suitable life partner, however, and like it or not (and he did not) the pressure mounted for him to do just that. On purely technical grounds there should have been no need. He was only the third son and his brothers fulfilled their dynastic duty by getting married and securing the succession by producing families of their own. From the royal standpoint what Edward did had become a genealogical irrelevance. But princes are expected to abide by established royal convention which in Britain, as Prince Philip observed, takes the family as its focus. Marriage was expected of him. There was no escaping that. It was his atavistic duty. And that made every seemingly 'suitable' date the subject of immediate attention.

The one girl who appeared to have everything a prince could wish for was Princess Martha-Louise, daughter of King Harald of Norway and, like Edward, a descendant of Queen Victoria. In the early Nineties Edward was going through a period of thinking that he ought to find a partner from another European royal family and Martha-Louise fitted the bill precisely. They also happened to like each other and when she moved to Britain to attend an equestrian training centre near Oxford in her attempt to reach Olympic standard, a serious romance looked a distinct possibility.

But Martha-Louise was a high-spirited girl determined to go her wayward way. As well as Edward, she had a boyfriend in Norway, professional windsurfer Per Gunnar Haugen, and was soon to embroil herself in an affair with her married riding instructor. Only her royal status saved her from an unladylike appearance in the British divorce courts.

Edward, meanwhile, was back on his own social round. Anastasia Cook, an attractive television journalist and former deb was just one pretty girl with whom he was linked. She met Edward in October 1990 at a ball at Luton Hoo, the magnificent Palladian mansion where the Queen and Prince Philip had spent part of their honeymoon. She entertained him and a group of friends for dinner at her parents' Wimbledon home. 'He's a friend and that's it,' she firmly declared as the drum of speculation started beating. He obviously was, because four years later she married Edward's closest friend, James Baker, whose father Richard is the former BBC newsreader.

Another girlfriend was Welsh-born Rhian-Anwen Roberts who met Edward in 1988 while she was an English student at Fitzwilliam College, Cambridge, and he was a production assistant with Lloyd Webber and was back at the university to start the famed *Chariots of Fire* charity race between Seb Coe and Steve Cram.

She was, said a friend, 'the girl who taught him not to be pompous with people. She is a very bright girl. She knew how to pop his balloon when he became pompous.'

She accompanied him to a Christmas party at Buckingham Palace and joined him for a Sandringham weekend during the Royal Family's New Year holiday in 1989, but once again the denials flew. Dark-haired Anwen, who became an investment banker with Goldman Sachs, insisted she was never involved with Edward, that she had another boyfriend at the time. The two are still close, however, and she is part of his Special Projects Group which devises new ways of raising money for the Duke of Edinburgh's Award Scheme.

The Canadian sportswoman Gail Greenough also had her moment in the frame. Having first met during the filming of *It's a Royal Knockout* they reconvened when he visited Canada in 1993 and she joined him at his lakeside base in Ontario and on a skiing holiday in Whistler, British Columbia. Four years older than the prince, in 1986 she became the first woman to win the title of Equestrian Show Jumper Champion after completing four clear rounds. Edward was very keen on her and she on him – to the extent that she broke off her engagement with Canadian video producer Steve Mahaney to be with him. She came over to England and stayed at Windsor and accompanied Edward to the Berkeley Square Ball in the heart of Mayfair. The geographical distance between them proved too great for the romance to sustain itself, however, and once again nothing came of it.

It was as if something or someone was holding Edward back and in a real sense this was true. It was largely due to the Duchess of York and the Princess of Wales.

Thirteen

Sisters-in-Law

PRINCE EDWARD DOES not hold his sisters-in-law the Princess of Wales and the Duchess of York in high regard.

Taking his cue from the Duke of Edinburgh, he deems them substantially responsible for many of the difficulties that have beset his family and so undermined their public standing.

The Duchess of York took the brunt of Prince Philip's displeasure. Even by his own standards, he was exceptionally brusque when she told him and the Queen that she was planning to leave Prince Andrew. He reminded her of her marital duty and insulted her by suggesting that if she really was going to leave she should book herself into a 'nunnery or looney bin'.

Edward admired his father immensely but not to the extent of trying to emulate that extraordinary bluntness. It was not in his nature. Nor was it his place – and Edward, with a keen sense of royalty and its obligations, always knew what his place was.

But if his reaction was muted, his point was clear. Members of the Royal Family, Edward once observed, have 'got to try to keep up some sort of appearance'. He is a man of fierce loyalty – to his family, and to the institution they embody. As far as he was concerned, Sarah and Diana had let the side down.

The Royal Family cannot just walk away from each other, and that was particularly true when it came to Diana. The Princess of Wales is a powerful force in the Royal Family and will remain so. No matter how her life develops she will always be the mother of a future king.

Almost alone amongst the Royal Family Edward was not taken in by her glamour. Unlike Prince Andrew, who in the early days, made a great fuss over Diana, Prince Edward was always wary of the seemingly malleable ingénue who so quickly captured the imagination of the world. She was the wife of his brother, the Prince of Wales. She was not necessarily his friend. He had been on board the Royal Yacht *Britannia*, anchored off Cowes on the Isle of Wight at the outset of Diana's romance with Charles. He had watched it develop at Balmoral Castle in Scotland later that summer. It was as if he sensed the trouble she would cause his elder brother and, by keeping her at arm's distance, he was readying himself for the problems that lay ahead.

In that, he was subconsciously taking his lead from Princess Anne. She had no need to wait upon events: she was indifferent to Diana from the very beginning. She treated the woman, who by marriage to her elder brother might have become her Queen, with withering disdain. She called her 'a silly girl'.

The situation came to an early head at the end of Ascot week in June, 1981, barely a month before Diana's marriage. Diana, who was already finding life on the inside of the Royal Family hard going, joined the royal party at Windsor Castle for the races and Prince Andrew's twenty-first birthday ball. Sensing Anne's apathy towards her and wanting to ingratiate herself, she ventured up to the nursery in the Queen's Tower where Anne was settling in with her son, Peter, who was three, and her four-week-old daughter, Zara. Diana, still only a Lady, gave the Princess the benefit of a full curtsey and declared: 'Ma'am, how wonderful to see you.'

Anne is contemptuous of pretension at the best of times. When she was struggling with two small children she had no time for it at all. She looked up at Diana – and looked straight through her. Diana, confronted by the searing force of Anne's scorn, fled the room.

If the clash was embarrassing, it was also all but inevitable. Edward had felt the tension building up for weeks. He could hardly miss it. Diana – highly strung, out of her depth, caught up in a situation over which she had no control – was fraying at the edges. But while the others were prepared to give her the benefit of all doubt, Anne was not. Self-contained and matter-of-fact to the point of ruthlessness, she had no sympathy for Diana's temperamental maunderings.

ther and son often attend the same functions in aid of the Duke of Edinburgh's Award and here
y arrive together for a performance of Shakespeare's *The Tempest* at the National Theatre.

m Andrew Lloyd-Webber's 'tea-boy', to Managing Director of his own company, Edward
ndsor has remained friends with all his showbusiness pals.

th former boss, Biddy Hayward (left) and Nicola Pagett.

With Sir Andrew and Lady Madeline Lloyd-Webber.

Some of the girls who mattered; Shelley Whitbourne with Captain Phillips' Badminton winner, *Lincoln*. Georgia May with Zara Phillips, Romy Adlington, Eleanor Weightman, or 'Munchkin' as Prince Edward called her, playing for the Cambridge University girls ice hockey team in 1986, Gail Greenough, Princess Martha Louise of Norway and actress Ruthie Henshall. One that didn't but was a pretty escort, Ulrika Jonsson

elley

Georgia May

Romy

Eleanor Weightman

Princess Martha-Louise

Gail Greenough

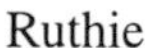

Ruthie

Ulrika

The picture that started it all, Sophie Rhys-Jones and Prince Edward at Queens Club in 1993.

A year later, Sophie and Edward together in public at a polo match in Windsor.

Sophie Rhys-Jones has come a long way from her parents modest farmhouse in Brenchley. She is now in the unprecedented position of being allowed to live with the Queen's youngest son in his Windsor Castle or Buckingham Palace apartments.

Prince Edward and the Princess of Wales at Viscount Linley's wedding to Serena Stanhope on the 8th October 1993.

Edward was more understanding. It would have been unusual if he had been otherwise. He had known Diana all his life. She was the 'girl next door' who had spent much of her early childhood at Park House, the ten-bedroom Victorian mansion only a couple of hundred yards from the gardens of Sandringham House, which Earl Spencer had rented from the Queen. Diana had been taken to tea parties at the 'big house'; Andrew and Edward had been brought over to play in her nursery. One afternoon at tea Edward had covered himself with honey, and after it had been scraped off, Diana's nanny, Janet Thompson, had watched her young charge engage in a high-spirited game of hide-and-seek in the corridor – with the Queen.

Even then, though, it was Andrew who got on with Diana, and she with him; she would later say that it was Andrew and not Charles she should have married.

Prince Edward felt more comfortable with Diana's eldest sister, Lady Sarah Spencer, who was nine years older than he was. Sarah was the first of Earl Spencer's daughters to go out with Prince Charles. The romance did not last ('Our relationship is totally platonic,' she had declared) but Edward continued to see her long after it was over. She often accompanied him to the cinema during his school holidays while Diana faded into the background of Edward's life. It was not until the fateful summer of 1980 that he renewed his acquaintance with her.

Edward had developed into a keen and competitive sailor and as usual was staying aboard *Britannia* when Diana joined the royal party as a guest of Lady Sarah Armstrong-Jones. At the time some members of the Royal Household felt that Diana had made friends with Sarah, three years her junior, in order to be invited on to the royal yacht. Once she was there she made a beeline for the Prince of Wales. The late Stephen Barry, his valet and confidante at the time, declared emphatically; 'She went after the Prince with single-minded determination. She wanted him – and she got him!'

Later that summer when Edward and the rest of the Royal Family repaired as usual to Balmoral, Diana followed and went to stay with her middle sister, Lady Jane Fellowes, whose husband was the Queen's assistant Private Secretary. They had a grace-and-favour cottage on the Balmoral estate three miles from the castle where Prince Charles was staying.

Lady Diana Spencer would spend much of her time walking about the estate hoping to meet the royal party enjoying a day's shooting. The ploy was obvious and successful and a few weeks later she was invited to spend four days at Balmoral castle itself.

Most of the ladies do not get up until after the guns have gone out at 9.30 but Diana was always up early. 'If you looked out of your window at a quarter to eight you would see her walking in the garden before breakfast', one of the guests recalled. 'And she made a great point of being around to see the guns off'.

Edward's bedroom happened to overlook the fountain where Diana would judiciously position herself on those carefully mapped-out early morning strolls. With Edward still in sleep-dominated adolescence, more often than not his footman would be opening his curtains on the new day as she was making her appearance beneath his window.

Throughout the rest of the day Diana would take every opportunity to extol the beauties of Balmoral. 'She would go around telling everybody how much she loved Balmoral and that it was such a magical place and how she loved it beyond imagination,' one of the guests recalled.

Charles was enchanted, for that was exactly the way he felt about the castle, its lochs and hills and burns and its teeming populations of deer and fish and birds. When he heard Diana echoing his own beliefs he thought he had found a kindred spirit and a destructive course of events was set in motion.

Edward might have thought no more about it – he had his own romantic interests to concern him at the time – were it not for the fact that when she visited Balmoral one year later, this time not as a young guest there for a brief excited stay, but as the wife of its future owner, she devoted as much vocal energy to saying how much she hated the place.

The turn around was remarkable, its implication disturbing. Armed with the evidence of his own ears he could hardly fail to draw an obvious conclusion. He also had other reasons to be apprehensive about the young woman who was proving to be more complex and manipulative than her public image ever suggested.

After her engagement to Prince Charles was announced, Diana moved into a suite of rooms at Buckingham Palace. They consisted of a bedroom, sitting room, bathroom and kitchen. They had previously been occupied by Edward's old Nanny, Mabel Anderson, and before that by Charles and Anne's much loved but ill-fated governess, 'Mispy' who had died there. The apartment was situated between Prince Andrew's and Prince Edward's brushing room where their valets pressed clothes and polished shoes. On the other side were their bedrooms.

Edward was away at Gordonstoun for much of the time Diana was staying there. She was ostensibly learning the royal ropes, but in fact was becoming increasingly overwhelmed by the situation she had swept herself into. She was irritable and dismissive of the Palace courtiers' attempts to interest her in her future role of Princess of Wales. When Charles's assistant Private Secretary Oliver Everett gave her James Pope-Hennessy's biography of Queen Mary and Georgina Battiscombe's authoritative account of Queen Alexandra, she waited until he had left the room before shouting, 'If he thinks I'm going to read those silly, boring books, then he's got another think coming'.

Her obvious unhappiness triggered her bulimia, that eating disorder caused by deep emotional disturbances in childhood, which erupted, not as she would later claim after her marriage, when she discovered her husband was seeing Camilla Parker Bowles, but before the wedding when he was not seeing her at all. The illness manifested itself in eating binges when she would gobble down two or three glass bowls filled with cereal and covered in cream, only to deliberately throw it up again.

But if Prince Edward was not there to see first hand the emotional disintegration of his future sister-in-law, he certainly picked up hints when he came back from school to Buckingham Palace that summer. He could hardly fail to notice that a number of the staff assigned to look after him were loaned out to the princess-to-be on temporary secondment.

Initially the staff had been taken with Lady Diana Spencer. Her ever more unpredictable behaviour, however, soon started to undermine her popularity. With Edward back from school and Prince Andrew on leave from the navy they had less time for her – much to her annoyance.

Prince Charles's valet remembers her frequently picking up the telephone and demanding to speak to members of staff whilst they were on duty in other royal residences. She would sometimes even use the Queen's private line, then known as the 'Windsor Line' which linked all the homes of the Queen's family to Windsor Castle without having to go through a switchboard.

Diana had no qualms about using this very private line to demand to speak to staff. In an age of instant worldwide telecommunications, Diana's behaviour now seems unremarkable, but it is worth recalling that at that time the British did not enjoy the easy access to telephones that they do today. Other people's 'phones were instruments to be treated with caution bordering on reverence. People were expected to ask very politely to make even a local call and the royal staff were appalled at Diana's effrontery in using the Queen's personal 'phone as if it was a public kiosk.

They were also less than enamoured by her demands when she was on it. Much to the surprise and annoyance of Princess Anne's butler, Diana expected their immediate attention when she rang Gatcombe Park. When she was put through, she complained she was lonely and wanted someone to come back to London to keep her company. It was embarrassing for the staff. It was also illustrative of the way, right from the start, Diana chose to ride unthinkingly over the royal system if and when it suited her.

Another indication of that determination came at the christening of Zara Phillips. Such occasions are a cornerstone of the Royal Family's routine, an essential part of the theatricality of their brand of monarchy; a moment when the whole family is on parade. It would never have occurred to Edward or any of his relations not to have turned out for one. Diana, however, chose not to attend. She had been telling friends beforehand that she had no intention of going but, either through a failure of manners or courage, it was not until forty-eight hours before the actual ceremony that she telephoned Princess Anne to inform her that she would not be there. Her excuse was that she was too busy preparing for the wedding ball that was being held in her honour that night. The tone of Anne's response would have chilled the Arctic.

Edward was astounded. It was simply not the way for members of the Royal Family to behave. But this was of no concern to Prince Edward at least not then. He had just left school. He was about to go to New Zealand. He was getting on with his own life. He was not going to get involved in the affairs of his elder brother (and future Sovereign). He kept his thoughts and reservations to himself.

Nor was it a case of 'I told you so' when relations between the Prince and Princess of Wales started to disintegrate only a few months after what the Archbishop of Canterbury, tuning into popular expectation if not private reality, chose to characterise as their 'fairytale' marriage. It certainly came as no surprise, however. He had caught glimpses of a side of Diana's character which the public, enraptured by her 'Madonna meets Mother Teresa image', had not seen.

When the marriage of the Prince and Princess of Wales finally and irretrievably collapsed, Edward felt enormous sympathy – for his brother, but also for Diana. It would be hard not to do so. Whatever her faults (and Diana's own extra-marital friendships certainly contributed to the breakdown of her marriage), she was obviously in some distress and therefore deserving of his family's compassion.

Underlying those personal considerations was his concern for the good name of the Royal Family. It was always one of his notable traits. As Biddy Hayward remarked, 'Edward is very, very loyal to his own family.'

His own actions had on occasion excited criticism and even controversy but if his behaviour had at times been a trifle odd – his loss of temper at the end of *It's a Royal Knockout* comes to mind – there was still that in-built awareness about the standards of public decorum expected of his position. He always has his eye on the royal ball. As he once put it to me when we were discussing the monarchy, 'I am a member of the Royal family.' That is a position he takes seriously. He is patriotic and takes a professional interest in the potency of Britain's national symbols – in its traditions, its monuments, its institutions.

For instance, the Royal Yacht attracts his specific attention. He said, 'In this country our greatest asset is *Britannia*. No other country in the world has anything to match *Britannia*. No country. Britain, although it is gradually declining in that sense, has always been a maritime power. It will always need to be a maritime power because we are an island. And *Britannia* harks back to that particular heritage, the naval heritage, which is a very strong heritage in this country.

'I've heard people saying, "Why don't they just drag *Britannia* up a beach somewhere and get tourists to go and look round if she's such an important part of Britain?" But they don't understand that by taking *Britannia* to wherever we want to in the world, we are taking Britain there. She is a symbol of Britain.

'The problem is 99 per cent of the people have never seen *Britannia* out of the country. They have never seen the effect she has when she goes to America, New Zealand, Hong Kong, the Far East, wherever. They have never seen the impact she has for this country. They have no concept of the amount of business that she does for Britain.

'They simply look at the cost and there is no straight equation for the amount of business that comes the other way. If you take *Britannia* out of the equation what is Britain going to do? She is just going to be on a lower par than anybody else in the world.'

For *Britannia* one could just as easily read Royal Family. In this convocation of metaphors, there was no doubt in Edward's mind which is the most potent. He said, 'The Queen as head of state is the symbol of the nation.'

Since earliest memory he has had it drummed into him that this embodiment of nationhood was to be cherished and looked up to and protected. It would have been out of character and training if he had been anything less than apprehensive when Diana began redefining the Royal Family to reflect her own personality. It grated against his sense of propriety. And the faster Diana spun her glamorous web, the further Edward distanced himself from her.

His relationship with the Duchess of York also became notably detached, although for different reasons and to a far greater extent.

Initially, Edward had got on well with the exuberant redhead. Everyone did. She was fun and open-hearted and brought a welcome breath of fresh air with her. She was not Edward's romantic type – she is much too jolly-hockey sticks for his taste –

but they certainly established a friendly rapport. On occasion Sarah would drive into Soho and join Prince Edward and Biddy Hayward for lunch at a nearby bistro. 'He was very fond of her,' Biddy recalled.

However her friendship with the handsome American oil trader Steve Wyatt and the enthusiastic way she appeared to revel in the trappings of her position alienated the Palace old guard. Sarah would steadfastly maintain that nothing had taken place between herself and Wyatt who, as she rightly said, was also a friend of her husband's. She also made the point that those very officials who were so quick to criticise her never offered her any help or guidance as she struggled to adapt to the peculiar demands of her royal role.

That did not help her case. Marital failings and romantic foibles are as much a part of life in royal circles as they are anywhere else – perhaps even more. But in much the same way as members of the royal circle are expected to know which way round the royal dinner table to pass the port, so they are required to maintain an outward appearance of decorum on the grounds that conventions must be observed if social chaos is to be avoided. The Duchess, they felt, stepped beyond the bounds of good behaviour. The Queen's former Private Secretary, Lord Charteris summed up their attitude when he described her as a 'vulgarian'.

It came down to a matter of style. Weighed on the scales of culpability, there was hardly any difference between the Princess of Wales and the Duchess of York. But while Diana somehow managed to remain above criticism, Sarah was unable to avoid it. Had she accepted the lot of a naval wife (after the separation she complained that she had only seen her husband for forty-four days in the previous year), stuck it out with Prince Andrew, forsaken her jet-setting friends and knuckled down to the often tedious round of official duties, the Palace guard, whatever their reservations about Sarah's suitability for her royal role, would have closed ranks around her. Instead she took the decision to try to break loose – and promptly found herself frozen out by the Palace machine.

There were to be no more lunches with Prince Edward.

It was very hard to escape the conclusion that here was the

Royal Family pulling itself apart – painfully, publicly, without purpose. One by one the marriages of the Queen's three older children, starting with the sister Edward was so fond of, had collapsed. It was a disastrous example to set before their youngest brother – a brother, moreover, who would have benefited enormously from the companionship and affection that a successful marriage would have brought him. With only a pattern of failure to refer to, however, it was hardly any wonder that Prince Edward, already inclined to keep his feelings in close check, shied away from any full-scale commitment.

It would take a special woman to break through his emotional barricades.

Fourteen

Sophie

IT WAS NOT Sophie Rhys-Jones Prince Edward was supposed to meet that morning at Queen's tennis club in London, but Britain's former number one player, Sue Barker. She was booked to appear with Edward at a photocall being held in aid of the Prince Edward Challenge which was raising money for local charities around Britain. It had been organised by MCM, the public relations company owned by Brian MacLaurin who described himself as a 'media manager'. MacLaurin recalled: 'I had arranged for Sue to come along and be photographed with Prince Edward, wearing the logo of each radio station that was involved in the challenge. That would have enabled me to generate publicity in the local newspapers for that radio station'. The night before, however, MacLaurin received a telephone call from Steven Hill, then head of sport at Sky News. He said, 'Brian, I can't let you have Sue Barker because as far as I am concerned, she has only one brand and that's Sky, so you can't have her for the radio stations'.

The involvement of a member of the Royal Family was no longer enough to override the commercial considerations of marketing images and brand identification. With less than twenty-four hours to go, MacLaurin did not have enough time to find a celebrity replacement for Barker. Driven by necessity, he press-ganged one of his own employees into coming along to be photographed, with Edward, in Barker's stead. The girl he chose was Sophie Rhys-Jones. Thus in effect it was Rupert Murdoch, the Australian-born media tycoon who owns Sky and is so distrusted by the Royal Family, who inadvertently brought about the meeting between Prince Edward and the woman who was to play such an important part in his life. 'That was the first time Prince Edward and Sophie met, out there on the Real Tennis court at Queen's club,' said MacLaurin.

If the attraction was instant it did not show. Edward, with a lifetime's experience of shielding his romantic feelings from public scrutiny, simply went through his professional paces and got on with the job at hand. Sophie, the well-trained PR executive, did what the photographer told her. She smiled her toothy grin. And when the photographer asked her to, she rested her arm on the Prince's shoulder. It was all very casual and innocent.

'I was there when Edward met her but I didn't notice any sparks fly,' said actor Robert Powell's wife, Babs.

They met again a few days later when Sophie accompanied her boss to Buckingham Palace for a breakfast meeting (croissants and coffee) to discuss the next stage of the Challenge's publicity campaign. As far as MacLaurin was concerned, it was purely a business meeting. He had the Prince Edward Challenge to organise and Sophie, in her capacity as a £20,000 a year junior executive, was detailed to help on the account.

For Edward and Sophie, however, the relationship very quickly moved on to a different and altogether more personal level. The electricity of mutual attraction had been generated. Edward had surreptitiously asked her for her telephone number that day they met at Queen's, but he was not the only one to take a shine to Sophie; so too did Michael O'Dwyer, the son of Edward's private secretary Lt Col Sean O'Dwyer. It was Edward who got there first, however, and a flurry of dates followed.

Sophie, an independent career girl with the experience and confidence to know when to follow her heart, responded to his princely attentions. Within a few weeks the couple were virtually living together.

Sophie was very much Edward's type. She was natural and unaffected, she had a zany sense of humour and was forever inventing imaginary newspaper headlines of the risqué tabloid variety (a picture of Edward fishing might provoke the remark, 'Show us your tackle, Eddie'). She was strong and blonde and, although she is shorter than she looks in photographs, very sporty. She also hailed from an unassuming environment, far removed from the formal splendour of the Royal Court but where Edward was emotionally more at home.

If Edward had found his emotional plane, the situation was much more complicated for Sophie. Nothing in her background could have prepared her for a romance with the son of her Sovereign.

Born in the Nuffield Maternity Home in Oxford on January 20th, 1965, she was the youngest of two children. Her father, Christopher, worked for a car firm and later exported tyres to Hungary. Her childhood home, where her parents still live, is an unpretentious farmhouse in Brenchley, Kent. When the romance first became public, it was valued at £160,000. One observer described it as 'frayed'.

Sophie's mother, Mary, took in typing to earn extra money for the family. At £4.50 an hour she would type documents on her word processor which she set up on the table in her yellow-painted kitchen.

By scrimping and saving, the Rhys-Jones' were able to send their daughter to Dulwich Preparatory School in Cranbrook, Kent, and then on to Kent College for Girls, a 'minor' public school in nearby Pembury where Sophie attended as a day pupil. Her friends remember her as 'vivacious and smart – but not too clever or bossy', and something of a classroom clown. She liked sport to the extent that she even enjoyed training.

Academically she did well until her teens, when parties took precedence over school work. She only managed six 'O' level passes, including art and religious education, not regarded as the most taxing of subjects. Her father was most disappointed with the results; Sophie did not share his concern. She had had enough of school and the measured, semi-suburban social life of Brenchley. She was in a hurry to grow up, leave home and move to London. Her parents vetoed that idea. They belong to a class and generation that places great store on academic achievement and refused to allow her to leave home until, as her father said, 'she was qualified in something'.

That meant two more years of study, this time at West Kent College, where she took 'O' level law, two 'A' levels and a secretarial course. It was not until 1983 that she was allowed to follow her own ambition and move to London, into a rented flat, sharing with a girlfriend. She got a job as a secretary at Quentin Bell PR and then went to work at Capital Radio. During this period she went out with chat show host Michael Parkinson's son, Andrew and a young man named Jeremy Barkley whom she called Jez and who remembered her as 'a fabulous girl'.

After three years at Capital, Sophie's determination to enjoy life took her to Switzerland where she worked for four months in the resort town of Crans Montana. She was exployed by Bladon Lines for £65 a week plus free board and helped to arrange the après ski entertainment. The work came easily to her. 'She was the life and soul of any party we had,' recalled Gareth Crump, the company's Alpine manager.

She was twenty-three years old, blonde, sporty and attractive and she did not lack for admirers in the easy-going atmosphere of the Alps. But rather than play the field, as so many chalet girls did, she settled into a steady relationship with an Australian ski-instructor. When he went back to Sydney at the end of the season, she went with him, but the affair did not last much longer than the journey – he wanted to settle down, she was chasing another destiny.

However, having got there, she decided to stay on for a while. She took a job with the Australian air freight company, Jet Services and, like many middle class English girls who make it Down Under, she set out to enjoy herself without too much concern for the future. Jonathan Miller, her boss at Jet Services, recalled, 'I think Sophie just wanted to let her hair down and have a good time.'

She fell easily into the Australian lifestyle of beaches and barbecues and evening visits to pubs and wine bars. She took up deep-sea diving and travelled north into the tropics of Queensland where the Great Barrier Reef provides some of the most spectacular underwater sights in the world. 'She liked to party,' said Miller.

But however pleasant it might have been, it was never going to be more than an interlude. After a few carefree months, Sophie returned to England and got down to the serious business of building her career.

For almost a year she was an events organiser for the Macmillan Nurses Appeal, the charity which raises money for the nurses who look after cancer sufferers. Then she was head-hunted by MacLaurin Communication and Media whose clients included the television presenter Noel Edmonds and his creation, Mr Blobby.

'She was recommended to me by Anita Hamilton, former head of promotions at Capital Radio,' MacLaurin recalled. 'She was lively, she was fun, she was knowledgeable and she was bright, so I hired her.' But not, he insists, to work on the Mr Blobby account. 'She never worked on Mr Blobby.' But she had once been photographed with Edmonds' television creation and that was enough for the headline writers to trumpet, 'Edward falls for Blobby's girl.'

Sophie was moving – and moving quickly – in to a glamorous world far removed from her perfectly ordinary middle class background.

'Let's face it, the Royal Family and the Rhys-Jones' are a world apart,' Christopher Rhys-Jones said, in a statement of the obvious.

That proved to be no obstacle on a personal level. As Michael Hobbs, the chairman of the Duke of Edinburgh Award Scheme, said, 'Sophie is a sensible, well-balanced person with her feet on the ground'. She has, observed Robert Powell, 'an ability to fit in wherever she is'.

For his part, Edward was determinedly egalitarian. Gordonstoun had been a very different school from the 'upper class reformatory' (as one housemaster had described it) of Charles's time and it had brought him into contact with people from a wide variety of backgrounds. The theatre had chipped away at the remaining edges of his upper class persona. Girls like Ruthie Henshall had loosened him up and shown him the way to be himself in a romantic situation. Sophie was his girlfriend and that, as far as he was concerned, was all there was to it.

As she negotiated the yawning social chasm that separated herself from her royal lover, Sophie clearly needed all the help she could get. The Royal Family, complete unto itself and protected by arcane ritual, is an intimidating institution that no woman of Edward's generation has joined successfully. Diana had been overwhelmed and had retreated into illness. Chefs and footmen had been made available to her but much to their bemusement, they were rarely called upon. Instead the Princess-to-be withdrew into self-imposed isolation and seldom asked anyone around to the Palace, even for tea.

Years later, she is stills fearful of what she perceives as the palace machinery, which she is afraid has the power to crush her. She is also aware of the animosity she has engendered among her estranged husband's influential circle of friends.

Sarah, conversely, had been over-excited by the outward trappings of royal life and lived it up, forever hosting champagne parties for her ever-widening circle of friends. By the time she realised her mistake it was too late and she was cast forever in the unattractive mould of 'Freebie Fergie'.

As later events would so clearly illustrate, neither woman was able to properly integrate into royal life. For that Charles and Andrew must shoulder a substantial share of the blame. There is no school for princesses, as Charles's valet, the late Stephen Barry remarked. It was up to the princes to help their wives to learn the royal rules and regulations. They were manifestly unsuccessful in their task. It was a failure that would cost them their marriages, a failure that Edward had no wish to repeat. Under his guidance, Sophie was set on a more cautious course towards her royal destination.

It was inevitable that he would attempt to maintain conditions of greatest secrecy, a natural consequence of his conviction that his romantic liaisons were of no one's business but his own. By observing what had happened to his brothers' girlfriends, Edward knew that anyone who had her name linked to his would, as he said, 'suffer a stigma for the rest of their lives'. In Sophie's case Edward's concern was heightened by his deep affection for her.

He went to elaborate lengths to protect her privacy and keep her name out of the newspapers. When he telephoned her at her office he used his old alias of 'Richard'. When he fetched her from her West London flat his detective would ring the doorbell and escort her to the car where Edward waited, unseen inside.

But no matter how hard he tried, no matter how many ruses and subterfuges he employed, he was not going to keep his romance a secret indefinitely. That he managed it for three months was an achievement. Much to his chagrin, the story was out and on the front pages shortly before Christmas, 1993. That the veil of secrecy was pulled back by the Murdoch-owned *News of the World* and, even worse, that the reporter was none other than Andrew Morton, only infuriated him further.

Morton had presumptuously walked into the West End offices of MCM one Friday afternoon, just as everyone was preparing to leave for the weekend and had confronted Sophie. Sophie, quite unprepared for the encounter, handled it as best she could. 'Prince Edward and I are good friends and we work together,' she said, avoiding eye contact with Morton. 'He is a private person and so am I. I have nothing more to add.'

When Sophie related what had happened to Edward as they drove to Windsor Castle that evening, two livid red spots appeared on his cheeks, a sure sign that he was angry. His temper was made worse on Sunday when Morton's story appeared, complete with a detailed schedule of the couple's movements over the previous few weeks. It reported that she had weekended at Windsor Castle, where she had lunched with the Queen, Prince Philip, Princess Anne and Commander Tim Laurence, as well as being served afternoon tea with the Duchess of York and her children, Beatrice and Eugenie.

The following day he took the most unusual step of denying that there was any impending engagement and pleading with the media to leave him alone so that his relationship with Sophie could develop in its own time. By choosing to handle the matter himself, rather than issuing a statement through Buckingham Palace, Edward (who no longer drew monies from the Civil List) was emphasising his status as a private citizen.

Interest in the young woman who had captured the romantic attention of the Queen's last unmarried child was predictably intense. Debrett's Peerage unearthed the fact that Sophie was the sixth cousin once removed of the 11th Viscount Molesworth, head of a large family with many collateral branches, one of which is Rhys-Jones, a piece of genealogical information which was news to the Rhys-Jones'. A host of acquaintances from Sophie's past materialised with a variety of information: that she wasn't really a strawberry blonde but a brunette, that she was well-known for growing her hair and cutting it short again, that she had sung in her school choir, that she had a lovely voice and never suffered from stage fright even when she had a solo to sing, that once she had set her sights on a man she would always see off the competition.

This probing into their background and recent past was most unnerving for the Rhys-Jones' who had never occupied centre stage in the nation's life and unlike both the Spencers and the Fergusons, had no experience of dealing with the Royal Family. They were, said Sophie's mother 'inundated' adding thankfully, 'but Prince Edward helped calm things down'.

Quietening Edward down was another matter. He wanted to know how Morton had found out about Sophie. It was Sarah Ferguson whom Edward thought was to blame.

Every Sunday when the Queen was in residence at Windsor Castle, the Duchess of York took her daughters to tea with 'Granny one'. It was the only opportunity the Queen had to see her grandchildren since the Duke of Edinburgh disapproved of Sarah staying at any of the royal homes. Shortly before the story of the romance broke, Sophie met Sarah at Windsor and the two girls started gossiping.

Edward had once been close to the Duchess, but he had come to believe that she had made a fool of his brother. Increasingly suspicious of his sister-in-law, he became convinced that she had leaked the information about Sophie to her press contacts, who included Andrew Morton.

Andrew Morton's source was, in fact, an employee, not a member of the Royal Family, but the criticism to which the Royal Family been subjected in recent years has produced a siege mentality breeding theories of conspiracy and betrayal. Sarah, who was unpopular with the senior courtiers, had long been the butt of every passing suspicion. This was one charge too many, however, and when she discovered that she was being accused, not only by Edward, but by the Royal Household itself she was incensed. It was unjust and untrue and she took her complaint to the Queen.

The Queen, who has remained very fond of her errant daughter-in-law, summoned Edward into her private sitting room and explained to him how unfair it was to accuse the Duchess of such disloyalty, especially as she was not in a position to defend herself. Edward, whose grasp of the niceties of royal protocol remains as sentient as ever immediately apologised to the Queen for any upset he had caused. As far as Edward and the Queen were concerned, it had been a small and minor family incident. For Sophie Rhys-Jones it was a fast lesson in the intrigues of Palace life. And by now Palace life was very much her life too. Although not officially resident at Buckingham Palace, come the morning, she was just as likely to leave for work from Edward's second floor apartment as she was from her own flat in West Kensington which she shares with a girlfriend.

That Edward should wish to have his girlfriend beside him as much as possible was perfectly natural. That the Queen should allow it to happen under her roof marked a significant change in attitude and approach. Never as straight-laced as her stately and often stern countenance might suggest, she had nevertheless been brought up to be acutely aware of what is seemly, and what is not. By old-fashioned convention, a young woman staying overnight in a gentleman's apartment most definitely fell into the latter category.

Both Sarah and Diana had moved into the Palace, but not until they were formally engaged. Even then they were carefully accommodated at the other end of the principal floor so that appearances could be maintained. Those strictures were set aside for Sophie. She was free to stay with Prince Edward wherever and whenever she wanted to.

It was an arrangement that survived its revelation. When she was photographed driving out of Buckingham Palace at 8 o'clock in the morning the obvious conclusion was drawn, but that did not prevent it happening again. She was photographed doing the same thing a few days later, and then again a few days after that until the paparazzi grew weary of the game and stopped doorstepping the Palace gates, leaving Edward and Sophie to continue the serious business of getting to know each other.

It was an eminently sensible way of familiarising Sophie with a forbidding family of enormous complexity. She was given her own pass which allowed her to come and go at Buckingham Palace as she pleased and she came to know the senior courtiers of the Royal Household who had made Diana's and particularly Sarah's lives so difficult.

The Princess of Wales and the Duchess of York only discovered how difficult royal life could be after they were engaged and already en route to the altar. Sophie was being given a careful and subtle induction, a fact which did not escape the notice of Diana and Sarah. Both would later complain (with more than an edge of resentment in their voices) that they had received no such help as they struggled to come to terms with their new situation.

Yet for all the support she was getting, it was nonetheless a wide gulf that Sophie had to bridge.

A strict and esoteric protocol governs all the royal family homes and mixing with people whose faces are famous but whose habits are unfamiliar can be bewildering. No one, for instance, is allowed to go to bed before the Queen or Princess Margaret. There is an order for entering the dining room at mealtimes and while the Queen Mother, the Queen and Princess Margaret can drink as much as they like (and on occasion do just that), anyone who is so foolish as to try and keep pace with them will find their bags packed and waiting in the hall the following morning. There are also little traps; the Queen keeps her own box of chocolates and fudge on the piano in the saloon and sometimes hovers in the gallery above to see if anyone surreptitiously takes one – and when they do makes a gleeful point of raising the matter at dinner.

The Queen has other little ways which can disconcert those who are not used to them. Romy Adlington recalled one night watching the Queen picking ticks off her corgis and throwing them into the fire. 'Each one made a spitting noise as it hit the flames', Adlington said. 'In the end it got too much for Prince Charles. He said, "Oh really! Do you have to do that here?" The Queen carried on!'

Sophie's first outing into a world so very different from the one she knew came when she was invited to join the Royal Family for the traditional Sandringham house party on New Year's Eve. Ever since Edward VII, Prince of Wales, acquired the Norfolk estate in 1862, the royal family have lavishly entertained in the mock Jacobean mansion that he built. Throughout the shooting season, house parties of up to twenty people are common. They are not easy affairs for an outsider. For a start, there is the matter of what to wear. Marina Ogilvy recalled: 'You have to change clothes at least four or five times a day. For shooting, for riding, for lunch, tea and dinner.' For Sophie, used to buying her clothes from chain stores like Whistles and Next, the problem of kitting herself out was only resolved by resorting to such country basics as a waxed shooting jacket and borrowing various dresses and hats (for church) from girlfriends.

She made it through the large and potent dry martinis mixed by an equerry and served before the black-tie dinner, and the mulled wine that helps ease in the New Year. She entered into the spirit of the 'first footing', when a footman in full livery is sent round to the front door which is opened by the Queen's page who then leads him through to greet the Royal Family, all of whom feign surprise at his supposedly unexpected arrival. She decided to pass over the opportunity of going riding with the Queen the following morning, but she was back on parade in time to join the men for a shooting lunch in one of the huts on the estate.

This is not the place to express any anti-bloodsport sentiments. Field sports, as the Royal Family calls them, are a vital part of Sandringham life and Sophie fell into the centuries old routine without complaint.

'The whole family stay out all afternoon, then come back and change for tea,' Marina explained. Tea is a formal affair served at five o'clock in the cream drawing room, untouched since the days of Edward VII's Queen, Alexandra. Sometimes the Queen, the Queen Mother and Princess Margaret play cards or finish the *Daily Telegraph* crossword and if there are any small children around, like Beatrice and Eugenie, this is the time they appear with their nanny for a family hour. Then the equerry mixes those lethal martinis and everyone goes upstairs to bath and change for dinner. After dinner, the Queen, Princess Anne and the Queen Mother are likely to gather around Princess Margaret at the piano for a sing-song.

It could have been a disaster for the PR girl from Brenchley. As it turned out, she survived the house party with her spirits intact. More importantly, she made a favourable impression on both

Prince Philip and the Queen. That is not always easy; if Philip is cantankerous, the Queen, cloaked in her majestic dignity, can be chillingly imperious in her disapproval, and her first appraisal of Sophie was disconcerting in the extreme. 'You wouldn't notice her in a crowd', was how the Queen described her.

That may not be a bad thing. After the egregiousness of her daughters-in-law, Diana and Sarah, Sophie's sensible and low-key approach to the situation was to be welcomed and the Queen gradually warmed to her.

If she had wished, the Queen could have terminated the affair, or at least made it very difficult to continue by making it clear to Prince Edward that she would not welcome Sophie in any of her royal homes. That she did not is a measure of her approval and Sophie became ever more assimilated into Edward's way of life.

Most weekends were spent together at Windsor where Edward feels most at home. 'If you see Prince Edward's rooms at Windsor, you know Edward,' says Malcolm Cockren, his chairman at Ardent. 'All the things he likes are there, he spends all his available free time there and Sophie stays with him.' They occupy the top floor of the Queen's Tower where the Prince and Princess of Wales stayed when they were still happy to be under the same roof. Situated above the old nursery suite, the apartment has two bedrooms, two bathrooms and a sitting room cum study. It also has a discreet entrance from what is called the 'dog door stairs' and commanding views across the East Terrace and down the Long Walk.

At Windsor Sophie and Edward were able to conduct their relationship without fuss and in privacy. Occasionally a long-lensed photographer would snap Sophie jogging out of King George IV gate, the nearest castle exit to the private apartments, but apart from lunch with the family after church on Sundays, they were left very much to their own devices.

According to friends they are very much soul mates, both intellectually and physically. Happier to stay at home in each other's company than run the risk of being stared at in restaurants, they share a love of cooking and are forever trying out new recipes. Confident in herself and comfortable around Edward, Sophie's main concern is the media and how they will choose to interpret her. She has remained as low-key as possible and has asked her close friends to do the same.

Edward and Sophie's determination that the relationship should not be jeopardised by over-exposure does mean that precautions have to be taken and sacrifices made. They were, for instance, able to take a skiing holiday together unnoticed in Canada, but Europe was a different matter. Earlier in their relationship they had scheduled a winter break in St Anton, Edward's favourite resort from childhood. When he discovered that Diana was going to the neighbouring resort of Lech with her sons, William and Harry, he cancelled the vacation. So many royals in such close proximity, he explained, would be an irresistible temptation to Europe's paparazzi.

If it was a nuisance to plain Edward Windsor, it was hardly an insoluble problem for Prince Edward and the couple took a romantic Highland break that Easter at Craigowan Lodge, five minutes walk from Balmoral Castle on the Queen's Scottish estate. Originally built for Queen Victoria's private seretaries, the house has been used as a weekend retreat by most of the Royal Family. The double-fronted 'honeymoon' house is small by royal standards and boasts only six bedrooms, and small staff quarters at the back. Inside, its tartan carpets and pine furniture are in keeping with the views over the Balmoral gardens. Philip hosts a small shooting party there before Christmas each year and Anne uses it when she takes her children out from Gordonstoun for the weekend. The Duke and Duchess of Kent spent their honeymoon there, as did Anne and Tim Laurence. It was where Charles took Diana for a pre-nuptial break, when the stress of her situation was first beginning to tell (but where she still managed to look at her most ingenuous in a patterned sweater with one black sheep and corduroy knee breeches).

In August Sophie was a guest aboard the Royal Yacht *Britannia* for Cowes week. She also started accompanying Edward on semi-official royal outings. They arrived together, for instance, with Princess Margaret, for the Suffolk wedding of his cousin, Lord Ivar Mountbatten (nephew of the late Earl Mountbatten of Burma who was killed by the IRA in 1979) to businesswoman Penny Thompson. They also arrived together at the nuptials of Edward's favourite cousin and childhood friend,

Lady Sarah Armstrong-Jones, to actor-turned-artist Daniel Chatto.

Slowly, carefully, by a route that had been denied both Diana and Sarah Ferguson, Sophie was being absorbed into the Royal Family. There were the occasional difficulties. On the Craigowan holiday a photographer armed with a long lens snapped the couple kissing. Edward, outraged as always by what he regarded as unwarranted intrusion, lodged a complaint with the Press Complaints Commission then recoiled at the press reaction (The *Sun* called him a pompous, petulant and precious prig), tried to withdraw his complaint, was told that he could not, and ended up receiving an apology from all the newspapers which had published the offending photograph, the *Sun* excepted. It was yet another salutory lesson that, even though he no longer enjoyed the financial benefits of the Civil List, as a member of the Royal Family circumspection was still the wisest course of action.

There were moments when Sophie, too, found it hard going. She gamely learned to waterski and sail at Cowes in full view of the press where her PR training saw her through. Away from the spotlight, however, the strain sometimes got the better of her. On occasion the Queen's personal staff found her unfriendly and condescending. They complained amongst themselves that although she was spending a great deal of time at Buckingham Palace and Windsor and was therefore availing herself of their services, she showed little appreciation for what they did for her. There was also the whisper in the staff corridors that Sophie was enjoying her new-found celebrity status just a little too much.

But this was nothing compared to the problems faced by Diana and Sarah, as they tried to come to terms with life on the inside of the gilded cage. And Sophie did at least have Edward to turn to. Like all couples there were moments when the effort of adjusting led to rows and disagreements and, in the summer of 1994, they came precariously close to parting. Edward became what one friend described as 'unnerved' by the speed at which the affair was developing. But if Edward was wracked with indecision (a not uncommon problem amongst male members of his family) Sophie remained coolly determined. She was not prepared to let the relationship flounder. When rumours of the rift became public she dismissed them as 'rubbish'. She was being elastic with the truth, but it did give her the breathing space she needed to get her relationship back on track again. The couple settled down again and shortly after Christmas of 1994, Sophie started working with Edward on the Duke of Edinburgh Award.

It was a job well within her capabilities, for by then Sophie's public relations skills were well honed. She also brought some worldly experience to the job.

Being Edward's girl made a substantial difference to her working life. As only the fifth employee of MCM, Sophie had been expected to put in long hours on her accounts. At various times they included the charity, Lifeline, a new adult-oriented radio station and disc-jockey Chris Tarrant. She would also help out with extra projects such as the Prince Edward Challenge. Sometimes her work carried over into the weekends. But her romance with the prince changed that. Explained MacLaurin; 'I negotiated a new contract with her whereby she works from Monday to Thursday night and Friday she has off. That enables her to have long weekends.'

Her work for the Duke of Edinburgh Award was also more low key than she had been used to. 'She is not involved in media relations,' said MacLaurin. Instead she concentrated on the altogether safer task of writing newsletters.

A change of office attitude accompanied the change in her work schedule. 'Nobody in the office is aware of what she is doing,' said MacLaurin. 'I do not want her to think that any of her colleagues, who of course all talk to the newspapers twenty-four hours a day, are responsible for anything that might get out. She does not tell anybody anything and we do not want her to tell anybody anything. She comes in and we call her Soph and that's it; she's one of the team.'

Many young women might have baulked at being the de facto fianceé without the benefit of an official engagement. But if Sophie had any reservations or complaints she prudently kept them to herself. Any romance with a member of the Royal Family is conducted on their terms. It was a case of putting up with it or getting out and Sophie had clearly decided to stay the course. Her romantic ambitions were firmly targeted on Edward.

Kevin Morley, the former managing director of Rover cars and a Charter Founder Member of the Duke of Edinburgh Award Scheme, observed, 'being from a PR background, she was fully aware of the real world. She knew what she was getting into.' The same might have been said about the Duchess of York who before her marriage to Prince Andrew had worked for a number of PR organisations.

Unlike Sarah, Sophie was careful not to upstage her royal paramour. She was there at his side if he wanted her there. She took up sailing and Real Tennis to please him. Should the situation so demand, however, she was quite happy to step out of the limelight.

Said Morley: 'They are confident in each other. They are able to operate very successfully as separate entities. They do not cling onto each other at parties and that requires a mature kind of relationship.'

Malcolm Cockren observed, 'She knows exactly when to take the back seat.'

For those who believe in such things, that is just the kind of woman Edward's Moonsign suggests he needs. According to astrologer Jonathan Cainer, Edward wants someone 'who sits contentedly in the department marked "spouse" and trusts you enough to know that you'll keep coming back, once you've gone off and been who you are to everyone else'.

More prosaically, this willingness to adhere to protocol's conventions was a most desirable credential from the Royal Family's point of view. The future of the British monarchy is not dependent on Edward's marital happiness but, after the tribulations and traumas that have engulfed the Royal Family since Diana burst on the scene, a period of quiet would not go amiss.

That is certainly what Edward wants. He was born into the most public family in the world and throughout his childhood and youth he of all the Queen's children was most keenly aware of his position and attendant privileges. But the Royal Marines and the theatre widened his perspective and he was no longer comfortable perched on the pedestal of his royal status. Like his sister, Princess Anne, he recognised the profound social changes taking place in his mother's realm and his need to change with them. Like Anne, he concluded that old-style royalty, with its pomp and privilege and isolated splendour, was no longer admirable or tenable. It is too removed, too self-content, too unworldly and too representative of an old and obsolete class system of which he strongly disapproves. Edward has assiduously set about recreating himself in a more egalitarian image befitting this decidedly less regal age. Prince Edward Antony Richard Louis, descendant of kings and emperors, changed himself into plain Mr Edward Windsor.

Prince Edward's choice of career is symbolic of the transformation he is so anxious to achieve. He is the child of the television age, brought up in its searching glare. It was the television programme *Royal Family* that introduced Edward to the public – and in so doing set in motion the process that has started to consume his family and its carefully polished reputation. Now he is looking to it to provide him with his professional future, not in the role of the performer he was born to be, but as a producer, directing the scenes and settings from the shadows of the background.

He carries this desire for privacy through into what has always been the most public of royal duties. By tradition royal marriages are matters of dynastic or political expedience, dressed up as national celebrations. In his own family, in his own generation, he has seen them become public fairytales which have twisted into the stuff of nightmares.

These are not roles Edward Windsor is interested in. He wants to pursue his own career at his own speed, in his own time, in his own way, without being weighed down by the burden of his royal birth. And he wants to get there with the woman of his own choice.

Bibliography

Beaton, Cecil & Strong, Roy, *Royal Portraits*, 1988 Thames & Hudson

Benson, Ross, *Charles The Untold Story*, 1993 Victor Gollancz

Eggar, Robin, *Commando, Survival of the Fittest*, 1994 John Murray

James, Paul, *Prince Edward, A life in the Spotlight*, 1992 Piatkus

Knockout: The Grand Charity Tournament, 1987 Collins

Lieven, Dominic, *Nicholas II Emperor of all the Russians*, 1994 Pimlico

Seward, Ingrid, *Royal Children of the Twentieth Century*, 1993 Harper Collins

Seward, Ingrid, *Sarah HRH The Duchess of York*, 1991 Harper Collins

H.R.H THE PRINCE EDWARD, C.V.O

Patronages and Official Appointments

Auckland Performing Arts Education Trust (New Zealand)	Patron
Cambridge Youth Theatre	Patron
The Children's Film Unit	President
City of Birmingham Symphony Orchestra and City of Birmingham Symphony Orchestra Chorus	Patron
Commonwealth Games Federation	President
The Duke of Edinburgh's Award International Association	Chairman of the International Council
The Duke of Edinburgh's Award International Foundation	Trustee
The Duke of Edinburgh's Award	Trustee
The Royal Exchange Theatre Company (Manchester)	Patron
Friends of Southwark Globe – International Shakespeare Globe Centre	Friend
Friends of the Wanganui Opera House (New Zealand)	Patron
The Globe Theatre (Regina, Saskatchewan, Canada)	Patron
Haddo House Hall Arts Trust (Aberdeen, Scotland)	Patron
London Mozart Players	Patron
National Youth Music Theatre	President
National Youth Orchestra of Scotland	Patron
National Youth Theatre of Great Britian	Patron
Ocean Youth Club	Patron
Scottish Badminton Union	Patron
The Royal Tournament	Patron

Index

Photo Credits

On The Palace balcony © Alpha
In the blue drawing room © Camera Press
With Mabel Anderson © Camera Press
At the *Blue Peter* studio © Camera Press
During the filming of *Royal Family* © Camera Press
At The Royal Tournament © Alpha
Prince Edward and Prince Andrew © Camera Press
At the Windsor Horse Show May 1969 © Alpha
The Royal Family in the gardens of Balmoral © Camera Press
At Badminton Horse Trials 1976 © Alpha
Edward in Toad of Toad Hall © Obee
Heatherdown school photograph © Obee
Prince Edward and Sarah Spencer © Tim Graham
Prince Edward and Susan Barrantes © Tim Graham
Prince Edward on his eighteenth birthday © Tim Graham
Prince Edward on the sea ice of McMurdo Sound © Camera Press
In Jesus College © Tim Graham
Playing rugby at Cambridge © Alpha
Sponsored cycle ride © Cambridge Newspapers Ltd
With the Royal Marines © London News Service
It's a Royal Knockout © Photographers International
With Sir Andrew Lloyd Webber © Alpha
With Biddy Hayward and Nicola Pagett © Alpha
Shelley Whitborn © Obee
Georgia May © Alpha
Romy Adlington © Alpha
Eleanor Weightman © Rex Features
Gail Greenough © Alpha
Princess Martha-Louise © Alpha
Ruthie Henshall © Alpha
Ulrika Jonsson © Alpha
With Sophie Rhys Jones at Queens Club © Alpha
With Sophie at Windsor © Alpha
Sophie Rhys Jones © Alpha
With the Princess of Wales © Joe Little